U.S. Business Law

Dongwook Lee, Esq.

-참고문헌-

Whittington & Delaney: Wiley CPA Regulation Exam Review -Regulation, John Wiley & Sons, Inc.

Les Wiletzky, Power Point Slides to Accompany Business Law, 5th Ed. Henry R. Cheeseman.

Roger E. Meiners et al.: The Legal Environment of Business, Thomson West

이상윤 :『영미법』(박영사, 2000)

이동욱 :『미국법정에 선 한국기업들』(세창출판사,2005)

이동욱 :『미국비즈니스법의 핵심』(세창출판사, 2007)

Table of Contents

Chapter 1

CONTRACT(K)

〈Formation of a contract 개념정리〉

Do we have a valid contract?		
Offer was created? • Objective • intent • communicated • subject matter • timing of performance • parties/participants • price • definite and clear about	➡ no ➡	No Offer • promises made in a jest • opinion • invitation for an offer • negotiation • general advertisement • inquiries • catalog, price tag • prediction • auction with reserve
⬇ yes ⬇	➡ even if offer was created, it can be terminated by	Termination of offer • timing out (lapse of time) • incapacity • revocation • express rejection/counteroffer • destruction of subject
Valid Acceptance? • Mirror image rule • Mail box rule • prescribed method of acceptance		• counter-offer or • mere inquiry
• communication • unilateral or bilateral	➡ no ➡	• no acceptance for silence or • Acceptance by silence or • crossing offer ➡ contract fails
• intent and knowledge • capacity		➡ contract fails
⬇ yes ⬇		
Consideration		no consideration
• bargained-for exchange • legal detriment • right to sue • output K/requirement K or consideration substitute	➡ no ➡	• illegal consideration • moral consideration • past consideration • illusory promise • pre-existing duty
• promissory estoppel • promise of donation to charity		➡ contract fails

 미국비즈니스법의 근원(Sources of U.S. business law)

• **Common Law(CL) :** "보통법" 혹은 "커먼로"라고 하며, 서비스에 관한 계약 및 토지에 관한 계약에 적용된다.

• **Uniform commercial code (UCC) : 미국의 법학자들이 만든 모델법안이며, 그중에서도 제2조**(Article II)는 상품의 거래에만 적용된다.

〈개념정리〉

Common Law	UCC Article 2
land, service contract	goods

Embedded contract : 대부분의 계약은 단순하게 service나 goods로 양분할 수 없다. 예를 들면 현대자동차에서 그랜져를 판매해도 자동차 판매 + 각종 A/S서비스를 약속한다. 이 경우, 판매의 주된 내용이 무엇인가를 살펴보아야 한다. 현대자동차의 경우 자동차 판매가 주가 된다. 따라서 UCC가 적용된다. 한편, 미장원에서 머리를 스타일링 하러갔다면 아무리 비싼 샴푸나 트리트먼트를 사용하더라도 서비스가 주가 되므로 common law가 적용된다.

따라서 계약내용을 분석할 때 UCC가 적용될 것인지, 보통법이 적용될 것인지 판단이 필요하다(Therefore in any analysis of a contract transaction, the first step is to determine whether UCC or common law is to be applicable)

2 Contract(K): legally enforceable agreement

계약이란 <u>법으로 강행이 가능한 합의(a legally enforceable agreement)</u>이다. 계약은 명시적(expressly)으로 하는 방법과 암묵적으로(impliedly) 하는 방법이 있다.

3 계약의 구성요건

• Mneumonic for the elements of contract.

- MA is mutual agreements of offer and acceptance (offer가 acceptance가 서로 일치),

 mutual agreement = meeting of minds and consent to act accordingly

- LOO is legality of objectives and means (목적과 수단이 합법적이어야 하며)
- C is capacity, consideration, concurrence, communication (법적능력, 약인, 동시성, 소통)
- I is with present intent and with no other defenses (의도가 있어야 하며 결격사유가 없어야 한다)

4 Offer : manifestation of an intent to K; manifested willingness to enter into a K

Offer란 상대방과 계약을 맺고 싶다는 의사표시(manifestation of an intent to K; manifested willingness to enter into a K) 즉, 계약을 맺겠다는 의사표시로 "청약" 이라고 한다. offer가 성립되기 위해서는

• Mneumonic: O: O-IC- SToPPP -DC-

- O is objective(객관적)
- I is intent(의도)
- C is communication(소통)
- S is subject matter (주제)
- TOP is timing of performance(시간)
- P is parties or participants(당사자)
- DC is definite and certain(clear) 명확성요건

1) **Objective** Test – **합리적인 사람이 상대방의 제안이 객관적이라고 생각해야 한다. 즉 객관성을 필요로 한다.(객관성, 주관적 의도와는 무관).**

EX Jamie says, "I offer to sell you, Tim, my Gallaway golf club for $1,000." This may be an offer, although Jamie actually might have been joking, as long as under the circumstances it was said, a reasonable person in Tim's position would think that Jamie was making an offer to sell her golf club.

2) **Intent** (present intent) **의도가 있어야 하고,**

3) **Communication 의사소통이 되어야 한다.**

EX1 Katie returned Tim his log dog unaware that Tim had placed an advertisement offering $1,000 rewards. Since the offer had not been communicated to Katie, there could be no mutual agreement. Therefore, there is no contract formed and Tim is not obligated to pay the reward.

EX2 What if Princess Pyeonggang proposed a marriage to Idiot Ondal in Koguryeo dialect and Ondal did not understand the dialect at all? Is the proposal a valid offer? 만일 평강공주가 바보 온달에게 고구려 방언으로 결혼하자고 프로프즈를 했고, 온달이 무슨 얘기인지 전혀 못 알아들었다면 이것은 offer로서 타당한가?

EX3 What if Princess Pyeonggang proposed a marriage to Idiot Ondal while she had a sleep disorder called sleepwalking? Is the proposal a valid offer?
평강공주가 잠꼬대로 바보 온달에게 결혼하자고 프로프즈를 했다면 이것은 offer로서 타당한가?

注意| An offer cannot be accepted if there is no knowledge of it. If the offeree acts without knowledge and learns of the offer later, her acts were not an acceptance. 아무리 offer를 해도 상대방이 모르면 꽝이다. 즉 notice와 knowledge가 생명이다. 극단적인 예로 A와 B사이에 가격만을 제외하고 서로 물건을 사고 파기로 합의한 상태에서 A가 10,000불에 팔겠다는 편지를 보내고 우연히 B도 10,000불에 사겠다는 편지를 발송했다면 서로 모르는 상태인 한 mutual assent부족으로 계약은 성립되지 않는다.(일부러 속이기 위해 가격을 같게 한다거나 동시에 같은 날짜에 발송하는 걸로 crossing offer가 있는 것처럼 fact를 만드는 등 속임수 문제가 많으니 주의가 필요하다)

EX After Joann, a miliatary servicewoman stationing in South Korea, heard the news that her 7-year old son Joe McGuire was missing, she posted a notice in the Korea Times as follows;

"Large Reward : Joe McGuire.
Last seen in Itaewon, Seoul, Korea, perhaps in company of a mysterious figure known only as "the Ferret." Anyone who supplies information leading to the rest and conviction of the "Ferret" will be paid "$10,000."

On the same day, Ben Wagner, an amateur detective and neighbor of Joann, without knowledge of the reward notice, began searching for Joe McGuire and the "Ferret" as a result of his own curiosity. One week later, Ben secured information which led to the arrest and later conviction of the kidnapper. During the trial on kidnapping, Ben found out about the reward and demanded $10,000 from Joann. What would be the result?

4) **Definite and clear** about **SToPP**[subject matter, time of performance, price,and participants].

EX Andrew asks Jack to fix the chandelier at Andrew's house within a week, at a price to be decided later. The offer will fail for indefiniteness of the price term.

5 No Offers(offer가 아닌 경우)

분명한 농담, 막연한 광고(Ex. While they last….), 청약의 유인, 사전문의나 협상, 의견표시는 offer가 아님.

• Mneumonic for non-offers : JOIN AICPA

- J is jokes or jests
- O is opinions
- I is inquiries
- N is negotiations
- A is advertisement
- I is invitation for an offer
- C is catalogs, price tags, price lists
- P is predictions
- A is auction with reserve

1) Promises made in apparent joke(농담)

2) Statement of opinions(의견표시) – is not an offer

EX A physician tells a patient that he will fully recover in a couple of months, but it actually took only two weeks. The physician's statement is only an opinion, not an offer.

3) Inquiries (문의)

EX How much would you charge for this golf club?

4) Preliminary negotiations (예비협상)

5) General advertisements(일반광고) ➡ 예외에 주의

〈개념정리〉

Exception to the ads - ads can be an offer if it is specific as to quantity, terms & indicates who can accept. 구체적인 물량, 조건, 자격을 명시해두면 그걸 따르는 순간 계약이 형성된다.

EX1 Starbucks Spreads Holiday Cheer With Tree Giveaway … The tree giveaway is first come, first served and supplies are limited to the 200 trees.

광고를 아주 제한적으로(Ex. 스타벅스에서는 휴일기념으로 나무를 무료로 나눠드립니다. 단 200 그루에 한정합니다) 할 경우 offer가 된다. ➡ 계약형성은 광고를 보고 performance를 하는 경우에 이루어진다. ➡ 즉 일종의 Unilateral contract이다.

EX2 우리 강아지를 찾아주면 $1,000 드립니다. ➡ completion of performance가 acceptance가 된다(UK).

6) Invitations for an offer, solicitation for an offer, invitation to a treat (광고에 대한 유인)

EX1 Tiger Woods asks Kyungju Choi, "What would you think my golf club is worth?" Choi says: "About $5,000." Woods says: "I accept your offer so I will sell it for $5,000." Under this circumstances, Choi never made an offer. However, when Woods said that he would accept, this is an actually an offer that Choi may accept or reject.

EX2 삽살 강아지 한 마리를 키우고 있던 주인1명이 잠재적 고객 4명에게 동시에 팔겠다는 의향을 나타내는 편지를 보낼 경우 1월15일까지 답장 달라고 한다면 이것은 offer일까, invitation for an offer일까?

EX3 위의 Ex2와 다른 내용은 동일하고 만일 강아지가 아닌 다이아몬드 1개를 갖고 있던 주인이라면?

7) Catalogues, Price tag[lists], (가격카달로그),

8) Predictions (예언)

9) Auction [auction with reserve] (제한적경매)

6 Creation of Offeror and Offeree

Offer is effective upon the receipt by the Offeree.
청약의 효력발생시기는Offeree에게 도달하는 순간에 발생한다. (도달주의 원칙)
편지, fax, e-mail,etc.

Offeror's risk is up until received by the offeree
따라서 도달하기 전에는 Offeror가 risk를 떠안게 된다.

7 Unilateral contract and bilateral contract

1) UK

A. an offer that expressly requires performance as the only means of acceptance. In other words, an offer for a unilateral K cannot be withdrawn once the offeree has begun to perform. UK에서는 performance 자체가 consideration인 것이다.

B. Communication of acceptance or the statement of performance not necessary. 즉 받아들인다고 하는 communication자체가 필요 없고 행동으로 보여주기만 하면 된다.

EX Michael says he will pay Jennifer if she will mow his lawn. Michael has made a UK. The moment Jennifer starts mowing, Michael's offer is accepted.

일단 performance를 시작하기만 하면 30초라도 상관없다.

But mere preparation is not enough to enforce UK 단순한 준비를 했다고 해서 UK라고 우길 수는 없다.

EX Michael이 자신의 집의 벽면과 지붕이 탈색되어 페인트칠을 새로 해야 하겠다고 생각하고, 페인트공인 John에게 집을 칠해달라고 전화를 하자, John은 페인트칠하는 데 사용할 붓을 사는 경우mere preparation.

반면 BK에서는 반드시 상대방에게 acceptance여부를 통보해주어야 하고, reasonably understand the offer as BK으로 알아먹어야 한다. 무조건 UK주장은 곤란하다.

2) BK offer that is not open as to the method of acceptance → must follow the specifically authorized method of acceptance to be valid.

EX Rebecca says Edward, "Will you agree to work for me for three months at $5,000 per month?" Edward replies, "Sure. I will start working from next Monday." This is a bilateral offer.

〈개념정리〉

Unilateral Contract(UK)	Bilateral Contract(BK)
promise to performance	promise to promise

8 Termination of Offer {Offer의 소멸}

Rule : Offeror is the king of the offer. He can cancel his offer anytime before acceptance.

Generally offeror may revoke offer at any time prior to the acceptance. offer를 취소하지 않겠다고 약속했어도 취소할 수 있다

The Offeree's(buyer's) power of acceptance was terminated by an effective revocation.

〈개념정리 : Termination of Offer〉

Is the offer terminated by?	➡ no ➡	Acceptanc possible
• Timing out	➡ lapse of reasonable time	➡ K fails
• Incapacity		➡ K fails
• Revocation of offer (must be communicated)	➡ If unilateral offer is accepted by performance, no revocation possible.	➡ K fails
• Express rejection and/or Counteroffer		➡ K fails ➡ K fails
• Destruction of subject	➡ Including death of the offeror before acceptance	➡ K fails

T is a lapse of reasonable Time after the offer is made, or the time expressly stated in the offer

EX What if Princess Pyeonggang proposed a marriage to Idiot Ondal and Ondal did not respond to her for more than a year? 평강공주가 온달에게 프로포즈를 했으나 1년이 넘도록 온달이 답이 없다면?

I is Incapacity or death of the offeror or offeree or seriously changed circumstances [illegality, impossibility, bankruptcy, insolvency, serious impracticability].

R is Revocation of the offer, communicated to the offeree, before the offer is accepted.

Rule : Revocation may be direct or indirect by oral, written or conducts. Revocation is generally effective when received by the offeree.

상대방에 acceptance하기 전에 revocation의사를 전하는 것이 가장 효율적. 직접 전달하는 것이 아니고 신문이나 친구 등을 통해 간접적으로 들어도 무방[구두, 서면, 액션 등으로 모두 가능]

E is Express Rejection and/or a counteroffer by the offeree.

EX1 평강공주가 결혼하자고 프로프즈를 하자, 온달이 "싫어"라고 대답한 경우

EX2 평강공주가 결혼하자고 프로프즈를 하자, 온달이 "싫어, 열쇠 세개 주면…"이라고 대답한 경우

EX3 평강공주가 결혼하자고 프로프즈를 하자, 온달이 "열쇠 세개 주면…"이라고 대답한 경우

D is Destruction of the Subject Matter of the K, or an intervening illegality, will terminate the offer by operation of law.

EX 가수 비가 카네기 홀에서 공연을 하기로 카네기홀 측과 계약을 했는데, 카네기홀이 테러분자들에 의해 폭파되어버린 경우, 계약의 주 대상인 subject matter의 파괴로 계약무효가 된다.

9 Counteroffer의 역할

〈개념정리〉

A counteroffer serves as both
① Terminating the original offer and
② Creating a new offer from the original offeree, thus
③ Reversing the former roles of the parties and
④ Giving the original offeror the right to accept or reject the new offer

Counteroffer는 original offer를 종결시킨다. 따라서 원래의 역할을 뒤바뀌게 하며 original offer를 한 자에게 새로운 offer를 거절 또는 수용할 권리를 주게 된다.

EX 하청업자가 7만 5천 불에 작업하겠다고 general contractor에게 bidding → general contractor는 5천 불만 깎아서 7만 불에 하자고 전화 → general contractor는 거절 또는 수용가능.

注意| **A mere inquiry≠counteroffer.**
Mere inquiry와 counteroffer는 다르다.
The test of whether the reply is a counteroffer or inquiry is whether a reasonable person would believe that the offer was being rejected.

EX Ann offers to sell her land for $30,000 and Earl asks Ann if she would accept $20,000 now and $10,000 plus 10% interest one year from now.

특히 offer와 acceptance가 유사한 것처럼 보이게 해놓고, "conditioned on ~ charges"등과 같은 경우는 counteroffer이므로 각별히 주의할 것.

ask if 혹은 ask whether 라는 문구가 들어있는 경우 대부분 mere inquiry이다.

10 Offer cannot be revoked when

일반적으로 offeror는 자유롭게 offer를 취소할 수 있는 king of offer이지만, 다음과 같이 취소를 할 수없는 경우도 있다.

1) consideration is paid in Option K

Option K : Offeror has promised to keep the offer open, and promise supported by consideration

Rule : Must be supported by consideration to keep the offer open : 아무리 option K처럼 보여도 consideration이 없으면 option K이 아니다. 속지말것!

EX Jennifer offers to sell her house to Robert at $100,000 and states she will keep the offer open for ten days if he pays $1,000. Robert pays $1,000 and one week later, Jennifer faxes Robert that she is revoking the offer. Robert then accepts the offer on the 8th day. An agreement has been formed because the offer was an option supported with consideration. The offer would not be revoked before ten days.

2) Performance already began under the UK.

3) Merchant's firm offer under the UCC, which is to be discussed under Sales.

11 Acceptance

1) Acceptance may be written, oral, or by conducts.

승낙이란 계약을 성립시키기 위해 Offeree가 Offer에 대한 동의의사를 표시하는 것이다. 의사표시 방법은 서면, 구두, 행동에 의해 가능하다.

EX 구두닦이 앞에 가서 아무 말하지 않고 구두를 올려놓을 경우 ➡ 행동에 의해 계약 성립.

2) For a valid **acceptance,** offeree must have **knowledge and intent** to accept the offer.

승낙은 offeree가 분명한 **knowledge and intent**가 있어야 한다.

3) Click-on agreements are legally enforceable when the offeree completes the contract online by clicking on the button that shows acceptance.

인터넷상으로 클릭을 하여 계약이 성립된 경우, offeree가 knowledge and intent를 갖고 있었다고 판단되어 acceptance로 본다.

12 Silence is not an acceptance.

침묵만 하고 있으면 acceptance가 되지 못한다.

Offeree is under no duty to reply.
Offeree가 청약에 대해 응답할 의무는 없다.
청약에 대해 offeree가 아무런 응답을 하지 않은 silence는 승낙이 되지 못한다.

EX What if Ondal proposes a marriage to Princess Pyeonggang and the Princess remains silent? ➡ no acceptance.

13 Acceptance by silence

1) Offeree intends to accept by silence and Offeror prescribes silence **[사전양해]**

2) Previous dealings imply acceptance**[사전거래]**.

3) Offeree Taking benefits **[혜택]**

4) Offeree has taken benefits of services or goods and exercised control over them when s/he had opportunity to reject them.

Offeree가 거절할 기회가 있었는데도 불구하고, Offeror가 제공하는 용역이나 재화의 benefit을 입은 경우, silence가 acceptance로 간주된다.

 Mirror Image Rule (완전일치의 원칙, 鏡像의 法則)

1) acceptance must be unequivocal and unconditional under the CL.

CL에 따르면 애매모호하지 않고 다른 조건을 달지 않고 acceptance를 해야 한다.

2) An acceptance which attempts to change terms of offer is a counteroffer.

Offer의 조건을 변경하려 할 경우 이는 Acceptance가 아니라 counteroffer이다.

3) A condition which does not change or add to the terms of the offer is not a counteroffer. **Offer에 내용변경이나 추가가 없는 경우 counteroffer가 아니다.**

注意| CL의 mirror image rule 과는 달리 UCC, 즉 sale of goods에서는 additional terms는 merchants들 끼리인 경우 당연히 acceptance가 되고, 서비스 거래에서는 주로 mere inquiry로 취급하는 경향이 늘고 있다.

 Mail Box Rule[MBR 발신주의(發信主義)]

1) If acceptance is made by methods specified in offer or by the same method used by the offeror, acceptance is effective when dispatched.

Offeree의 Acceptance는 Offeree가 발송시(on dispatch)에 효력이 발생한다. Offer가 살아 있는 한, Acceptance는 Offeror가 이를 반드시 수령할 필요는 없다.

2) Other method of acceptance is considered effective when actually received by the offeror.

3) If acceptance is valid by dispatch, a lost or delayed acceptance is correctly mailed but never arrive. valid acceptance.

EX 우체부의 실수로 잘못 배달된 경우

4) The acceptance of a contract is effective upon being mailed, unless the contract provides otherwise.

16 Exception to the Mailbox Rule(Mailbox rule의 예외)

1) Rejection, then acceptance : 먼저 도달하는 것이 효과 발생.

If the offeree mails a rejection(changes her mind) and then send an acceptance, the MBR does not apply. 거절을 먼저하고 난 뒤에는 MBR이 적용되지 않는다. 그리고 rejection이든 acceptance이든 먼저 도착하는 게 이긴다.

2) Acceptance, then rejection : → Acceptance효력 발생. 단, rejection이 먼저 도착하고 offeror가 이에 rely한 경우는 rejection효력 발생 → within reasonable period of time 이내에 acceptance letter를 발송

3) <u>단 communicaiton요건이 있을 경우 반드시 그 방법을 따라야 한다.</u>
(Ex. Please notify me by Friday금요일까지 서면으로 보내서 상대방이 받아보아야 함).

4) <u>offeror가 구체적인 'authorized notification'을 요구하는 경우 그 방법만이 유일하</u>

다. ➡ authorized notification 방법이 아닌 MBR을 통해 답을 보내온 경우 이를 무시하고 offer를 취소가능하다.

EX1 Acceptance must be received to be effective.

EX2 Acceptance shall be not be effective until actually received.

5) Option deadlines - MBR Not Applicable. Acceptance must be received by option deadline.

데드라인이 있으면 반드시 그 데드라인을 지켜야 한다.

Rule : Under the option K, the so-called MBR does not apply to the exercise of options. In such cases, acceptance is effective when received by the offeree.

[option K에서는 MBR도 적용되지 않는다. 오직 하나, 약속시간까지 약속을 완전히 이행하는 것 이외에는 소용없다]

6) **Late acceptance does not create a K.** It is a counteroffer and a valid K is formed only if original offeror then accepts. 데드라인을 넘겨 도착한 acceptance는 무효다.

〈개념정리〉

☑ standard acceptance

offeror	offer	
	⬇ yes ⬇	exception : specified communication 요건이 있으면 그 것을 따라야 한다.
offeree	acceptance	receipt of effective acceptance

☑ Lost Acceptance

offeror	offer	※ Even if the acceptance is lost, it is okay immediately upon dispatch only if acceptance mirrors the offer under mailbox rule.
	⬇ yes/no ⬇	
offeree	acceptance dispatched and lost	acceptance lost

☑ Rejection trumped by earlier acceptance

offeror	offer	➡ receipt of effective acceptance
	⬇ yes/no ⬇	
offeree	rejection dispatched first but another acceptance arrived earlier	➡ receipt of ineffective rejection by the offeror

☑ Rejection trumped by later acceptance

offeror	offer	
	⬇ yes/no ⬇	➡ whichever arrives earlier wins. Mailbox rule does not apply.
offeree	rejection dispatched first, then acceptance dispatched.	

17 Consideration or consideration substitute

Forms - Performance, Forbearance, Promise to Perform., Promise to forebear.

Issues - is action a K or a gift? A gift does not ask for anything in return. In a K you get something in return.

계약구성의 필수요소로서 적어도 consideration 혹은 consideration substitue의 일부분이 반드시 포함되어야 한다.

〈개념정리〉

Consideration	Consideration substitute	**No consideration**
① bargained-for exchange	① promissory estoppel	ⓐ illegal consideration
② legal detriment	② promise of donation to charity	ⓑ moral consideration
③ right to sue		ⓒ past consideration
④ requirement K		ⓓ pre-existing duty
⑤ output K		ⓔ illusory promise

1) bargained-for exchange[상대적 거래관계]

약인이란 약속을 하는 사람(promisor)이 입은 손실(detriment) 또는 약속을 받는 사람(promisee)이 받는 이익(benefit)이다.

2) Legal detriment [법적인 손실] either doing something that you did not have to do or not doing something that you had a right to do. Adequacy of consideration is not relevant. 법적으로 의무가 없는데도 실행을 한다거나, 법적으로 할 수 있는 권리가 있는데도 불구하고, 하지 않는 것.

EX1 만일 원래 담배를 피우지 않는 30세의 아들에게 어머니가 연말까지 담배를 피우지 않으면 $1,000을 준다고 약속했다면?

Consideration은 경제적으로 판단하는 게 아니라 법적으로 판단하는 것이므로 금액의 유사성이나 consideration의 적정성 등은 상관없다.

Q

만일 경찰관 Police officer가 도박과 마약혐의로 구속된 적이 있었던 연예인 H에게 "만약 도박과 마약을 1년간만 하지 않으면 $1,000을 주겠다"라고 말한다면 consideration이 있는가?

3) **Consideration as the Right to Sue** : honest and reasonable belief in a valid claim = compromise among the parties

소송을 안한다거나 소송의 가능성이 있다고 믿고서 이를 않는 조건으로서 타협을 하는 것도 consideration이라고 볼 수 있으므로 주의할 것

4) **Requirement Ks/Output Ks** : a K for the sale of goods can state quantity in terms of the Buyer's requirements or Seller's output.

Requirements K generally present adequate consideration on both sides of the K because one party is bound to supply the goods, and the other has lost her right to buy goods from another source. Requirements K는 상대방에서 서로 구속이 되고, 다른 상대방에게 구입할 기회를 포기하게 되므로 적절한 consideration이 있다고 본다.

5) Promissory Estoppel as consideration substitute

[약속에 의한 禁反言]

Promissory estoppel may become a consideration substitute and renders promise enforceable … promissor is estopped from asserting the lack of consideration. Promise, reliance that is reasonable, foreseeable, detrimental, and enforcement necessary to avoid injustice.

Consideration이 없더라도 대체효과를 나타내며 약속을 해준 사람은 consideration이 없다는 이유로 계약관계가 없다고 주장 못한다.

〈개념정리〉

> • **Elements of the Promissory estoppel**
> 1) Detrimental reliance on the promise 약속에 대한 detrimental reliance
> 2) Reasonable and forseeable reliance 합리적이고 예측 가능한 의존
> 3) damages or injustice may result if not enforced. 만일 이행을 하지 않으면 damages나 injustice가 발생

Promissory estoppel allows a party to recover on a promise even though that promise was made without consideration. Essentially it prevents, or estops, a person from arguing that his or her promise should not be upheld. It also requires that reliance on the promise was reasonable, and that the person trying to enforce the promise actually relied on the promise to his or her detriment. The precise legal requirements for promissory estoppel may vary between jurisdictions.

EX An employer orally promises to pay an employee a monthly amount for the remainder of her life as retirement. If the employee reasonably relies on the promise and retires, the employer will likely be estopped, based on the doctrine of promissory estoppel, from reneging on his promise to pay a monthly retirement payment.

6) **Promise to donate to charity** is enforceable based on public policy reasons. 증여약속은 일반적으로 consideration이 없다. 그러나 자선단체(교회, 병원, 학교 등)에 증여하기로 한 약속은 공익의 차원에서 구속력을 갖게 된다.

EX When Oprah Winfrey, the richest woman in the world, promised to donate $100 million to Korea University at the ceremony of her honorary doctorate, the school committee reasonably and in good faith relied on the promise and incurred expenses.

18 No consideration

〈개념정리〉

1) illegal consideration

2) Past consideration general rule, is not consideration.

3) Moral Obligation is not bargained-for exchange

물에 빠진 사람을 구해주었더니 감사의 표시로 내일 사무실을 찾아오면 100만원을 사례금으로 준다고 했을 경우, comfort and affection에 대한 감사의 표시 등은 moral obligation이나 gift에 해당하고, consideration이 아니다.

4) **Preexisting Duty Rule [PEDR], Pre**–existing contractual or statutory duty rule – Promise to pay someone to do something for which he or she is already obligated to do is unenforceable. CL performance of pre–existing duty is not consideration.

어떤 당사자가 이미 자신이 법적으로나 계약상 의무가 있는 일을 하거나 할 것을 약속하는 경우, 손실이 없기 때문에 consideration이 되지 못한다.

EX1 Agreement to pay police officer $300 to recover the solen goods is unenforceable.

EX2 Fredrick is an auditor of Semiconductor Company. Donna is a potential investor of the company and offers Fredrick to pay $1,000 if he performs a professional quality audit of Semiconductor Company. The $1,000 is in addition to the fee Fredrick will get from Semiconductor. Are there any considerations for the additional $1,000?

5) **Illusory promise** : A promise that pledges nothing, because it is vague or because the promisor can choose whether or not to honor it. Such promises are not legally binding.

EX If you get a new job and promise to work for three years, unless you resign sooner, you have not made a valid contract and can resign or be fired at any time

 K modification[Modification of K]계약내용의 변경

〈개념정리〉

	CL	UCC
applicable to	land, service K	goods
when K is to be modified	new consideration is needed	only good faith is sufficient

1) Under the CL, K modification needs new consideration on both sides to be legally binding. CL에서는 체결된 계약이 수정되기 위해서는 양쪽 당사자 모두에게 새로운 약인이 필요하다.

EX Personal service K.

2) Under UCC, a K modification for the sale of goods is enforceable if made in GF, even without consideration. 그러나 UCC에서는 good faith만 있으면 된다.

 Defenses to the formation of a K. 계약형성의 결격사유

• Mneumonic: MUFFIN fails K

다음의 문제가 생기면 계약이 생겨나지 않게 된다.

- **M**-Mistakes
- **U**-Unconscionability, undue influence, duress of the underlying transaction
- **F**-Failure of consideration or seriously changed circumstances
- **F**-frauds [statute of frauds]
- **I**-fraudulent inducement of the underlying K through infancy, incapacity, illegality, etc,
- **N**on-existence[absence] of reality of consent

1) Mistake – a wrongful understanding of a fact that is not present in the agreement

A. **Unilateral mistake** of material fact

(1) generally courts are reluctant to allow a party to avoid a K for a mistake made only by one party. 원칙상 한쪽의 착오를 이유로 계약취소 불가

(2) **Exceptions - palpable (obvious) mistakes.**

Mistakes discovered before significant reliance by the other party. In all unilateral mistake situations, if the non-mistaken party knows or should have known of the other party's mistake, he will not be permitted to snap up the bargain and take advantage of the mistaken party.

注意| 만약 룰을 한쪽이 간접적으로 알고 있었다면(직접 들은 게 아니고 신문 등이나 제3자를 통해 알게 되어도 무관) 다른 쪽은 claim 주장 못한다. 즉 상대방을 이용하지 마라!

B. Bilateral mistake[Mutual Mistake]

(1) **Mutual mistake about material subject matters** [existence, identity, important characteristics]
중요사항에 대하여 쌍방 간 착오를 일으켰을 경우 이를 이유로 계약취소 가능(voidable)

(2) mistake about the value of subject matter is not grounds for voiding a K. 중요하지 않은 사항의 가격이나 가치에 대한 착오는 계약취소사유가 되지 못한다.

EX Mistake about the fair market value of land.

〈개념정리〉

Mistakes		
Mistakes	**Unilateral Mistake**	
	Minor mistake	➡ does not affect K formation
	Palpable(obvious) mistake	➡ the other non-mistaken party cannot take advantage of the mistake
	Bilateral(Mutual) Mistake	
	on minor issues	➡ does not affect K formation
	on material issues	➡ K fails

2) Unconscionability [부당계약]

Unconscionability는 계약당시에 결정되며 법원에서는 bargaining power의 불균형(disparities)와 심각한 위배(significant deviation), 강압성 정도를 보고 결정한다.

Unconscionability of a K is determined at the time the parties entered into the agreement. A court will consider

A. disparities in the bargaining power and
협상력의 큰 차이

B. significant deviation from what otherwise would be considered a reasonable contract and.
합리적인 계약관계에서 지나친 괴리여부

C. Unfair surprise & oppressive terms are tested as of the time the agreement was made. 강압적 조항 존재여부

EX Adhesion K(상호협상가능성이 전혀 없는 take it or leave it 성격의 계약) : 예. 전기, 가스, 수도 계약

3) Undue Influence[mental coercion]

A. Occurs through abuse of fiduciary relationship[close relationship] (e.g. CPA, attorney, guardian, trustee) 정신적 강박은 주로 신뢰관계를 저버리는 상황에서 발생한다.

B. normally cause agreement to be voidable. 취소가능하다.

4) Duress [물리적 강박]

〈개념정리〉

economic duress	duress	extreme duress
⬇	⬇	⬇
no excuse	voidable	void

A. Any wrongful threats or acts of violence or extreme pressure
(물리적 힘을 사용하거나 위협)

B. Generally ordinary duress creates voidable agreement. 강박에 의해 체결된 계약은 voidable.

C. Extreme duress causes agreement to be void.
심한 duress는 계약이 void(무효)가 된다.

D. Personal Duress/Economic Duress - personal or physical duress but not economic duress is a basis for avoiding an agreement
개인적인 강박이나 물리적인 강박은 계약 취소원인이 되지만 경제적인 애로는 인정되지 않는다.

5) Failure of consideration or seriously changed circumstances

[consideration 결여 또는 심각한 상황변화]

Serious Changes in weather conditions, economic conditions, etc., that cause hardship to one party will create voidable Ks.

계약의 기초가 되는 상황(기후, 경제여건 등)이 심각하게 변화되어 계약을 강행할 경우 상대방에게 손실이 심각하게 가혹해진 경우(예컨대 사업이 망하는 경우) 계약취소 가능.

EX 쓰나미, 총파업, 지진 등

6) Failure under Statue of Frauds. 사기방지법의 서면기재 요건을 충족하지 못하는 경우

A. 대부분의 계약은 서면이 아닌 구두로(orally)도 enforceable하나, 몇 가지 계약들은 그 성격상 서면으로 작성되어야하고, 당사자가 반드시 서명하여야 함.

• Menumonic : MY F* LEGS

• M(marriage in consideration of)

注意 | 결혼당사자간의 혼전계약(prenuptial agreement, PNA)뿐만 아니라, 예비 시아버지-며느리간의 결혼조건과 관련한 계약도 서면으로 해야 한다.

• **Y** (a K that cannot be completed within a year)

注意 1 | a BK, which BY ITS EXPRESS TERMS is not capable of complete performance within one year from its execution, must be evidenced by a signed writing.

EX a 5-year employment K is within the SOF.

注意 2 | 단, 1년 이내에 시행될 가능성이 조금이라도 있다면 SOF의 적용을 받지 않는다.

• **F** is finders' fee arrangement :

注意 | 서면으로 해둔 뒤에 최종 계약closing까지 가지 않으면 한 푼도 못 받는다]

• **L** (land K)

注意 1 | 특히 토지거래에서 매매가격이 기재되어 있지 않으면 즉시 위반이 된다. lease periods for longer than 1 year, must be in writing signed by the party to be charged, or signed by her agent whose authority to sign must be in a writing signed by the principal.

注意 2 | 단, UCC의 적용을 받는 상품매매에서는 가격이 기재되어 있지 않아도 reasonable price가 적용된다.

• **E** (exector's promise to pay the debts of the estate from his personal funds)유언집행인이 체결한 계약

• **G**(goods $500 or more)

• **S** (suretyship or guarantee)보증계약에 보증인의 서명없는 경우 채권자가 보증인의 보증계약을 이행하라고 할 수 없다.

B. **SWAP** Exception to the SOF

$500 이상의 상품판매에 관한 Oral K라도 다음의 경우엔 SOF가 적용되지 않고 약속이행 강제가능하다.

(1) Oral K for **specially manufactured** or unique goods not suitable for ordinary sale enforcible when the seller has begun substantially to perform. [특수목적 제작품]

(2) **Written confirmation** between merchants-one party may send signed written confirmation stating terms of oral agreement to the other party within reasonable time, then the non-signing party must object within 10 days or the K is enforceable[상인간의 구두거래내용 확인서].

(3) **Admission in court** : 계약의 이행을 요구하는 당사자가 법정에서의 변론이나 증언 등에 의하여 계약이 체결되었음을 인정한 경우

(4) **Performed** : received and accepted goods(서면계약서 없어도 상품을 수령하거나 상품의 대금을 지급한 경우 계약이 형성된 것으로 본다. 즉 한번 받고 나면 책임지라는 원칙)

C. Other Issues in the SOF

doctrine of Part performance[부동산과 관련된 part performance의 법리] - equity will intervene & decree specific performance of an oral K of the sale of land when

① buyer takes physical possession & pays all or a substantial part of the payment [점유+지불]

② buyer takes physical possession & makes substantial improvements(점유+개선)

D. writing forms

- need not to be written in a single document 계약조건을 담은 문서로서 당사자들의 서명이 있는 문서가 반드시 하나일 필요는 없다. 예를 들어 A와 B가 구두계약을 맺고서 각자의 서명의 담은 문서를 서로에게 보냈을 경우 각각 상대방에게 이행하라고 촉구 할 수 있다.

7) Infancy : K with minors(K with a minor)미성년자 계약관련 주의사항

A. 미성년자와의 계약은 valid가 대원칙

B. A minor may contract, but agreement is voidable by the minor. A minor may disaffirm his K on the ground that he lacked capacity, but the party contracting with him may not. 미성년자는 자신이 미성년이라는 이유로 계약을 무효화할 수 있으나 미성년자와 계약을 맺은 당사자는 미성년을 이유로 무효화할 수 없다.

EX 미성년자 Boy가 오토바이 한대를 성인인 Seller에게서 사기로 계약을 맺었는데 Seller는 나중에 delivery직전에 다른 성인을 데리고 오기 전에는 계약이행을 못하겠다고 주장할 경우 미성년자인 Boy가 이긴다.

C. Disaffirm = repudiate (계약의 취소)

A minor may disaffirm the K at any time until a reasonable time after reaching majority age. 미성연자는 계약체결순간부터 성년이 된 이후 합리적인 시간 내에 언제든지 계약을 취소할 수 있다.

EX 미성년자일 때 K 계약을 맺었는데 나중에 18살이 되면 400$를 준다고 했다가, 실제 18살이 되자 $300 만 주겠다고 한 경우 $300이 적용가격이다

D. 단 미성년자의 necessities(생필품)과 관련한 경우에는 계약성립인정.

A minor is liable for necessaries furnished for him.

EX1 Food, clothing, shelter, education, etc.

EX2 눈보라를 피하기 위해 16세인 미성년자가 호텔에 급히 들어가자 평상시 $50인 숙박료를 주인이 갑자기 $100로 인상한 경우 → $50만 법적으로 인정된다.

The infant is not liable for the K price, but for the reasonable value of the necessaries furnished.

> **注意|** 계약이 아직 이행(non-executory)되지 않은 상태라면 미성년자는 그 계약을 이행하지 않고, 계약을 취소할 수 있다. 그러나 이미 이행되어 미성년자에게 제공이 되었다면, 미성년자는 자신이 제공받은 것에 대한 합리적인 대가(reasonable value)에 대한 책임을 부담하고 계약을 취소할 수 있다. 미성년자는 K price에 책임이 없고, reasonable value of the necessaries furnished에 책임.

E. ratifying[계약의 추인]계약의 추인은 취소할 수 있는 계약을 취소하지 않겠다는 의사표시로 성년이 된 이후부터 미성년인 상태에서 체결한 계약을 추인하는 것.

F. 꼭 necessity가 아니더라도 미성년자가 사용해서 혜택을 봤다면 그 금액만큼 제하고 주인은 돌려줄 수 있다.

EX 미성년자가 중고자동차를 $1,000 불에 사서 두 달간 이용했는데 나중에 두 달만에 고장이 나자 주인에게 되돌려주며 원금반환을 주장했을 경우 주인은 원금에서 사용한 이용료만큼을 제하고 나머지만 돌려줘도 된다.

8) Incapacity[Incompetency]

〈개념정리〉

contract signed by the incompetent before adjudication	contract signed by the incompetent after adjudication
voidable	void

A. 법원에 의해 insanity(incompetent)로 판결된 사람에 의해 판결이전에 맺은 계약은 취소가능(voidable)

B. 법원에 의해 insanity(incompetent)로 판결 받은 사람에 의해 판결이후 체결한 계약은 무효(void)

9) Illegality of the subject matter[불법계약]

A. Agreements are unenforceable if illegal or violate the public policy. 불법계약이나 공공정책에 위배되는 계약은 이행불가 (Ex. 도박관련 대금지불 계약)

B. When one party is innocent, s/he will be given relief. But when both parties are guilty, neither will be aided by court. 쌍방이 과실일 경우, 법원은 도와주지 않는 것이 원칙.

C. types of illegal K unenforceable

(1) agreement to commit the crime or the solicitation of the crime. 범죄계약, 범죄교사계약

(2) agreement not to press criminal charges for consideration. 댓가를 받고 형사상 고소 또는 고발을 하지 않기로 하는 계약

(3) Services rendered without licenses(무면허 서비스 계약) 공익보호 목적 for the protection of public interest

- 의사, 변호사, 회계사, 부동산 중개사 자격증 보호

EX 치과나 성형외과의사 등이 의사면허증 없이 수술해준다면 돈을 안줘도 된다.

(4) revenue-seeking statute. Ex. Liquor license

(5) usury for greater than legally determined interest 법에서 정한 이자율 상한선 초과징수

〈개념정리〉

voidable K	void
K with minors/infants (voidable by the minor only)	Illegal K
K by undue influence	K by extreme duress
K by duress	K after adjudication
K with unconscionability	
K before adjudication	

10) Non-existence(Absence) of Reality of Consent

A. Fraud(사기) : fraud의 elements는 Plaintiff가 입증하여야 한다.

〈개념정리〉

Fraud	Constructive fraud = gross negligence	Innocent mistakes
misrepresenation of materials facts	좌동	misrepresentation of minor facts
intent to deceive, intent to mislead, or scienter	reckless disregard of truth	fault or negligence
reasonable reliance	좌동	
injury or damage	좌동	
causation	좌동	
rescission of K, damage 등의 remedy 청구가능	rescission of K, damage 등의 remedy 청구가능	rescission of K, damage 등의 remedy 청구 불가

(1) Misrepresentation of material facts [중요사실에 대한 부실표기]

注意 1 | layperson opinion, sales puffing, prophecy, sales talks 일반인의 의견, 세일즈 목적상의 과장, 예언 등은 이에 해당되지 않는다.

注意 2 | layperson's opinion does not constitute fraud, but expert opinion does constitute fraud. 일반인이 아닌 전문가 의견은(audit opinion, appraisal value) 등은 사기의 구성요소가 될 수 있다.

EX appraisal value of the diamond

(2) Intent to mislead - "scienter" [기망의 의도 또는 고의성] : Knowledge of falsity and deceptive intent

(3) Reasonable reliance [상대방의 합리적인 신뢰]

(4) resulting Injuries [손해발생]

(5) causation [인과관계]

B. Types of Fraud[사기의 종류]

(1) fraudulent inducement[= fraud in the inducement] 계약의 협상과정에서 사기로서 계약내용에 대하여 기망을 한 경우, 이렇게 체결된 계약은 취소가능(voidable)

EX 연예인이 팬들이 몰리면서 사인을 해달라고 하길래 사인해주었더니 나중에 보니 대출금 계약서인 걸로 밝혀졌을 때 무효

(2) fraud in the execution : 계약의 체결과정에서 사기를 당하여 내용을 잘 모르고 계약서에 서명을 한 경우, 또는 계약을 한다는 사실은 알았지만 전혀 내용이 다른 서류를 서명한 경우[void]

C. Remedies for Fraud

(1) affirm and sue for damages under tort of deceit. 계약을 취소하지 않고 손해배상을 받을 수 있다.

(2) rescind the K and sue for damages that resulted from fraud. 계약을 취소하고 손해배상을 받을 수 있다.

D. Constructive Fraud or gross negligence

Fraud의 elements중 intent to mislead[scienter]대신 Reckless disregard of the truth라는 점을 제외하고는 fraud와 동일하다.

E. Innocent(Negligent) Misrepresentation

(1) Fraud의 요건 중 intent to mislead[scienter]대신 fault 또는 negligent (부주의)를 요건으로 한다.

(2) Remedies for Innocent Misrepresentation

Rescission of the K(계약취소), Return of all benefits to the relevant parties(모든 혜택 반환), But no right for damage claims for the aggrieved party(innocent misrepresentation 을 이유로 상대방에게 손해배상을 청구할 수 없다)

21 Other Issues

1) Parol Evidence Rule [PER] affects terms of K, not formation.

Rule - when parties have agreed to a written K as the final expression of their agreement, evidence of a prior or contemporaneous agreement (written or oral) cannot be used to vary the terms of that written K. where there is complete integration, no extrinsic evidence is permitted

당사자들이 최종적이고 완전한 의도를 가진 서면계약을 체결하였다면 법원은 그 서면계약 이전에 체결된 구두, 또는 서면계약, 또는 그 서면과 동시에 체결된 구두계약을 그 서면계약의 선결조건을 다투기 위한 증거(contradicting evidence) 로 받아들이지 않는다.

〈개념정리〉

	oral	written
past(prior or precedent) evidence	X	X
present(concurrent) evidence	X	O (finally integrated written expression)
future(subsequent) evidence	O	O

2) Exception to the PER

A. to show **condition precedent**. 해당계약의 성립을 위하여 선행조건이 있음을 설명하기 위하여

B. to show **invalidity(inconsistency)** of Ks between parties because of fraud, duress, mistake, failure of consideration. 계약 성립의 결격사유 존재

C. to explain the intended meaning's **ambiguity**
서면계약 내용 중 일부의 애매성을 설명하기 위하여

D. UCC1-205 PER의 또 다른 예외로서 **trade usage(trade terminology) 또는 의미를 분명하게 해주는 과거의 거래경력(the meaning of disputed terms)은** 인정된다. Trade usage can contradict or supplement the written K

3) PER Not applicable to subsequent transactions

최종적이고 완전한 의도를 가진 서면계약을 체결하였다 하더라도 당사자들은 그 서면계약을 수정할 수 있는데 그 서면계약의 조건을 타투기 위해 수정된 계약(subsequent K)을 증거로 사용가능.

EX Mark and Nancy have a complete written employment K. Later, Mark and Nancy orally modify the K with M agreeing to pay more and Nancy agreeing to work more hours on duties. The oral evidence is allowed because it arose subsequent to the written K and those modified terms are additional to the existing K.

4) Contracting On-line

When one individual makes Ks over the internet, basic rules of K law still apply. 일반계약법상의 원칙이 전자거래에도 적용된다.

22 Assignment and Delegation

〈용어정리〉

Assignor(양도인) = a Party to K who later transfers his/her rights to another or an Individual who transfers a title, claim, property, interest, or right to another person.

Assignee(양수인) = an Individual to whom a title, claim, property, interest, or right has been transferred. The assignee stands in the shoes of the assignor. The assignee of K rights is entitled to enforce them to the same extent the assignor would have been.

Obligor[채무자] = An individual or company that owes debt to another individual or company (the creditor), as a result of borrowing or issuing bonds. also called debtor.

Obligee[채권자] = Obliging party (bond holder, creditor, lender, insurance policy holder, etc.) in whose favor a promise is made or an obligation is entered into by an obligor, under the terms of an agreement. Also called promisee or creditor.

Mortgagor[저당권 설정자] = The borrower in a mortgage agreement. Sometimes spelled mortgager.

Mortgagee = The creditor or lender in a mortgage agreement.

룰 정리 Rules of AOR and DoD

1) An AOR generally extinguish any rights of assignment, but a DOD does not relieve the delegator of his duties.

[AOR]

A. The assignee has exclusive right of performance. Assignment를 하고 난 뒤에는 assignor의 권리는 소멸되고, assignee의 배타적 권리만 남게 된다.

B. If the obligor has notice of assignment, s/he must pay the assignee, not the assignor. 채무자는 assignment에 대한 내용을 알았을 경우 assignor가 아닌 assignee에게 이행하여야 한다.

C. If assignee release obligor, then assignor is also released. Assignor가 obligor에 대한 권리를 assignee에게 이전하고 난 뒤에 assignee가 obligor를 release하게 되면 assignor도 release가 된다.

〈개념정리〉

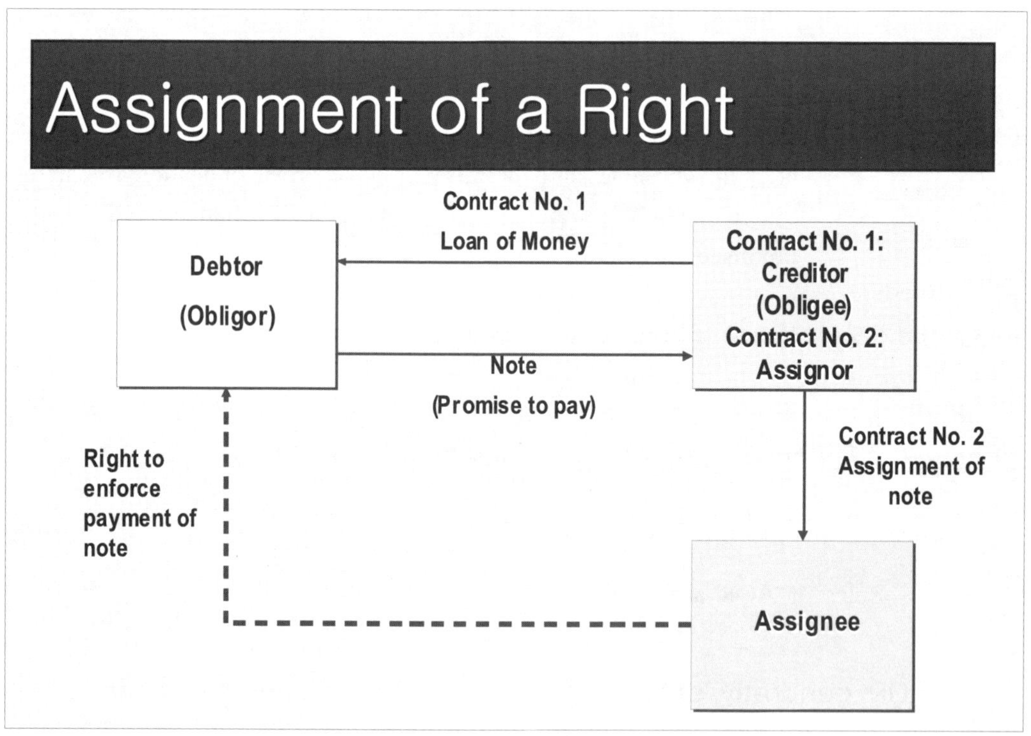

(출처 : Les Wiletzky, *Power Point Slides to Accompany Business Law*, 5th Ed. Henry R. Cheeseman)

[DOD]

(1) **The delegator remains secondarily & personally liable.** → When a duty is delegated to a delegate, the delegator remains liable if the delegatee fail to perform. **Delegation does not relieve the delegator of contract duties or liability for breach.**
즉 한번 책임지겠다고 한 (delegatee)는 다른 사람에게 책임을 넘겨도 계속해서 secondarily liable하다.

〈개념정리〉

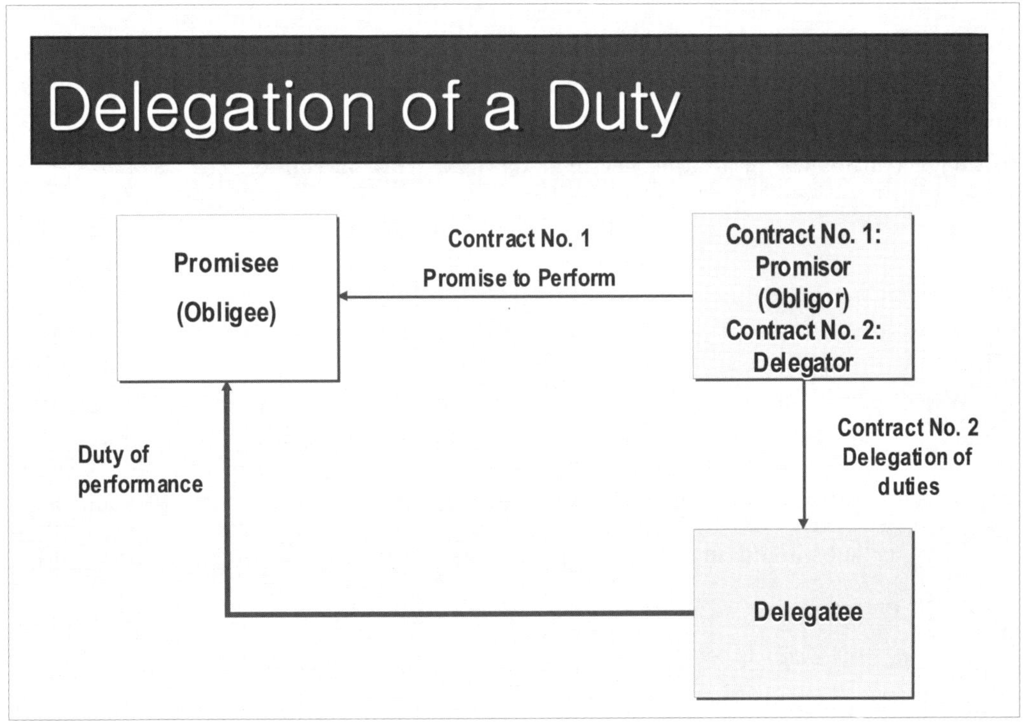

(참고 : Les Wiletzky, *Power Point Slides to Accompany Business Law*, 5th Ed. Henry R. Cheeseman)

2) Assignment of rights[AOR] and Delegation of duties[DOD] are transferable in almost all the K.

대부분의 계약에서 권리와 의무는 제3자에게 이전 가능

注意 | Exception to the AOR and DOD

a) An assignment of right is barred if it will **substantially/materially change the obligor's duty or risk** 의무 관련사항이나 위험을 확 바꾸는 권리양도는 곤란

EX (CL) 작은가게 A와 제조업체 B간 전량 납부계약조건이 있었는데 대형체인점인C가 A의 권리를 양도받은 경우, A한테 있던 B의 의무(약 20개)가 C(약 5천개)에게로 이전됨으로써 B의 책임과 의무의 변화가 커지는 경우.
(UCC)만약 수량이 너무 unreasonably disproportionate 하지 않으면 무방하다.

b) Contract involving **too unique personal services, trust or confidences**. 계약의 특성상 이전이 불가능

EX Malpractice K

3) 예외

A. Novation occurs when one of the original parties to the K is released and a new party is substituted in his or her position. Novation requires consent of all the three parties.

Novation(계약갱신, 更契)은 delegator를 의무에서 벗어나게 하고, delegatee만이 의무를 지게 되는데 delegator, delegatee, the 3P의 동의가 필요하다.

EX Alex owes Becky money and all parties agree that Charlie will pay the money to Becky, not Alex. Becky's consideration to Charlie is agreeing to release Alex from his obligations and Alex's consideration is providing the new debtor, Charlie.

B. Contractual substitution(계약대체) : an existing contract is extinguished and a new contract brought into being in its place."… the substitution for an existing contract of a new contract either between the same or different parties."

C. An assignment is a transfer of a right(or obligation) of one person to another. Assignment differs from novation in so much that the parties to the contract do not change - privity of contract still exists between the parties. The consent of the third contracting part is not necessary. So, a party to a contract (the assignor) is able to transfer the benefit of a performance he is to receive under that contract to another person (the assignee) who is able to enforce performance in his own right, without the consent of the other party (the debtor).

D. **Generally, no consideration is needed for AOR.**

Gratuitous assignments - it is possible to make a gratuitous assignment but they are generally **freely revocable** without any consideration.

일반적으로 AOR에는 consideration이 필요 없다. 단, gratuitous assignment는 자유롭게 취소가능하다.

〈개념정리〉

Novation	Contractual substitution	Aassignment
경계. 갱계(당사자 교체 또는 계약갱신의 의미로 사용)	계약대체	권리이전/의무이전
takes place by the intervention of a new debtor, where another person becomes a debtor instead of a former debtor, and is accepted by the creditor, who thereupon discharges the first debtor. (채무자 당사자 교체) → 제3자의 동의필요 takes place without the intervention of any new person, where a debtor contracts a new engagement with his creditor, in consideration of being liberated from the former. (기존의 당사자는 그대로 유지하면서 계약의 성격만 변경)	The parties to a contract may agree to substitute another contract in its place. Once they so agree, they are no longer required to perform under the first contract. Instead, they are required to perform under the substitute contract. 계약당사자는 그대로 유지되고 계약의 내용만 바뀌는 것	Assignment differs from novation in so much that **the parties to the contract do not change** - privity of contract still exists between the parties. **The consent of the third contracting part is not necessary.** So, a party to a contract (the assignor) is able to transfer the benefit of a performance he is to receive under that contract to another person (the assignee) who is able to enforce performance in his own right, without the consent of the other party (the debtor). 계약당사자는 변경 없고, 제3자가 합의할 필요도 없음. 계약당사자는 자유롭게 자신의 권리를 다른 사람의 동의 없이 이전가능

23 Third-Party Bebeficiary {3PB} Charts

〈용어정리〉

1) **Intended beneficiary : the one whom the contracting parties intended to give rights when signing the K.** Only intended beneficiary can maintain an action against contracting parties for nonperformance.

EX Susan and Tom enter into a K for Susan to sell and Tom to buy Susan's car. The K provides that Tom is to pay the price to Susan's son as a wedding present. In such a case, Susan's son is an intended 3PB.

2) Intended beneficiaries are classified as

a) **creditor beneficiary** : a debtor contracts with second party to pay the debt owed to creditor. 채무자가 채권자에 대한 채무를 변제하기 위하여 제3자와 계약을 체결하면서 채무자가 받을 수 있는 대가를 채권자에게 지급하도록 함으로써, 채권자는 제3자로부터 어떤 대가를 지급받을 수 있는 권리를 갖게 된다.

〈개념정리〉

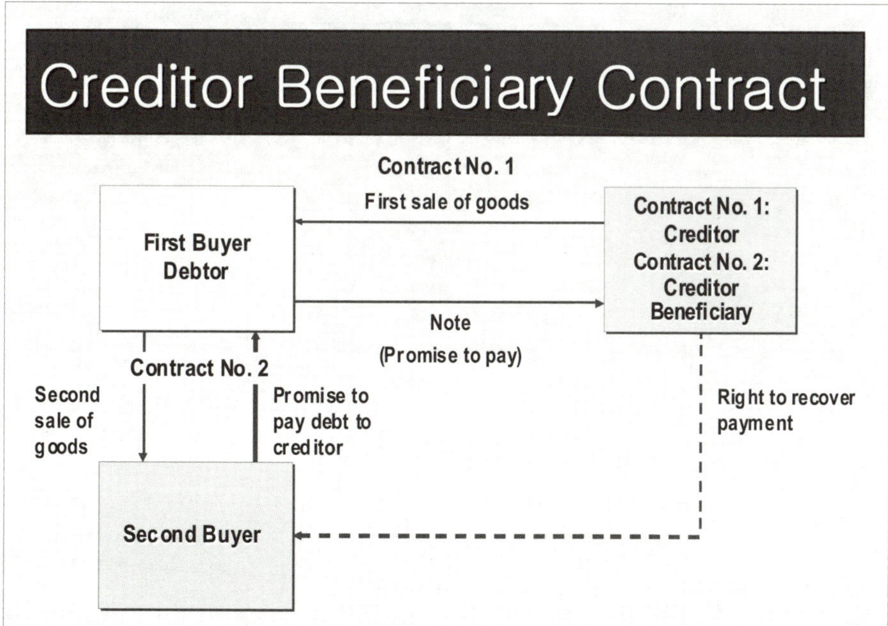

(출처 : Les Wiletzky, *Power Point Slides to Accompany Business Law*, 5th Ed. Henry R. Cheeseman)

EX 황태덕장 가게를 운영하는 황씨(45세)는 Buyer의 구매제안을 받게 되자 오랜 고민 끝에 자신의 가게를 10억 원에 팔고, 그 대신 자신이 60세가 될 때까지 15년간 S보험에 자신의 이름으로 되어있는 생명보험을 계속 유지해 대납을 해달라고 요구함. Buyer가 이에 동의한 경우, Buyer는 황씨가 이뻐서 선물처럼 보험을 들어준 것이 아니라 계약의 일부분으로서 들어준 것이고, 이 경우 황씨는 intended creditor beneficiary임.

b) **donee beneficiary** : 계약의 일방당사자(promisor)가 donee beneficiary에 재화나 서비스를 공급하기로 약속하고, 그 대가는 계약의 상대방인 promisee에게 지급하기로 계약하게 되면 donee beneficiary는 promisor로부터 계약에서 정한 재화나 service를 받을 수 있는 권리를 갖게 된다. Donee beneficiary can proceed against the promisor only.

〈개념정리〉

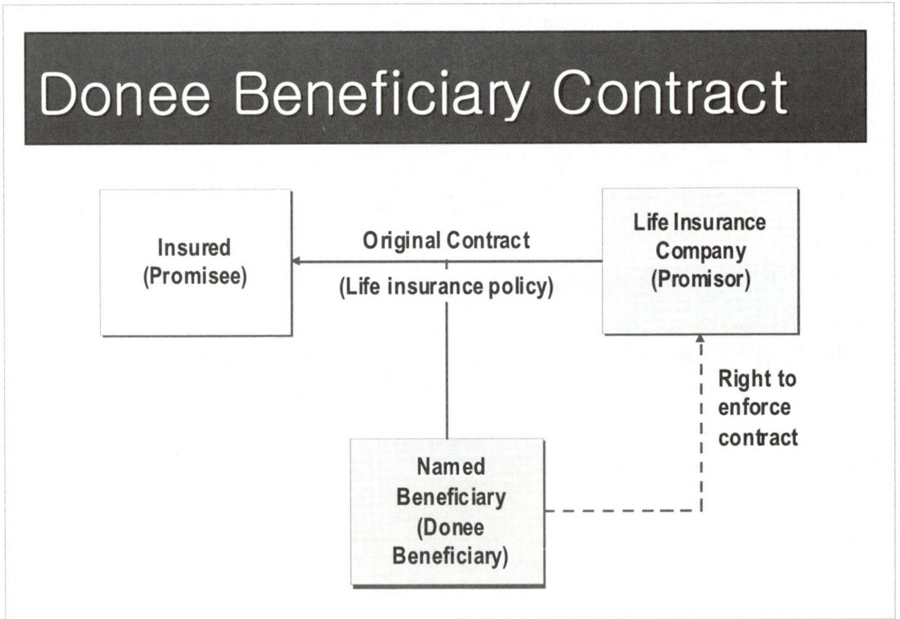

(출처 : Les Wiletzky, *Power Point Slides to Accompany Business Law*, 5th Ed. Henry R. Cheeseman)

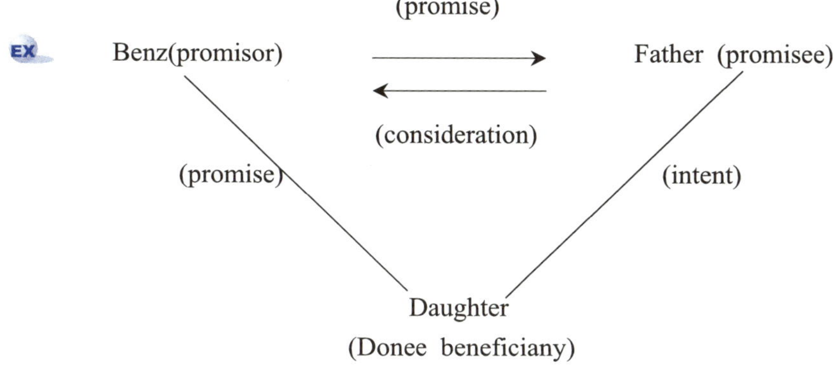

EX 아버지가 딸의 졸업식 선물로 벤츠 한 대를 선물하려고 주문하였을 경우, 딸은 intended donee beneficiary가 된다. 아버지는 언제라도 선물을 받을 대상자인 딸이 마음에 들지 않을 경우 다른 사람에게로 벤츠를 선물할 수 있다. 딸은 이 경우 아버지를 상대로 소송할 수 없다. 단, Benz 회사가 잘못했을 경우 소송을 제기하는 것은 가능하다.

3) **Incidental 3PB** (windfall receiver) : no rights under the K. 계약에서 의도되지 않고 우연히 사실상 이익을 보게 되는 자로 계약상의 권리를 취득하는 것은 아니다.

EX 현대건설과 KBS 방송국이 행복도시에 KBS 신사옥을 설치하기로 하였는데 이를 엿들은 L이 신사옥 설치 예정지 바로 옆에 초대형 주차장 설비를 완성함. 이 경우 KBS 혹은 현대건설 측이 계약을 진행할 경우 L은 incidental 3rd party beneficiary가 된다. 그러나 KBS 혹은 현대건설 측이 계약을 진행하지 않기로 한 경우, L은 어느 쪽에도 소송제기를 할 수 없다.

24 Performance - duty to perform may depend upon a condition.

1) Condition precedent[선행조건] : 조건이 성취되어야 계약상의 권리와 의무가 발생

EX Baker agrees to plant trees on a specified land once Carl removes the old waste boxes from the land.

2) Condition subsequent[후행조건] : 조건이 성취되면 권리와 의무가 소멸되거나 변경된다.

EX Margaret agrees to rent Natham a certain home until Margaret finds a buyer.

3) Substantial performance doctrine [실질적 이행 원칙]

A. works only to excuse buildings & CONSTRUCTION Ks.
건설관련 계약에서만 적용되는 원칙

B. If there has been GF effort to comply with the K and there has been substantial performance, then the performance is satisfied, although the deviations are minor breach of the K.
계약의 일방 당사자가 중요하지 않은 계약부분을 위반하였더라도 신의성실원칙에 입각하여 계약의 중요한 본질적인 부분을 이행하여 계약의 원래목적을 달성하였다면 그 당사자는 상대방에게 계약을 이행하라고 할 수 있다는 원칙.

EX The defendant learned that some of the pipe, instead of being made in Reading, was Cohoes piping. The Defendant asked the plaintiff via the architect to do the work all over again supported by the perfect tender rule. Because the pipes had already been encased within the walls except in a few places where it had to be exposed, to replace the Cohoes Pipe with the contracted for Reading Pipe would have meant more than the substitution of other pipe. Plaintiff would have had to demolish at great expense of substantial parts of the completed structure. The plaintiff left the work untouched, and asked for a certificate that the final payment was due (arguing substantial performance). Jacob & Youngs v. Kent(1921)

25 Discharge of Contract

〈개념정리〉

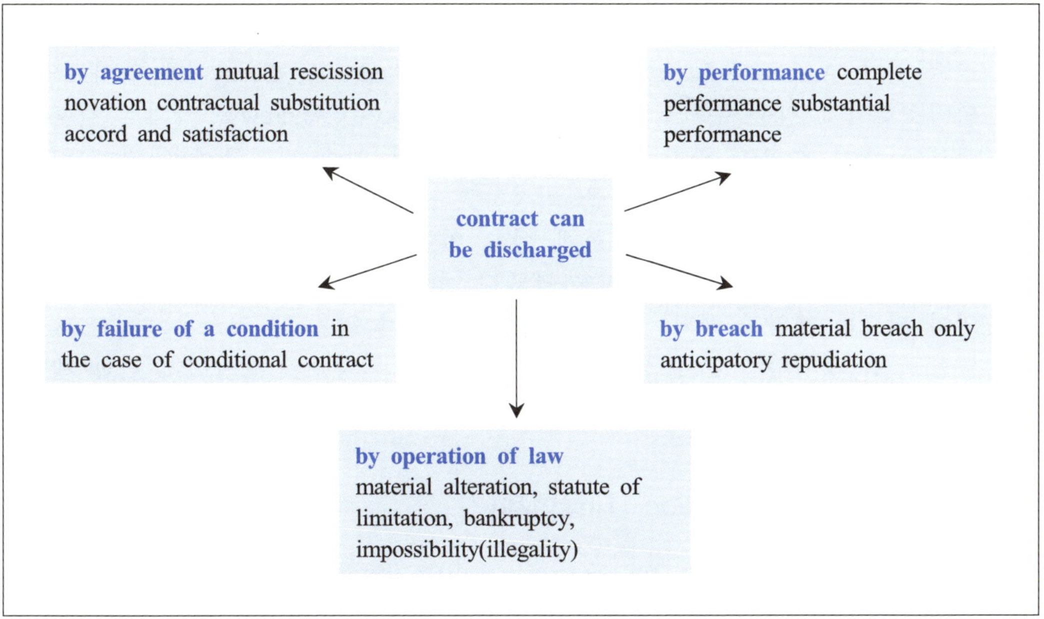

1) Both parties may mutually agree to rescind K.

계약의 합의해제 : 계약을 해제하면 당사자들은 원상회복의무를 부담한다.

2) Novation[更契 계약당사자 갱신]

An agreement between both parties to an existing K to the substitution of a new party. It excuses the contracted performance of the party who is replaced.

EX Tom purchases Jane's land and assumes her mortgage with the Bank. Jane, the original mortgagor, is still liable unless a novation has occurred.

EX Susan contracts to build a house for John, but then gets a more profitable job to construct a building for Tom. Susan asks John if it is okay to substitute Jack to build the house. The parties agree to substitute Jack and release Susan. ➡ novation

3) Contractual substitution

EX 유부남인 Andrew가 새로운 여자친구 Cathy를 만나 그녀의 집으로 들어가 살기로 하면서, Andrew와 Becky는 이혼을 하였다. Andrew는 Becky에게 위자료와 생활비조로 1억 원을 주기로 합의했고, 대신 Becky는 Andrew를 상대로 결혼파탄 사유에 대한 소송을 하지 않기로 했다. 그런데 Andrew는 Becky에게 차일피일 미루며 위자료와 생활비 지급을 거절하였다. 그러자 Becky는 자신이 못 받을 위자료와 생활비를 대신하여 현재 살고 있는 집(소유주는 Andrew의 이름으로 되어있음)을 대상으로 전세계약을 맺었다. 즉, Becky가 세입자로 Andrew가 집주인이 되도록 계약을 맺되, 전세금은 Becky가 1억 원을 낸 것으로 하는 그런 계약을 맺은 것이다. ➡ 이 경우 실제 원 계약은 위자료와 생활비에 관한 계약이었지만, Andrew와 Becky의 합의에 의해 전세계약으로 계약 대체가 된 것이다.

4) Accord and Satisfaction [대물변제]

A mutual consent to discharge the obligation and fulfillment of the legal consideration which binds the parties to the agreement. For example, a satisfaction agreed upon between a debtor and payee

EX1 If a debtor tenders a check in the amount of $5,000 marked "payment in full" and if the debtor honestly contends that he only properly owes $5,000, the tender of a check in this amount, if accepted, could establish an accord and satisfaction.

EX2 A widow has an automobile accident but is mentally unable to cope with a lawsuit because her husband has just died. She gratefully accepts the offer of a close family friend to talk to the other driver, who has been threatening a lawsuit. The friend convinces the other driver that both drivers are at fault to some extent. The friend offers to pay the other driver $500 in damages in exchange for a written statement that he will not make any claim against the widow for damages resulting from the accident. The family friend and the other driver each sign a copy of the statement for the other, and when the payment is made, the accord and satisfaction is complete. If the other driver then sues the widow for more money on account of the accident, the widow could show that she agreed to let his friend negotiate an accord and satisfaction, and the court would deny relief.

5) by Objectively Serious Changes of circumstances(serious impracticability) or by performance becoming objectively illegal or impossible(illegality or impossibility).
이행이 객관적으로 불가능하게 해지거나 불법이 되는 경우

But mere fact of performance becoming more costly or less profitable does not excuse performance.
그러나 약간 비용부담이 많아지거나 수익성이 떨어진다고 해서 계약이행을 중단해서는 안된다.

6) By Breach of K[BOK]

계약의 일방이 계약을 심각하게 위반한 경우 상대방은 계약상의 의무를 면하게 된다.

7) Anticipatory Repudiation(anticipatory breach)先行的 履行拒絶

AR is a statement that the repudiating party will not perform made prior to the time that performance was due.

EX Sculptor Laura contracts with Mayor Han on Jan 1st to deliver a complete torso of Mayor Han by Jan 30th for $100,000. But Laura changed her mind after receiving a Jan. 15th order from President Lee who asked her to complete his torso by Jan 29th for $500,000. Laura repudiates her contract with Mayor Han on Jan 16th by telling him unequivocally and positively that she would never be able to complete Mayor Han's torso by Jan 30th. Under this situation, Mayor Han can

① sue without waiting for the time of performance; 즉시소송
② wait for the performance date to sue(i.e. waiting until Jan. 30th); 만기까지 기다리거나
③ rescind the contract; or 계약취소 혹은
④ attempt to cure the breach(i.e. hire another sculptor) and sue Laura. 소송 및 계약위반에 따른 해결책 강구 가능.

A. The AR must be positive and unequivocal. An expression as to future inability to perform is not breach by repudiation. 확정적인 의사표시(express and unequivocal indication)가 아니고, 막연하게 돈을 더 올려 달란다거나 하는 경우에는 AR이 성립안된다.

EX 집짓기로 계약해서 진행 중에 건축업자가 비용을 더 올려달라고 하는 것은 merely asked for more money for its Performance .

注意 1 | Prospective inability to perform(막연하게 일을 못하게 될 것 같은 경우)은 anticipatory repudiation과는 다르다.

注意 2 | Remedy for AR under the CL : 일반적인 계약위반으로 보아 상대방(aggrieved party)은 계약을 즉시 취소하거나, 손해배상을 청구하거나, 합리적 기간 동안 이행을 거절한 자가 마음을 바꾸는 것을 기다리는 방법이 있다.

EX John agrees to convey and Mary agrees to pay for the land on April 1st. On Feb 1, Mary learns that John has already sold the land to Tom. Mary can sue before April 1st, or she may wait and sue on April 1st.

注意 3 | Remedy for AR under the UCC : Upon the ground of insecurity, the aggrieved party may demand adequate assurance.
UCC에서는 AR에 대한 통보를 받고 불안할 경우 확고한 이행보장(adequate assurance)을 요구할 수 있다

26 Remedies.

〈개념정리〉

<table>
<tr><td colspan="5">remedies</td></tr>
<tr><td colspan="3">at law</td><td colspan="2">in equity</td></tr>
<tr><td colspan="3">compensatory damages
(for money damages)</td><td>injunction(injunction al relief)</td><td>specific performance</td></tr>
<tr><td>disputed damages</td><td>undisputed damages
=
liquidated damage</td><td>punitive damages =
exemplary damages</td><td>Ex. temporary restraining order; entry ban; departure ban</td><td>applicable for highly unusual and unique goods; for real property transactions;</td></tr>
</table>

1) Damages

A. Money damages(compensatory damages손해배상)

(1) actual damages 실제 발생한 손해

(2) Foreseeable damages 예측 가능한 손해

(3) Mitigation duty : Non-breaching party has a duty to mitigate the damages.

EX Jack contracts to fix Mary's car. After Jack begins work, Mary breaches and says "Stop."Jack cannot continue to work and incur more costs, for example by putting in more parts and labor.

B. Punitive damages [징벌적 손해배상]Monetary compensation awarded to an injured party that goes beyond that which is necessary to compensate the individual for losses and that is intended to punish the wrongdoer. Punitive damages, also known as exemplary damages, may be awarded by the trier of fact (a jury or a judge) in addition to actual damages, which compensate a plaintiff for the losses suffered due to the harm caused by the defendant. Punitive damages are a way of punishing the defendant in a civil lawsuit and are based on the theory that the interests of society and the individual harmed can be met by imposing additional damages on the defendant.

Punitive damages are generally not allowed in K law. 고의적 불법행위에만 적용되고 계약법에서는 일반적으로 적용하지 않는다.

C. Liquidated damages [손해배상액의 약정] = disputed damages

(1) Agreed-upon provision in a K to set the amount of damages in advance if breach occurs. 계약위반에 대비하여 손해배상액을 상호합의에 의하여 미리 계약서에 정해두는 것.

(2) Not enforceable if punitive 징벌적 약정조항은 적용곤란하다. 손해배상액은 합리적인 수준에 한하여야 한다.

(3) For the sale of goods under UCC, if K has no provision for liquidated damages, seller may retain deposit up to $500 when defaults.

2) Equity

A. Injuction(금지명령)

an equitable remedy in the form of a court order, whereby a party is required to do, or to refrain from doing, certain acts. The party that fails to adhere to the injunction faces civil or criminal penalties and may have to pay damages or accept sanctions for failing to follow the court's order. In some cases, breaches of injunctions are considered serious criminal offences that merit arrest and possible prison sentences

B. Specific performance(특정이행 명령)

An order of the court which requires a party to perform a specific act, usually what is stated in a contract. While specific performance can be in the form of any type of forced action, it is usually used to complete a previously established transaction, thus being the most effective remedy in protecting the expectation interest of the innocent party to a contract.

Equitable remedies such as specific performance and injunctional relief are available only when

① There is a valid contract,
② The conditions are satisfied,
③ The legal remedy is inadequate
④ Mutuality of remedy exists(i.e. each party of the contract would have a right to enforce it should occasions arise)

27 Statute of Limitation [SOL제소기간의 경과 = 소멸시효]

1) Bars suits if not brought within statutory period.

SOL 이란 법정 기간 내에 소송을 제기하지 않으면 그 이후로는 소송을 제기할 수 없도록 하는 것

2) SOL begins to run from the time when the cause of action (e.g. breach) accrues. 계약위반이 발생하는 순간부터 SOL이 적용된다.

CL와UCC의 차이(개념정리)

	CL	UCC	Remarks
applied to	land, services, etc.	Goods[tangible and movable]	
definiteness	Must contain all the material terms on STOPPP(subject, timing of performance, price, participants(parties)	UCC gap-filler rule(additional terms ok for open Delivery, Price, Time, quantity) Exception: Requirement K, output K.	
Delivery method	Mail Box Rule	Same method, Similar method, or Reasonable method	
Delivery of performance	Perfect tender(exact performance, mirror image rule)	1) perfect tender among non-merchants 2) non-conforming goods acceptable among merchants	
K modification	New consideration necessary	good faith will be sufficient. additional terms in the acceptance are part of the contract unless : - The offer expressly limits the acceptance to the terms in the offer The acceptance requires acceptance of the additional terms - The offeror does not object to the additional terms, or - The additional terms materially alter the contract	
Irrevocable offers	Option K	IMFO(irrevocable merchant firm offer)	
Counteroffer	Acceptance must be a mirror image offer. Otherwise counteroffer rejects and terminates the offer	1) Ok if not materially alter the terms of the offer 2) OK if offeror does not object within reasonable time after reviewing the acceptance	
Acceptance by silence	No contract is formed	K formed unless it is objected within reasonable period of time	

Chapter 2

Sales of Goods

In order to determine if CL or UCC applies, look at what is the
CL와 UCC 중 어느 것이 적용될지 여부에 대해서는

- Predominant factor 중요한 요소
- Gravamen of the injury [i.e. was P injured by the service or the good] 불평원인
- Broker = service even if finds buyer for seller's goods 중개인 여부 등을 보고 파악한다.

1) Definition of Goods and the Application of the UCC

A. goods = tangible and movable property[有形動産]

The sales of goods do not include sales of investment securities, accounts receivable, K rights, artworks, copyrights, or patents. 유가증권, 어음, 계약상의 권리, 예술작품, 저작권, 특허 등은 UCC 가 적용되지 않는다.

B. Article 2 of the UCC is applicable for the contracts for the sales of goods while CL generally applies to Ks for services and land transactions.

상품(goods)매매계약에서는 UCC 2조가 적용되는 것을 원칙으로 하며 UCC에 정해진 바가 없으면 CL가 적용된다.

2) Definiteness

A. Under CL, an Offer shall be definite and clear about STOPP[subject matter, time of performance, price,and participants].

Under UCC, however, open terms[missing terms] OK.

UCC 에서는 definite and certain요건이 없어져 계약이행기간이 분명하게 명시되지 않아도 된다.

3) Delivery Method, Price, and Time

Under UCC, open delivery, open price, open time[duration] ok, only if supported by good faith. 즉 D.P.T가 명시되지 않아도 계약이 성립될 수 있다.

4) Merchant

A. A Merchant is …

A Merchant is defined as someone who
① regularly deals in goods of the kind at issue
② holds out to have special knowledge about the goods. 상인이란 특정상품을 정기적으로 취급하고, 해당상품에 대해 전문지식을 갖고 있다고 내세우는 사람이다.

B. UCC applies whether the sale is between consumers or merchants. But be always careful about the deals involving merchants. 일반적으로 상품에 관한 거래는 UCC가 적용되는 것이 원칙이나, 상인에 관한 거래는 예외조항이 많으므로 주의를 요함.

C. Irrevocable Merchant's Firm Offer (IMFO Rule, UCC2-205) : Offer for sale of goods cannot be revoked for a reasonable time up to 3 months, if supported by signed written promise "to keep offer open" by a merchant.

〈개념정리〉

 IMFO rule

An offer by

① merchant to buy or sell

② goods in a

③ signed writing which by its terms give

④ assurance that it will be held open

⑤ revocation is impossible for lack of consideration. binding even without consideration
Merchant가 상품매매에 대하여 서명된 문서로 offer를 하면서 일정기간동안 청약이 유효하다고 명시하는 경우에는 그 기간동안(3개월이내)에는 청약을 철회할 수 없다.

〈개념정리〉

CL option K	Unenforceable without consideration, if without consideration, it is revocable (the language does not prevent the promisor from revoking the offer) 장사들 간이 아니고, goods도 아니고 consideration이 없다면 취소안하겠다고 했어도 취소가능
IMFO	Enforceable without consideration. → irrevocable

1 Acceptance

1) Additionalterms to K

<Mirror Image Rule v.s. Additional Terms>

A. Mirror image rule[CL] - additional words kill the K unless supported by separate

Consideration. CL에서는 mirror image rule에 따라 추가조건이 있으면 별도의 consideration이 있지 않는 한 계약이 소멸된다.

B. Under UCC 2-207, for the sale of goods among the merchants, additional terms in the acceptance are included in the contract unless
   (1) the additional terms are material change
   (2) the offer expressly limits acceptance to the terms of the offer
   (3) the offeror objects within a reasonable time.
   UCC에서는 원래 original offer랑 약간 달라도 상인들끼리의 sale of goods에 관한 것이라면 심각한 변화, 명백한 조건제한, 합리적 시간 내에 이루어지진 것이라면 추가조건을 허용한다.

<MBR v.s. SSR Methods>

C. Mail box rule[CL] - 발송주의

D. If acceptance is made by <u>specific</u> method in the offer or the <u>same</u> method used by the offeror, the acceptance is valid when sent under the CL. Acceptance is also valid when dispatched if <u>reasonable</u> method used in the UCC.
Offeror가 정한 구체적 방법이나 Offeror가 정한 동일한 방법으로 acceptance를 하거나 UCC상의 합리적인 방법이라면 유효.

2 Nonconforming Goods

1) Perfect Tender Rule : Under the CL, perfect tender is required[Mirror image rule]

CL에서는 완전일치 원칙

Under the UCC, the general rule also requires perfect tender if among non-merchants.
상인간이 아닌 일반인의 경우에도 완전일치 원칙

If seller sends[ships] <u>nonconforming goods</u>, acceptance & breach[general rule]불일치

상품을 보내면 발송과 동시에 계약 성립, 수령, 및 계약위반

일반인이 주문한 것이라면 거부가능. 즉 must가 아니고 may reject가 된다.

상인들 간에는 additional terms는 must accept이다.

2) K modification

A. Under the CL, new consideration is required on both sides for modification.

B. Under the UCC, good faith is required for modification without consideration. UCC에서는 consideration이 없더라도 GF만 있으면 가능하다.

C. 기본적으로 상품판매에 관한 계약수정은 형식에 별로 구애받지 않는다.

EX 볼펜 500자루를 보험업자 전국대회에 납품하기로 했는데 사정상 400 자루만 납품하기로 서로 구두로 합의한 경우 ➡ 문제없음.

D. UCC2-209 : If the original K must have been in writing, then the modification must ALSO be in writing. 주의 : 2-209 : 만일 원래의 계약이 서면으로 되어있다면, 계약내용의 수정도 서면으로 이루어져야 한다 ➡ 현재 이 규정은 거의 사문화 되었음.

흔히 "전화로 수정하기로 동의했다(agreed to modify by telephone)" 나 "구두로 수정하기로 동의했다(orally agreed to modify)"등의 문구를 넣어 오답을 유도하므로 주의할 것

〈개념정리〉

oral	written
telephone, tell, dial, speak, say 등의 문구가 온다.	fax, telex, telegram, e-mail, mail, post, dispatch, send, text message 등의 문구가 온다.
Question : 만일 레이져 광선으로 상대방에게 offer나 acceptance를 보냈다면?	

3) Cure

A Seller who fails to make a perfect tender will be given an option of curing. 2 situations:

A. Time for performance has not yet expired - seller is not obligated to try again but may cure to avoid being sued for breach 만기 전에 위반사실이 발견된 경우

B. Time for performance has expired in limited situation. ➡ a seller has an option of curing even after the K delivery date 만기 이후에 라도 특별히 cure를 해주어야 할 사정이 있는 경우

(1) The rule of perfect tender is softened by the rules allowing the S to cure the defect by giving reasonable notice of an intention to cure and making a new tender of conforming goods within the time originally provided for performance 고치겠다는 의향을 전달해야 한다, 약속 기일 내에 고치겠다는 의향을 전달 안하면 계약위반인 것이다.

(2) Where the buyer rejects a tender that the S reasonably believed would be acceptable with or without money allowance, the seller, upon reasonable notification to the buyer, has a further reasonable time beyond the original K time within which to make a conforming tender. ➡ therefore the buyer may reject the goods delivered, but s/he MUST give the seller an opportunity to cure 고칠 합리적인 시간을 가질 권리가 생겨난다 ➡ 고칠 시간을 줘야 한다.

注意| 다가오는 일요일 오후 1시에 파티가 있을 예정이어서 3시까지 농심 라면 1,000개를 배달해주면 1,000달러 주겠다고 식당주인 A가 슈퍼마켓 주인B에게 연락

① B가 배달업자 C를 시켜서 농심라면700개와 삼양라면 300개를 배달 ➠ A는 reject한 후 breach로 B를 sue 할 수 있나? ➠ Yes! B의 행위는 acceptance of the order(offer)and breach

② B가 배달업자 C를 시켜서 농심라면700개와 삼양라면 300개를 배달하면서 쪽지를 보냄. '농심라면 재고가 부족해서 삼양라면 300개를 대신 보내니, 이를 대신 받으면 좋겠다. 가격은 동일하다'
➠ A는 reject한 후 breach로 B를 sue 할 수 있나?
➠ No! B의 행위는 counteroffer
➠ A는 accept하거나 reject할 수 있다. reject하더라도 no additional remedy

상기 두 가지 사례의 차이점을 잘 알고 있어야 한다. Offer에 명시된 것과는 다른 wrong good을 shipment한 경우,

☞ 아무런 설명 없이 wrong good을 shipment했다면 offer에 대한 acceptance와 동시에 성립된 계약조건에 관한 breach가 된다(상기 첫번째 사례).

☞ 관련하여, 위 사례에서와 같이 농심라면 700개와 삼양라면300개를 배달한 경우, 농심라면 700개에 대하여는 정당한 계약이행이 성립하는가? No, 전체에 대한 breach 성립.

3 Product Liability

〈개념정리〉

Warranty of title	Express warranty	Implied warranty (by the merchants only)
① must be free from lien, theft, and other encumbrances related with the ownership	① affirmation flowing from the free will of the seller	① implied warranty of merchantability for general ordinary purpose
② cannot be disclaimed by the wordings such as "as is."	② can be disclaimed by the wordings such as "as is" and it may become the basis of bargain	② implied warranty of fitness for particular purpose
	③ Limitations on consequential damages for personal injuries are presumed to be unconscionable if consumer goods.	

1) Warranties of Title

A. Seller warrants good title, rightful transfer, and freedom from any security interest, infringement, or lien about which the buyer has no knowledge or has no reason to know.
매도인이 상품을 판매할 경우 유효한 소유권(good title), 정당한 이전(rightful transfer)이 가능하며, 담보나 법률위반 등에 걸리지 않는 다는 것[즉 buyer가 알지 못하는 불법사항은 없다] 을 warrant해야 함.

B. Can not be disclaimed only by specific language such as "as is." "as is"등과 같은 용어로 warranty of title의무를 피해갈 수 없다.

2) Express warranty (written or oral)

A. An affirmation of fact or promise made

(1) by the seller to the buyer

(2) relating to the goods that

B. Becomes part of the basis of the bargain(UCC2-313)

(1) sales talks, puffing, or sales opinion do not create warranty. 상인들의 과장광고는 해당되지 않는다.

(2) does not require buyer's reliance
Buyer가 굳이 믿고 의존하지 않아도 된다.

(3) Intent to create warranty does not matter.
Intent는 warranty와는 상관없다.

(4) Seller may be a merchant or non-merchant. 판매자는 상인일 수도 아닐 수도 있다.

3) Implied Warranty

[발생요건 : seller가 merchant이어야 한다]

A. Implied Warranty of merchantability for general ordinary purpose

The sellers who are also merchants guarantee that goods are fit for ordinary purpose and that goods are properly packaged and labled. 상인이 제품이 만들어진 통상적인 목적에 부합하고, 제대로 포장 및 레이블이 되었다는warranty.

B. Implied Warranty of Fitness for particular purpose

The seller knows of the particular purpose for which the goods are required and further knows that the buyer relies on his skills and knowledge.
판매자가 제품이 판매되는 목적을 정확히 알고 있고, 특히 상대방이 자신의 기술과 지식에 의존하고 있다는 것을 아는 경우

EX When Jennifer went to Sherwin-Williams Painter's shop, she asked John, the salesperson in the shop, to select a paint that would protect the dining table from getting wet on a rainy day.

C. can be extended to a buyer's family and also guests in the home who may be reasonably expected to use and/or be affected by the goods and who are injured.

EX 딸의 집에 간 친정어머니가 식기세척기를 사용하던 중에 오작동으로 인하여 고급영국산 식기가 모두 깨져버린 경우 친정어머니도 seller를 상대로 소송제기 가능하다.

4) Disclaimer(담보책임의 면책조항)

A. warranty of title can be disclaimed only by specific language, but cannot e disclaimed by the term "as is."

EX Seller가 $500 물건을 buyer에게 "hot stuff"이라면서 $10에게 팔 경우(즉, 훔친 것임을 암시) 이런 내용을 서면으로 설명해둘 경우 seller는 warranty of title책임을 지지 못한다.

B. Express Warranty

(1) "as is" 또는 " with faults" 등의 흠결을 나타내는 문구를 그대로 두고 판매해도 가능함.

EX 광고에서 실제물품은 샘플과 약간 다를 수도 있습니다.

(2) 서면이나 구두(written or oral)로도 가능함.

(3) buyer's inspecton opportunity가 있었는지, 혹은 검사권한을 포기한 적이 있었는지 여부도 담보책임의 기준이 된다.

C. Limitations on consequential damages for personal injuries are presumed to be unconscionable if consumer goods. 만약 소비제품을 사용하다가 다친 것 (personal injuries)에 대해 제조회사가 면책을 주장하려 하거나 자신들의 책임 한계를 제한하려 하는 것은 unconscionable하므로 무효이다.

4 Torts

Any wrongdoing for which an action for damages may be brought.

EX negligence, strict liability, intentional torts

1) Negligence

definition : careless act or omission that causes harm to another and for which the law entitles the injured party to compensation

EX ⓐ failing to provide adequate warning about the dangers in a product

ⓑ giving negligent professional advice such as in the case of an accountant, doctor, engineer or lawyer

ⓒ injuries caused to a plaintiff by the careless driving of the defendant's delivery driver

ⓓ in the case of bar owners, serving alcohol to intoxicated persons who later injure themselves or others due to their state of drunkness.

2) Elements to prove Negligence

A. Duty of reasonable care [합리적인 주의의무]

B. Breach of the duty[의무위반] insufficient instruction

C. Causation[인과관계]

D. Damages or injuries[손해 또는 상해]

3) Privity of K is not required because the suit is not based on the K. Torts상의 negligence책임을 묻게 될 때 직접적인 계약상의 privity는 불필요하다.

One sure sign of the personal nature of contracts is that no one but one of the parties can go to court and enforce the contract even if the contract was to operate to a third party's benefit. This is known as the "privity of contract" rule

Today, however, if you buy a toaster and it blows up, your injured neighbor who is over for breakfast can sue the manufacturer, though she is not in privity of contract with the manufacturer.

4) Defense to Negligence Charges.

The two most common defense in a N actions are contributory N and assumption of risk.

A. Contributory N where plaintiffs totally barred since he helped cause accident. [기여과실] 원고도 잘못이 있어 사고유발에 도움이 되었을 경우, 보상못받는다는 원칙

B. Comparative N - if P is guilty of any fault jury assigns percentages. [비교과실]원고의 잘못이 일부 있어도 비례책임을 묻는 원칙

5 Strict Liability

1) 엄격책임의 대상

원래는 ultrahazardous activity(Ex. 폭약, 독극물 등)과 inherently vicious animal(예. 맹견) 과 서비스업종인 Common carrier(운송업자), innkeeper(숙박업자)등 이 고객의 물건에 입힌 손해에 대해 예외적으로 인정했으나 최근 들어 제조물제조업자

(manufacturer)와 판매업자(commercial distributor)에게도 그 범위가 확대되어 고객보호에 치중.

> • Landmark Case : *Grimshaw v. Ford Motor Co.*
>
> The California Court of Appeals held that Ford was guilty on every issue in the appeal. Top officials of Ford were found guilty of not taking possible injuries or death to users of their vehicles into account when deciding to install bladders at a cost of $20.9 million

2) Common carriers are allowed to limit liability to dollar amount specified in the K. **운송업자는 엄격책임의 대상이 되기는 하지만 자신의 책임한도를 계약서에 정할 수 있다.**

3) Elements of SL

A. Strict duty applicable by the operation of law to sellers, manufacturers, lessor, etc.

(1) 제조업자, 판매자, 리스업자 등에게

(2) 법규에 의해 부과되는 엄격한 의무

B. Breach of such duty :

- products were ① defective when sold and
  제품이 판매되는 순간부터 이미 defective한 상태이었으며
  ② the product reached the consumer without serious changes.
  심각한 변경상태 없이 소비자에게 도달.

C. Actual and proximate causation of Plaintiff's injuries
인과관계

D. Damages to the P's person or property

The defect was unreasonably dangerous to the plaintiff for ① design defect, ② manufacturing defect, & ③ inadequate warning defect. 디자인, 제조, 경고상의 defect를 이유

Q

McDonald가게에서 뜨거운 커피를 쏟아 화상을 입은 할머니가 McDonald가게를 상대로 소송을 제기한 사건은 SL요건에 충족될까?

McDonalds had a "reasonable and customary" responsibility to provide safe products. In this case, a liquid that is not so hot that it can cause life-threatening injuries (if she drank coffee that hot, it could have caused death). McDonald's breached that duty be heating their coffee to a high temperature. The coffee temperature, as it was served, directly caused that amount of damage. The damages were actual : 2nd & 3rd degree burns to the legs & groin.

注意 | **e) Defense to SL**

SL로 문제를 제기하면, negligence(comparative negligence, contributory negligence), disclaimer등은 해당사항 없으니 답안에서 먼저 지우고 다른 답안을 찾아보라. 그러나 Assumption of risk 와 product misuse등은 defense가 될 수 있다.

Transfer of Property Rights.

1) Good faith purchaser or good faith purchaser for value

definition : a good faith purchaser is a purchaser who gives value for an asset in good faith and without knowledge of adverse claims called also good faith purchaser for value. If a party having voidable title transfers goods to a good faith purchaser for value, the latter obtains good title. 돈을 제대로 지불한 (for value)선의의 구매자(good faith purchaser)는 voidable title을 취득한 경우에도 유효한 소유권(good title)을 취득가능.

- Abel took his malfunctioning notebook computer to Del's computer sales and repair shop in Bloomington for repair. Del told Abel it would take a week to repair the computer.
- Before the week was up, Del sold the computer to Charlie, who came into Del''s shop looking for a good used computer for a reasonable price and had no reason to suspect that the computer was only for repair in the shop
- When Charlie attempted to pawn the computer, a routine check disclosed that it was reported stolen.
- Abel has demanded return of the computer.
- Charlie comes to you to determine his legal rights.

Question : Is Charlie a good faith purchaser for value?

2) Examples of **voidable title.**

A. goods paid for with a check subsequently dishonored

B. goods obtained by fraud, mistake, duress, or undue influence

C. goods obtained from minors.

D. Stolen product's owner(e.g. thief) does not have a voidable title, but void title.

7 Entrustment(위탁)

1) If a person entrusts possession of goods to a merchant, who deals in the same goods, a good-faith purchaser for value obtains title to these goods, unless there s/he has a knowledge or a reason to know that this merchant does not own the goods.

만일 특정해당상품을 취급하는 상인에게 어떤 사람이 물건을 위탁하였다면, good-faith 에 입각하여 정당한 가격을 지불하고 산 다른 사람은 해당 물건에 대한 title을 갖게 된다. 단, 선의의 구매자가 해당 상품이 그 상인의 것이 아니라는 것을 알았거나, 알만한 이유가 있을 때는 예외로 한다.

2) The person who entrusted the goods to the merchant can recover only monetary damages from the merchant. **또한 그 물건을 위탁한 원소유주(original owner)는 상인으로부터 금전적인 손해배상만 청구가능하다.**

8 Passage of Title through confirmation of existence and identification

1) Passage of title cannot take place until goods exist and have been identified.

있지도 않은 물건을 팔수는 없다.

해리포터의 작가 조앤 K 롤링은 앞으로 3년뒤 새로운 해리포터의 연작물을 쓰기로 결심했는데 이를 들은 TOY 제작사에서 롤링의 새로운 소설이 완성된 뒤 1년 이내에 소설에 근거한 미니어처 장난감을 만들기로 결정함.

한편 TOY 제작사는 TOY'RUS 장난감 백화점에 미니어처 장난감을 미리 입도선매하지 않겠냐며 제안을 한 뒤에 백화점 측으로부터 돈을 받을 경우 장난감의 title은? 장난감이 완성되어 생겨날 때까지는 Passage of title이 이루어지지 않는다. 또한 장난감이 다 제작되어 탄생될 때까지는 TOY 제작사는 돈 받을 권리를 제3자에게 이전양도할 수도 없다. **an assignment of future rights to arise from future contracts[즉 현재 있지도 않은 계약에 대해서는 미래양도 불가**

1) Whether justified or not, if a buyer rejects the goods shipped or if a buyer makes a justified revocation of acceptance, the title reverts to the seller.

정당한 이유로 거부한 게 받아들여지면 또는 Buyer가 수령을 거부하면 정당성여부를 떠나 물건의 title은 Seller에게 되돌아간다.

9 Risk of Loss(손실부담)

definition : Probability that one will have to bear the costs associated with a damage, destruction, injury, or an inability to locate documents, goods, or other property.

Risk of Loss arises after the K has been performed but before Buyer receives the goods, the goods are damaged or destroyed & neither the Buyer or the Seller is to blame

계약이행과정에서 buyer가 물건을 인수하기 전에 물건이 손상(damages)되었고, buyer나 seller모두 책임이 없을 경우, 누가 손실(loss)을 부담해야 하는가에 관한 문제이다.

注意| Risk of loss(손실부담)을 누가 질 것인가 하는 문제는 물건에 대한 title과는 무관하다. Breach가 일어났는지 안일어났는지가 중요하다.

Mitigating Duty : Aggrieved (or non-breaching) party's obligation to make reasonable efforts to limit additional losses, after a damaging event (or a breach of contract) has occurred. Failure in this duty may prevent the aggrieeved party from obtaining compensation for avoidable losses. In insurance contracts, Claimant must take all reasonable steps to minimize their losses. And the. Plaintiff cannot accumulate losses.

- *Flewelling v. Blue Cross Life Ins. Co. of Canada.*

Claimant unable to return to work due to chronic fatigue. Claimant refused treatment. Award damages only to the point in time that the Court finds the Plaintiff's symptoms would have been resolved had she followed medical advice

EX 만일 물품전달을 by train으로 하기로 계약을 했는데 철도종사자들의 총파업으로 인하여 seller가 트럭으로 물건을 전달할 경우 이를 buyer는 거부할 수 없다. 또한 seller는 철도총파업을 이유로 가만히 앉아있어서는 안된다.

1) FOB Contracts

<u>**A. FOB seller's place of business or FOB Shipping Point**</u>-if the seller ship the goods in the manner provided in section 2-504 and bear the expense and risk of putting them into the possession of the carrier, the risk in such **a case passes to the buyer when** the goods are duly **delivered to the carrier**.

FOB판매자 주소 조건에서는 매도자가 운송기관(carrier)에게만 물건을 가져다주면 그 다음은 buyer책임이다. 즉 제조업체가 물건을 만들어 선박에 싣기만 하면, 설령 배가 난파되어도 매수인 책임이다.

B. **FOB buyer's place of business or FOB Destination Point**-the seller is responsible at his own risk and expense for tendering conforming goods to the buyer at the named destination in the K. ➡ **The risk of loss does not pass until the goods are tendered to the buyer** at the named destination.

FOB 매수인 주소 조건에서는 매도자가 목적지에 있는 매수인의 주소에까지 안전하게 전달해야만 한다. 즉, 제조업체가 물건을 만들어 선박에 실어 보낸 뒤 난파가 되면 제조업체가 책임을 져야한다.

2) If shipping terms are **not specified,** then the seller generally discharges his obligation to the buyer only if the seller ① **make the conforming goods available to the buyer's disposition** and ② giving the buyer the reasonable notice to enable the buyer to take possession and accepts.

선적방법이 명시되어있지 않은 경우 conforming goods를 buyer가 가져갈 수 있도록 준비한 다음 이 사실을 적절하게 통지만 하면 매도인의 의무는 소멸된다.

3) Non-Carrier Case

A. Agreement of the parties controls 별도의 합의문이 있는지 여부를 확인하고,

B. ROL passes upon delivery of document of title. 소유권을 나타내는 문서**(document of title)가 있는 경우, 문서양도가 이루어질 때 ROL도 따라간다.**

C. Breach - **breaching party** is liable for any uninsured loss even though breach is unrelated to the problem 잘못한 측이 책임을 져야 한다.

4) Merchant or No-Merchant

A. ROL shifts from a merchant seller to the buyer on the buyer's receipt of goods. 상인이 물건을 팔 경우 매입자가 확실히 물건을 잡아야 **(physical possession)** 손실위험이 이전이 된다.

B. If non-merchant Seller, ROL shifts when he tenders the goods. Tender meaning seller has made the goods available to the buyer(UCC2-319) 상인이 아닌 사람이 물건을 팔 경우, 매도인이 판매를 하는 시점(made available)에 ROL이 이전된다.

"made available"이라는 용어대신 "tendered delivery"등의 용어를 사용하기도 하므로 주의할 것

5) Sale or return contract (SORK)§ 2-326

Under the UCC where delivered goods may be returned by the seller even though they conform to the K. The transaction is a sale or return K if the goods are delivered primarily for resale. (주목적이 매수인이 다른 고객에게 되파는 것(resale)이며 팔다가 다 못 팔 경우 매도인에게 반환가능)

The **ROL passes to the buyer after s/he takes delivery**. If the goods are returned to the seller, the risk remains on the buyer while the goods are in transit. 매도인에게 반환되는 동안 매수인이 위험부담.

6) Sale on approval contract (SOAK)§ 2-326

Goods held on approval are not subject to the claims of the buyer's creditors until acceptance : Seller는 잠재적인 매수인에게 상품을 보내고 이를 매수인이 사용해 본 뒤 마음에 들지 않으면 반환할 수 있는 계약.

The ROL on seller until Buyer accepts the goods.

매수인이 물건을 accept할 때까지 seller책임이다.

7) Cash against delivery(CAD), collection on delivery, or collection against delivery (COD) 현금박치기 거래

Buyer has **no right to inspect** the goods until payment is made. Buyer has **the right to reject the nonconforming goods** after the payment. COD조건으로 물품을 매입한자는 대금을 지급하기 전에는 상품을 검사하거나 인도받을 수 없지만, 만일 대금지불 후 상품인수한 뒤 nonconforming goods인 것이 밝혀질 경우 수령을 거절할 수 있다.

8) UN Convention on Contracts for the International Sales of Goods

국제상품거래에 관한 UN 협약에 따르면, 매도인이 운송을 위해 첫 번째 운송업자(first carrier)에게 상품을 인도하는 순간 ROL이 매수인에게 이전된다.

 SOL[statute of limitation, 소멸시효, 시효기간]

A statute of limitations is a statute that sets forth the maximum period of time, after certain events, that legal proceedings based on those events may be initiated.

1) **SOL for sale of goods is 4 years** and any action for breach must be commenced within this period.

법정기간이 4년 이내에 소송을 제기하지 않으면 그 이후로는 소송을 제기할 수 없다. 4년 내에 소송을 시작하기만 하면 되고, 소송이 4년 내에 종료될 필요는 없다.

2) SOL begins running when the BOK(breach of the contract) occurs. 계약위반이 되는 순간부터 SOL은 적용된다. 계약위반을 발견하는 순간(Not the discovery of breach)이 아니라는 점에서 주의할 것.

3) Parties may agree to reduce **not less than one year**, but may not extend it over four years. SOL을 합의에 의해 4년 이하로 줄일 수는 있지만 1년 미만으로는 줄일 수 없고, 4년 이상으로 연장할 수도 없다.

11 Remedies

1) Seller's Remedies

A. Right to cure the nonconformity : nonconformity에 대한 치유권을 seller는 갖고 있으며 nonconformity란 매도인이 이행한 상품이 계약내용과 차이가 있는 것

B. Cure of the nonconforming goods must be made within the reasonable period of time within original time of the K. nonconforming goods의 cure는 원 계약기간 중의 합리적 시간 내에 이루어져야 한다.

C. Notice requirement(통보의무) : Seller must notify the buyer of his intent to cure. Seller는 cure하겠다는 의향을 buyer에게 밝혀야 한다.

D. A buyer cannot cancel the entire K because of a defect in one installment if the defect can be cured. 납품계약이 있을 경우 일부 품목이 잘못 전달되었다고 해서 Seller가 cure 가능한데도 buyer가 전 품목을 반환하려고 하는 것은 곤란하다.

Eg. Forest Products v. White Lumber Sales : a deviation in plywood thickness does not substantially impair the value of whole K. Nonconformity could be cured by a price adjustment.

2) Damage Rules for Sale of Goods – Who breached & who has the goods& whether or not, resale is possible

A. Seller's damages with resale = incidental damages + the difference between the resale price and the K price

매수인이 상품을 수령하기 전에 부당하게 상품수령을 거부하거나 매도인의 계약이행 시작 전에 계약을 위반한 경우 매도인은 제3자에게 재판매(resale)하고 부대비용(incidental damages)과 함께 재판매가격과 계약가격간의 차액을 보상받을 수 있다.

B. 만일 resale을 한다면 commercially reasonable한 방법을 사용해야 하고, public sale과 private sale이 가능한데 특히 private sale을 할 경우에는 매수인에게 반드시 통지해야 하는 의무(notice requirement)가 있다.

C. Seller's damages without resale

(1) The difference between the market price at the time of tender and K price + incidental damages minus expenses saved due to the buyer's breach. 만일 buyer가 물건의 인수거절 또는 계약자체를 부인하면 이행의 제공시점의 시장가격(market price at the time of tender)과 계약가격간의 차액에 부대비용(incidental damages)을 더하고, buyer의 계약위반에 따라 절약된 비용을 차감한 금액을 받을 수 있다.

(2) Consequential damages[간접적 손해]

① Seller generally cannot recover consequential damages. 매도인은 일반적으로 간접적 손해비용을 받을 수 없으나, 예외적으로 매도인이 volume seller로 인정될 경우 또는 유사한 상황의 경우, 계약위반으로 <u>상실된 이익(lost profit)</u>을 간접적 손해로서 인정받을 수 있다.

EX A전자제품가게에서 Buyer에게 계약금 $300받고 $2,500짜리 워키토키 주문을 받았는데 일본공장에서 갖고 오는 원금은 $1,000 일 경우 - the amount of the difference between the market price and the production cost and reasonable overhead and incidental cost를 받을 수 있다. because under the circumstances, the lost profit is the only measure of damages.

(3) The seller can recover the full K price

• Mneumonic : A STUD deserves Full K Price

- the buyer accepted the goods
- The seller's right to stop the delivery
- destroyed **after the ROL had** transfered **to the buyer**
- unable to resell the identified goods.

Seller가 계약액 전액을 보상받는 경우는 다음과 같다.

① when the buyer **accepted** the goods 매수인이 계약의 대상물을 인수한 경우

② The seller has a right to **stop the delivery**. 만일 buyer가 계약자체를 부인하거나 위반하였을 경우 seller는 상품 인도를 중지할 수 있는 권리

③ the seller is **unable to resell** the identified goods.

④ Conforming goods are destroyed **after the ROL had transferred to the buyer**. 위험부담이 buyer에게 넘어간 뒤에 상품이 손상된 경우 재판매가 불가능한 경우

3) Buyer's Remedies

A. Rejection(수령거절)

(1) a buyer **may reject** nonconforming goods. 매수인은 nonconforming goods를 거절할 수 있다.

(2) Buyer has a duty of care after rejection. 매수인의 **보관주의 의무**

① a buyer must care for goods until returned. 돌려줄 때까지 매수인이 상품을 잘 보관해야 할 의무가 있다.

② If goods are perishable or threatened with decline in value, buyer must make reasonable efforts to sell.
특히 상품이 부식성이거나 가치하락의 가능성이 클 경우, 매수인은 처분을 하기위해 노력해야 한다.

③ If buyer is a merchant, s/he must follow reasonable instruction of seller. 특히

매수인이 상인인 경우 매도인의 지시사항을 잘 준수해야 한다.

(3) a buyer has a right to inspect goods with reasonable notice within reasonable time before acceptance or payment.
매수인은 적절한 통보를 거쳐 검사할 권리를 갖는다.

B. Acceptance of Nonconforming goods 수령

Buyer may accept nonconforming goods. In such a case, buyer must pay the K price, but may still recover damages. 계약서 내용과 일치하지 않는 상품이라도 buyer는 수령가능하며 그 경우 차액을 배상받을 수 있다.

즉, 계약내용과 일치하지 않는 상품을 받았다고 해서 buyer가 손해배상권리까지 포기하는 것은 아니다.

C. Revocation of Acceptance[수령철회]

(1) Buyer may revoke acceptance in a reasonable time

① S/he accepted the goods expecting the nonconformity will be cured. Nonconformity가 치유될 수 있다고 기대하면서 수령한 경우

② S/he accepted because of difficulty of discovering defects 하자를 발견하기 어려워 모르고서 수령한 경우

③ S/he accepted because seller assured conformity 판매자의 상품에 하자가 없다는 확언(assurance)을 믿고서 수령한 경우

D. Right of Cover(대체물의 구매권)

(1) Buyer can buy substitute goods from another seller and ask for the damages for the difference between the cover cost and K price plus incidental damages and consequential damages. 매수인은 다른 매도인으로부터 대체물을 구매하고, 계약가격과 대체물간의 차액 + 부대비용 + 간접적 손해를 청구할 수 있다.

E. Specific Performance [구체적 이행명령]

Buyer may obtain specific performance if goods are **unique and highly unusual**. 주의해야 할 사항으로, enforcement의 대전제는 feasible해야 한다는 점이다. 따라서 비록 unique goods라고 하더라도 이미 BFP에게 팔려서 더 이상 goods 자체가 없는 경우라면 SP의 청구가 불가능하다.

EX Simon contracts to sell Beatrice an antique Benz car of which only one exists. If Simon later refuses to go through with the K, Beatrice may require Simon to sell her the unique car under the remedy of specific performance.

〈개념정리〉

Unique goods ➡	Specific performance가 가능하다
Unique service ➡	Specific performance가 가능하다

a personal service/an employment K is not specifically enforcible. →

① money damages are generally available

② it is impossible for courts to properly supervise service K by the order of specific performance.

참고 **Replevin(동산물 점유회복 소송)** Replevin, sometimes known as "claim and delivery", is an old-fashioned legal remedy in which a court requires a defendant to return specific goods to the plaintiff at the outset of the action. Although rarely used, replevin can be a very powerful weapon in a case where somebody is wrongly holding your property, because it deprives the defendant of the use of your property while the case is awaiting trial, which increases the likelihood of a quick settlement.

계약의 목적물이 특정(earmarked; identified)된 이후에 매수인에게 인정되는 구제수단으로서, 매도인에게 또는 계약의 목적물을 불법적으로 압류 또는 취득한 자에게 매수인이 특정된 계약의 목적물을 인도하라고 요구하는 것을 말함. 매수인이 대체물을 구매(cover)할 수 있는 경우에는 인정되지 않음.

Chapter 3 Commercial Paper

참고

savings account	checking account
passbook or bankbook	checkbook
interest-bearing	no interest
none	monthly bank statement
real name	real names for checks, drafts, etc.

Application of Laws(법률의 적용)

1) Negotiable instrument : UCC Article3 applies.

유동성이 있는 (negotiable) 증서는 UCC3조 적용

2) Nonnegotiable instrument : ordinary K law applies.

유동성이 없는 증서는 일반 계약법 적용

Negotiable Instrument의 정의

1) 일정한 금전의 무조건적인 지급을 약속(promise to pay) 또는 지급명령(order to pay)이 기재된 증서를 의미한다.

A special form of K unconditionally calling for the payment of money.

2) Commercial paper = negotiable instrument 사실 양자는 엄밀하게 말하면 약간의 차이가 있으나 편의상 같은 것으로 보고 이 과목을 이해하는 것이 좋다.

3) 권면(券面 face of the instrument)을 보고 negotiable 인지 아니면 nonnegotiable instrument인지를 구분할 수 있어야 한다.

Types of commercial papers

〈개념정리〉

	parties	remarks		parties	remarks
draft	drawer(발행인) drawee(지급인) payee(수취인)	① bill of exchange(환어음) = a negotiable discount security with a face value payable at a date in the future. ② pay to the order of (지급명령)	Note (promissory note) = an unconditional promise by the note maker to pay at a specified future time, a certain amount of money to a designated person or to the bearer	promisor (maker) and payee	① "I promise to pay~~" ② also called promissory demand note
check	drawer(발행인) drawee(지급인) payee(수취인)	① special type of draft ② pay to ~~	(negotiable) certificate of deposit = Receipts issued by banks as evidence of a deposit for a stated period of time at a stated rate of interest payable to bearer	issuer of CD bearer ※보통 무기명식 (소지인식)이 많다.	① Special type of Note ② 금융기관이 지급약속을 하는 문구가 있다. Ex. We certify that~~ ; it certifies that~~~

If it is not clear whether the instrument is draft or note, holder may treat it as either.

1) Draft

A. Drawer, Drawee, Payee 와 같은 **3 parties**로 구성되어있다.

> March 26, 2009
> To : ABC Corporation
> On March 26, 2009, pay to the order of Andrea Gorbachev $100,000 plus 10% annual interest from March 26, 2010.
>
> (signed) Kathy Taimie

(Kathy Taimie가 drawer 이며, ABC회사(drawee)에게 Andrea Gorbachev(payee)에게 지불을 하라는 내용의 draft임).

2) Check

A. 3 **parties, 즉 drawer, drawee 와 drawee**로 구성된다.

B. 수표를 **발행하는 사람이 drawer**이다.

C. drawee는 은행이다.

D. **발행일자(issuance date)**만 있으면 되고, payment date는 필요하지 않다.

E. **Payable on demand가 특징**이어서 요구를 하면 언제라도 지불을 하여야 한다.

F. 만일 수표발행 일자를 현재날짜보다 너무 아주 뒤로 기재할 경우(즉 **postdated) payable on demand**가 되지 못한다.

EX 현재 발행일이 2007년 1월13일인데 2017년 1월 13일로 발행했다면, 2017년 해당 날짜가 될 때까지 그 수표는 negotiability를 잃게 된다.

3) Note[= promissory note]

A. **2 parties , 즉 promisor[maker]와 payee 로 구성된다.**

B. 지불을 약속하는 쪽이 promisor[maker]이고 돈을 받는 쪽이payee이다.

> Jan. 13, 2007
>
> I promise to pay to the order of Andrea Gorbachev[payee] $100,000 plus 10% annual interest on Jan 13, 2008.
>
> Timothy Kane[maker]

C. Note에 단순하게 "Pay to A"라고만 쓰여 있으면 non-negotiable해진다. 반드시 "pay to the order of ~~~"라고 해야 한다.

D. Note의 문구에 secured by conditional sales contract등이 있다고 해서 nonnegotiable해지는 것은 아니다. note로서의 요건만 충족되면 negotiable해진다.

4) certificate of deposit

When you put money in a savings account, you can draw it out at any time. In a certificate of deposit, you agree to leave it in the bank for a certain period of time. They pay slightly higher interest because they know that money will be there for 3 months, 6 months, 1 year, etc. If you draw it out early, they reduce your interest.

금융기관에서 지불을 약속하는 special type of note이다. 일정기간이 지나면 금융기관이 지불을 약속하게 되므로 promisor가 되고, 특정기간동안 맡겨둠에 따라 이자가 약간 높으며, 대부분의 CD는 유동성이 높은 게 특징이다.

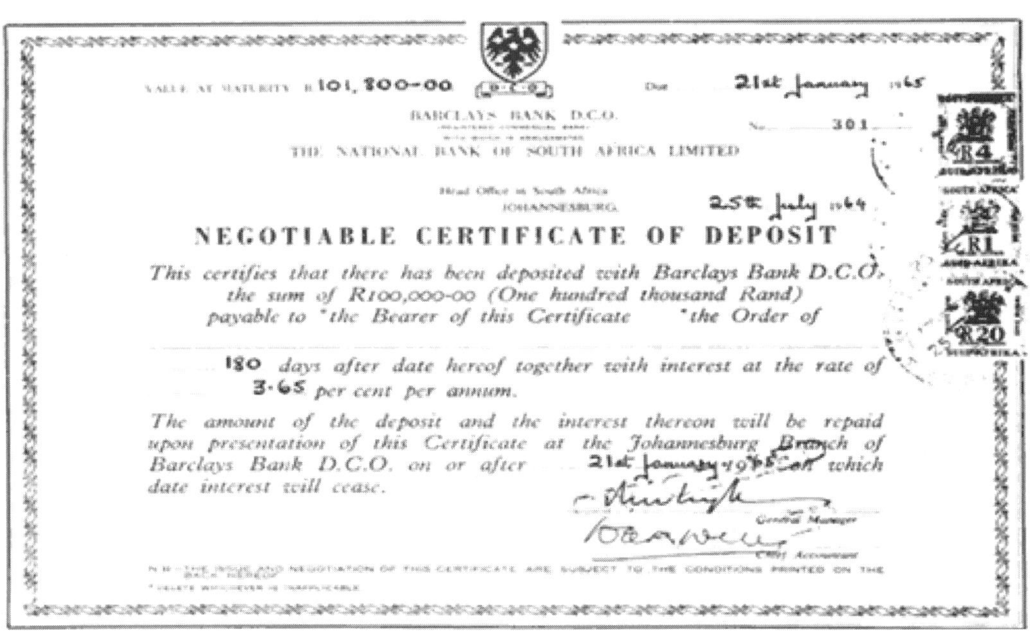

VALUE AT MATURITY R101,800-00 Due 21st January 1965

BARCLAYS BANK D.C.O.

No. 301

THE NATIONAL BANK OF SOUTH AFRICA LIMITED

Head Office in South Africa
JOHANNESBURG. 25th July 1964

NEGOTIABLE CERTIFICATE OF DEPOSIT

*This certifies that there has been deposited with Barclays Bank D.C.O. the sum of R100,000-00 (One hundred thousand Rand) payable to *the Bearer of this Certificate *the Order of*

180 days after date hereof together with interest at the rate of 3·65 per cent per annum.

The amount of the deposit and the interest thereon will be repaid upon presentation of this Certificate at the Johannesburg Branch of Barclays Bank D.C.O. on or after 21st January 1965 on which date interest will cease.

General Manager

Chief Accountant

NEGOTIABLE FLOATING RATE CERTIFICATE OF DEPOSIT

THE CHO-HEUNG BANK, LTD.

(Incorporated in Korea with limited liability)

LONDON BRANCH

Plantation House, 31-35 Fenchurch Street, [illegible]

SPECIMEN

U.S.$ 500,000

[illegible] 16th May, 1984

Certificate No: 0000

[illegible] Date 19th May, 1988

The Cho-Heung Bank, Ltd. certifies that the sum [illegible] UNITED STATES DOLLARS has been deposited with its London Branch upon terms that it is payable to bearer on surrender [illegible] Certificate, [illegible] bank, at the office of such Branch at the above address on the Interest Payment Date (as defined on the [illegible] (in the event that either of the options referred to on the reverse hereof are exercised) the Interest Payment Date [illegible] deposit will accrue from the date hereof to maturity at a rate to be calculated as provided on the reverse hereof and [illegible] Interest Payment Date. A record of an interest payment endorsed hereon and initialled by an authorised officer of the said London [illegible] be [illegible] evidence of the discharge of the obligations of The Cho-Heung Bank, Ltd. in respect of the interest payment in question.

Payments of principal and interest [illegible] be made without deduction of United Kingdom, Korean or other taxes upon presentation of this Certificate at the said London Branch by draft or telegraphic transfer on New York.

The obligations of The Cho-Heung Bank, Ltd. shall be solely in accordance with this Certificate and shall be governed by English law.

For and on behalf of
The Cho-Heung Bank, Ltd.

Authorised Signatory

4 Requirements of Negotiability

All the following requirements must be on the **FACE of instrument.**
유통성의 여부는 증서의 앞면(face)에 다음의 요건이 모두 반드시(must) 충족되어야 한다.

• Mneumonic : WOSSUP for Negotiability

- **W**riting
- **O**der or bearer
- **S**igned
- **S**um certain(fixed amount).
- **U**nconditionally payable on demand or at a definite time
- **P**ayable in currency

Detailed Requirements of Negotiability

1) Writing [be written] 증서는 문서의 형태로 되어있어야 한다.

2) Order or bearer[be payable to order or to bearer, unless it is a check]

A. 주의 "To A" 라고 하면 non-negotiable이 된다.

Draft나 note를 막론하고 단순하게 "pay to 홍길동(John Doe or Jane Doe) "이라고 하면 negotiate가 안되고, "pay to 홍길동 or order(기명식)," "pay to the order of 홍길동," 이라고 반드시 해야 한다[(statutory terms of art).

"To A's Order", "To A's Assigns", " To A or order"

EX A draft written "pay to Ghildong Hong" is not negotiable. This statement destroys negotiability because the draft is not payable "to the order of Ghildong Hong."

B. bearer[무기명]식의 경우 "to bearer," "to Ghildong Hong or bear," "to cash," "to the order or cash"이라고 한다.

C. **예외적으로 수표check의 경우 "pay to 홍길동"이라고 해도 negotiable 하다.**

〈개념정리〉

	설명	예
bearer paper(무기명식 증서 = 소지인식 증서)	instrument에 권리를 가진 사람의 이름을 기재하지 않고 증서를 갖고 있는 사람(즉, 소지인)을 권리자로 인정	pay to bearer, pay to cash, pay to John Doe or bearer, pay to the order of bearer, pay to the order of cash
order paper (기명식 증서)	instrument에 권리를 가진 특정인의 이름을 기재하여 그 사람 혹은 그가 지시하는 사람을 권리자로 인정	pay to the order of John Doe ※Check의 경우에만 예외적으로 pay to John Doe or pay to the order of John Doe 가능

3) Signed[be signed by maker of note or drawer of draft] : Sign can be ANY authentication, such as initials, nickname, rubber stamp … **발행인의 서명이 있어야 되고, 여하한 형태의 서명도 가능하다.**

4) Sum certain[fixed amount in money]

A. 반드시 금전이어야 하며, 다른 물건 등을 지급해서는 안된다.

B. 외화(foreign currency)도 무방하다.

C. 원금(principal)의 금액만 확정적으로 하고, 이자(interest), 추심비용(collection fee), 변호사 비용(attorney's fee)은 확정하지 않고 (변동금리의 가능성 등으로 인하여) variable amount로 해도 무방하다.

D. 금리는 누가 보더라도 객관적으로 알 수 있는 금리면 모두 가능.

注意1 | When adding interest, it must be clear enough to be indicated.

注意2 | "with interest" means judgment rate (statutory rate of the Usury act)

4) Unconditionally payable on demand or at a definite time

무조건적인 지불약속(promise to pay or order to pay)을 해야 한다

A. 즉 어떤 조건이 발생하면(subject to agreements) 지급하겠다는 등의 문구가 함께 있으면 nonnegotiable해진다.

If accompanied by conditions, nonnegotiable. Then K law applies

EX (X) : "If", "As long as", "Unless"
I, Kathy Taimie, promise to pay to the order of Andrea Gorbachev $10,000 if the car delivered to me is well-functioning.

Q

Does the term "90 days after my death" make the commercial paper non-negotiable?
Answer : Yes. Although death is certain, it is not a fixed time that easily can be determined just by looking at the instrument. Thus, there cannot be a HDC of that instrument.

B. 그러나 다음 사항은 기재해도 **negotiability**를 해치지 않는다.

(1) 발행목적 **(issuing purpose)**

EX for the purpose of renovating the Barnes Jewish Hospital in St. Louis.

(2) 발행이유나 근거계약 명시(referral to another **agreement**)

(3) 담보물을 통해 담보가 되어있다는 내용의 기재
[secured by **mortgagor** collaterals]

(4) 필요시 추가담보 제공의사[additional **collateral**]

(5) 지급이 특정펀드로부터 이루어진다는 내용[payment from particular **funds**]

C. 그러나 IOU(채무증서, I owe you)는 채무를 인정하는 것일 뿐 negotiable하지 않다.

5) Payable in currency

Amount must be set **"purely" currency**, not mixed with goods

 Interpretation of Ambiguities in Negotiable Instrument

1) Contradictory Terms

A. 증서상의 같은 내용에 대해 문자와 숫자가 일치하지 않을 경우 문자에 따른다 (**words control over figures**)

B. 인쇄물보다는 타이핑한 것이, 타이핑한 것보다는 수기(손으로 쓴 것)로 한 것이 이긴다.

Handwritten > Typewritten > Printed terms

2) Omissions

날짜(date), 이자(interest rate), 약인(consideration), 발행장소(place of issuance)는 기재되지 않아도 negotiable하다.

Postdated[선일자 수표] or Antedated[후일자 수표]

1) postdated 수표에 대해서는 해당날짜가 될 때까지 은행은 지급하지 못한다.

2) 만일 은행이 실수로 postdated check을 해당날짜가 되기 전에 미리 지급했다면, 은행은 책임지지 않는다.

3) 단, 발행인[drawer]이 별도의 문서에 수표를 미리 지급하지 말라고 통보(notify)했는데도 은행이 postdated check을 지급했다면 책임을 져야한다.

Negotiation

Commercial paper만의 독특한 양도방법을 negotiation이라고 한다.

1) 2 Methods of negotiation이 있다.

A. Negotiating **bearer paper** may be negotiated by **delivery** alone.
Negotiation of bearer instrument is accomplished by delivery of the instrument to the trustee. Once the transfer has possession, he qualifies as a holder.
무기명증서는 교부(전달)만 하면 된다.

B. Negotiating **order paper** requires both **endorsement** by **transfer and delivery** of instrument[resulting in **possession**]. For order instrument, negotiation is accomplished by delivery of the instrument to the payee named on the instrument. Any further negotiation requires that the payee endorse and deliver the instrument to the transferee. 기명증서는 배서와 교부(전달에 따른 소지)가 있어야 한다.

〈개념정리〉

bear paper(bearer instrument) ➡	delivery alone
order paper(order instrument) ➡	delivery and endorsement(resulting in possession)

C. The recipient of the negotiating instrument is called a "holder." 교부된 증서를 받는 사람을 holder라고 한다.

D. 소지인이 Holder in due course[HDC]요건을 충족하게 되면 transferor보다 더 큰 권리를 갖게 된다.

2) Assignment occurs when the transfer does not meet all requirements of negotiation. Negotiation 의 요건을 충족하지 못하면 assignment라고 한다.

8 Types of Endorsement

〈개념정리〉

Blank endorsement	Restrictive endorsement	Special endorsement	qualified endorsement
Simplest endorsement, consisting of only the holder's signature. It generally converts "order" paper to "bearer" form. 백지배서라고 하며, negotiable instrument의 앞면에 이름이 나온 사람이 바로 뒷면에 배서를 하는 것(이렇게 배서를 할 경우 order paper가 bear paper로 바뀐다)	In addition to holder's signature, includes a restriction on how the paper may be used by transferee. Most common wording is "For Deposit Only." The transferee bank must apply the check to the holder's deposit account. 제한적 배서 : 배서를 하면서 돈의 사용용처 등에 대해 구체적인 목적을 기재하는 것	This endorsement specifically names the next holder and requires his/her/its endorsement for further negotiation. Usual wording is "Pay to [the order of] TRANSFEREE NAME." 특정인 지명배서 : 받을 사람의 이름을 구체적으로 기재하고 난 뒤에 배서하는 것	an attempt by the endorser to escape general liability if the negotiable instrument is dishonored. Wording might include the words "without recourse." There is a legitimate purpose for this form, but if you see it on a check deposited by your customer, you should check with management before accepting the deposit. 한정배서 : 수표가 중간에 문제점이 생겨도 소구책임은 지지 않겠다는 의미의 배서

1) blank endorsement(백지 배서)

A. Does not specify any endorsee(**endorser's signature only on the back**). 증서의 뒷면에 피배서인을 특별히 정하지 않고, 배서인이 뒷면에 서명만 하면 된다.

B. **Converts order paper into bearer paper**. Bearer paper needs only delivery order paper에 백지 배서를 하게 되면 무기명 증서(즉, 소지인 증서)가 된다.

EX Andrea endorses a check in blank that had been made payable to his order. He lost it and Baker found it and delivered it to Charlie. Charlie is a valid holder since Baker's endorsement is not required.

2) Special endorsement(특별배서 = 기명식 배서)

A. **Indicates specific person to whom endorser wishes to negotiate the instrument. Further negotiation is possible.**
배서인이 배서를 하면서 피배서인을 특정한 뒤 자신의 서명을 하는 것을 기명식 배서라 한다. 피배서인은 그 다음사람에게 또다시 배서를 해줄 수 있다.

B. 이 경우 "pay to the order of John Doe"라고 하지 않고, "**pay to John Doe, [signature] Endoser's name**"이면 된다.

EX On the back of a check payable to the order of John Doe, he signs as follows : Pay to John Doe, (signed) Andrea Gorbachev.

C. Bearer paper may be converted into order paper by use of special endorsement. 무기명증서(bearer paper) 에 기명식 배서(special endorsement)를 하면 지시증서(order paper)가 된다.

EX A check made out to cash is delivered to John Doe. John Doe writes on the back : Pay to Andrea, (signed) John Doe.
Until this special endorsement is made, this instrument was bearer paper.

D. If last endorsement on the instrument is a blank endorsement, any holder may convert that bearer paper into order paper by writing "Pay to John Doe," above that blank endorsement. 마지막 배서가 백지식인 경우에는 소지인 누구라도 **그 백지식 배서위에 "pay to 홍길동" 이라고 기재하여 그 증서를 지시증서(order paper)로 만들 수 있다.**

3) Restrictive Endorsement

A. Requires endorsee to comply with certain conditions.
특정 요건에 반드시 따르도록 강요하는 조건부 배서

EX1 For deposit only, John Doe

EX2 Pay to John Doe only if he completes the renovation works of the shop to my satisfaction by the end of 2007.

B. Endorsement cannot prohibit subsequent negotiation.
배서를 한다고 해서 더 이상 negotiation이 되지 않도록 할 수는 없다.

EX Pay to John Doe only. John Doe has become a new endorsee, but it does not stop John Doe from further endorsing or further negotiations.

3) Qualified Endorsements[무담보 배서]

A. 일반적으로 배서인은 피배서인에게 부도가 발생할 경우 소구의무(일종의 보증책임)를 부담하는데, qualified endorsement(무담보 배서)를 하면 자신의 소구의무를 면할 수 있다.

B. 보통 **"without recourse"**라는 문구를 집어넣음으로써 무담보배서가 된다.
without recourse. no promise or guarantee of payment on dishonor.

9 Holder in Due Course[HDC]

definition : one holding a check or promissory note, received for value (he/she paid for it), in good faith, and with no suspicion that it might be no good, claimed by another, overdue, or previously dishonored (a bank had refused to pay since the account was overdrawn). A HDC is entitled to payment on negotiable instrument despite most defenses that maker or drawer of the instrument may have.

HDC는 유통증권의 발행인이 갖고 있는 항변사유(또는 결격사유)에도 불구하고 지금을 받을 수 있는 권리를 확보하게 된 자를 의미한다. 발행인은 HDC에게 인적항변 사유(personal defenses)를 가지고 지급을 거절할 수 있다.

〈개념정리〉

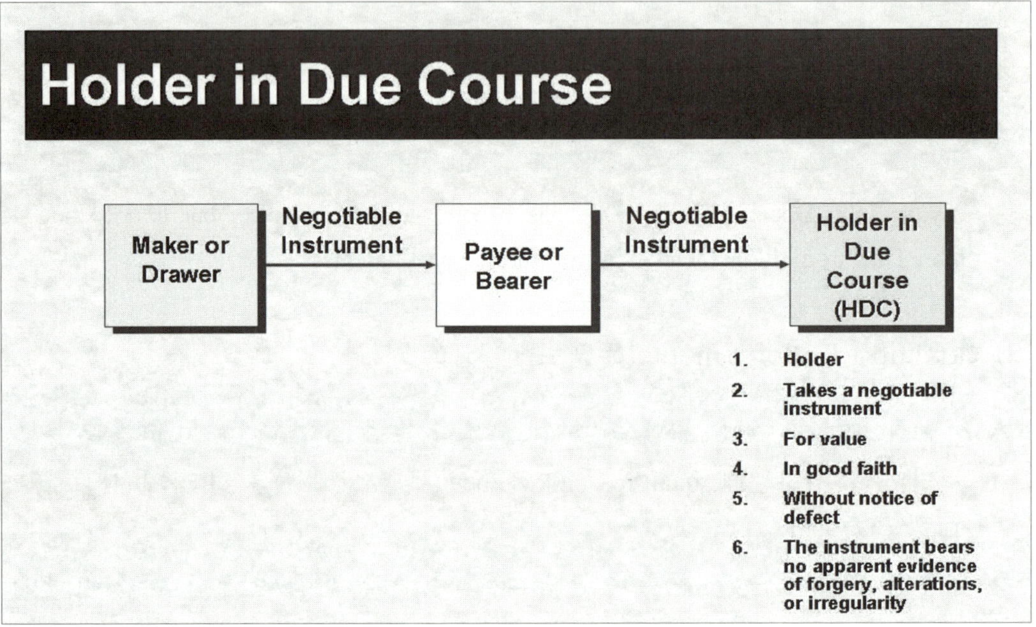

• Mneumonic : **END ODD GF**, but **Pay Value** to be a HDC

To be a HDC of the note, When a note is to become

- endorsed,
- negotiated
- & delivered (END), the transferee must take the note
- without any notice of any ODD(overdue, dishonored, or defenses), must be
- in GF
- pay value for the note
- and there should be no real defenses.

Note가 endorse되고, negotiate & deliver 되기 위해서는 good faith로 ODD사항에 대한 notice없이 pay value를 해야 한다. 또한 real defense가 없어야 한다.

1) Be a **holder** of properly **endorsed, negotiated,** and **delivered** instrument. 소지인이란 유통성 있는 증서를 negotiation에 의해 취득한 자를 의미

2) Without Notice of **ODD**[overdue, dishonored, or defenses or claims to it.

A. **객관적 기준(objective standard)**에 의하여 소지인이 발행인의 책임에 영향을 미치는 사실이 있다는 것을 몰랐고, 알 수도 없이(does not know or has no reason to know) 증권을 취득해야 한다.

B. Defenses or claims forgery, material or questionable alteration.
위조, 상당한 수정이거나 신뢰성에 의문이 가는 변조는 Defenses가 된다.

C. Postdated or antedated 여부는 발행인의 책임에 영향을 미치지 않는다. defense가 되지는 못한다.

D. 이자를 제때 지불하지 못했다고 해서[default in payment of interest] 발행인의 책임에 영향을 주지 못한다. defense가 되지는 못한다.

E. If one acquires notice after becoming a holder and giving value, s/he may still become a HDC.
소지인이 HDC의 지위를 취득한 이후에 발행인의 책임에 영향을 미치는 사실을 알게 되었을 경우 이미 pay value를 했다면 HDC의 지위에 아무런 영향이 없다. 즉, HDC가 되기 위해 notice가 있었는지 여부는 증권이 배서, 또는 교부되어 소지인이 되고 pay value를 하는 시점이다.

3) take in **good faith**

GF = subjective honesty in fact and reasonable commercial standards of fair dealing.

4) **pay value for instrument**

소지인이 증권의 대가를 지불했을 것

A. pay or perform agreed consideration 합의된 consideration을 이행할 것

B. promise to perform/give in the future is not value until performed. 미래에 이행하겠다고 약속하는 것은 value가 되지 못한다.

C. 과거의 채권변제, 다른 유통증권을 주고 다른 증권을 취득하는 경우, 증권을 담보목적으로 취득하는 경우 등은 모두 pay value에 해당한다.

〈개념정리〉

under K law	under commercial paper law
past consideration 인정안됨	past consideration 인정됨
future consideration 인정됨	future consideration (or executory promise)인정안됨

D. value does not have to be for equal or for full amount of instrument 증서와 등가(等價) 또는 전액(全額)을 꼭 지불할 필요는 없다.

Rights of a HDC against Personal Defenses

Personal defenses are assertable against ordinary holders and assignee of K rights to avoid payment. **A transfer of a negotiable instrument to a HDC cuts off all personal** defenses against a HDC. Personal defense가 있으면 ordinary holder에게는 지불을 거절할 항변사유가 되지만, HDC는 personal defense가 있다하더라도 지급을 거절할 수가 없다.

1) Theft by holder or subsequent holder after theft

2) **Illegality** personal defense if sate law makes transaction voidable but real defense if state law makes the transaction void. 주법에 근거하여 해당 transaction을 voidable하게 할 수 있다면 personal defense이지만, 만일 void하게 할 수 있다면 real defense가 된다.

3) Mental Incapacity

注意| minor의 경우는 제외된다.

주법에 근거하여 해당 transaction을 voidable하게 할 수 있다면 personal defense이지만, 만일 void하게 할 수 있다면 real defense가 된다.

4) Duress or undue influence

강박(ordinary duress)의 경우 대부분 voidable하므로 personal defense에 그치나, 심각한 강박(extreme duress)의 경우 real defense가 된다.

5) Fraudulent inducement or fraud in inducement

When signing a negotiable instrument induced by misrepresentation.
속아서 서명한 경우

6) Unauthorized Completion 부당보충

EX John이 수표에 금액을 적지 않고 Timothy 에게 주면서 $500 범위 내에서 교과서 사는데 보태 쓰라했는데 만일 Timothy 이 수표에 $50,000 이라고 적어서 Ann에게 준 경우, Timothy는 부당보충을 한 것이 된다. 만일 Amy가 HDC라면 John은 꼼짝없이 $50,000을 모두 지불하여야 한다.

7) Nondelivery 미교부

유통증권을 발행하기 위해서는 증권의 용지에 서명을 하고 이를 수취인에게 교부하여야 하는데 서명을 하였으나 이를 아직 교부하지 않은 상태에서 분실 또는 도난한 경우.

8) Prior payment 기지급

발행인 또는 인수인이 유통증권에 대해 지급을 했으나 그 유통증권을 회수하거나 취소하지 않았는데 다른 사람이 지급을 요구한 경우. 그러나 이는 personal defense이므로 발행인/인수인은 HDC에게 지급의 의무가 있다.

9) Failure or Lack of Consideration : 약인의 결여 또는

10) **Breach of <u>K</u> [including breach of warranty]**계약의 위반 : 유통증권을 발행한 근거가 되는 계약을 상대방이 위반한 경우 발행인은 "계약위반"이라고 항변할 수 있다.

11 Rights of a HDC against Real Defenses

물적 항변을 의미하며 HDC라 할지라도 이에 대항하지 못한다.

Transferee is **<u>subject to "real" defense</u>** that might arise. The real defense can beat HDC.

• Mneumonic : IBM FAILED HDC in R&D

HDC can be trumped by

- infancy or minority,
- Bankruptcy
- Material alteration
- Forgery
- Fraud in execution
- Illegality
- Extreme duress
- Incapatiy
- Real Defense

Note가 endorse되고, negotiate & deliver 되기 위해서는 good faith로 ODD사항에 대한 notice없이 pay value를 해야 한다. 또한 real defense가 없어야 한다.

1) Infancy or minority

발행인이 미성년자인 경우 물적 항변이 된다.

2) Bankruptcy : 발행인이 파산하여 채무면제(discharge)를 받은 경우 real defense가 된다.

3) Material Alternation

중요한 내용의 변조란 권한 없는 자가 유통증권 상의 기재 내용 중 **금액(amount), 날짜(days), 이자(interest) 등을 변경.**

A. Partial defense only : 중요한 내용의 변조란
부분적 항변에 그치므로 변조되기 이전의 조건에 따라 HDC는 지급을 받을 수 있다.

4) Forgery

위조란 권한 없는 자가 타인의 서명을 위조하여 유통증권을 발행하는 행위. 서명을 위조당한 자에게 유통증권에 대한 책임을 물을 수 없지만, 위조된 서명을 위조한 자(forger)의 서명으로 보아, 위조한 자에게 책임을 물을 수 있다.

5) Fraud in Execution

발행(서명)을 하는데 있어서의 사기행위

6) Illegality

personal defense if sate law makes transaction voidable but real defense if state law makes the transaction void. 주법에 근거하여 해당 transaction을 voidable하게 할 수 있다면 personal defense이지만, 만일 void하게 할 수 있다면 real defense가 된다.

7) Extreme Duress

보통강박(ordinary duress)은 personal defense에 그쳤지만 극심한 강박(extreme duress)는 real defense가 된다.

8) Incapacity : **행위무능력자[incompetent person]가 서명한 경우에 해당**

Holder through HDC[Shelter Doctrine or Shelter Rule]

1) Shelter Doctrine

A holder who takes a negotiable instrument from a HDC as a gift (no value), or even if the holder had knowledge that the instrument was overdue, or with knowledge

that there exist defenses to the payment of the negotiable instrument - nevertheless has the same rights as a HDC under the Shelter Doctrine. It is, however, in line with the concept of marketability and free transferability of negotiable instruments, as well as with contract law, which provides that assignees acquire the rights of assignors. The shelter principle extends the HDC benefits, and it is designed to aid the HDC in readily disposing of the instrument. Anyone, no matter how far removed from an HDC, who can trace his title ultimately back to an HDC comes within the shelter principle. Normally, a person who acquires an instrument from an HDC or from someone with HDC rights receives HDC rights on the legal theory that the transferee of an instrument receives at least the rights that the transferor had.

HDC로부터 유통증권을 취득하여 소지인의 요건은 충족하지만 나머지 HDC의 요건을 충족시키지 못해 HDC가 될 수 없는 자(holder through HDC)의 경우 HDC와 동일한 권리를 갖게 된다.

2) reacquisition exception

A person who earlier participated in the activity giving rise to the alleged defense, or as a prior holder of the instrument with notice that it was ODD. (He cannot enhance his position by re-taking the instrument from a HDC). Persons who formerly held instruments cannot improve their positions by later reacquiring them from HDCs(reacquisition exception).

HDC가 아닌 자가 HDC에게서 일단 배서, 교부하였다가 증서를 HDC로부터 다시 취득하는 경우로서 증서를 재취득한 자는 처음에 이 증서를 취득했을 때의 지위를 갖는다.

3) **Fraud or illegality exception** : 사기나 위법행위에 관여했던 자는 HDC로 인정받지 못한다.

13 Liability of Parties

〈개념정리〉

contractual liability	primary liability	note maker	payment liability
	secondary liability	draft drawer	secondary liability
warranty liability	transfer liability	for good title, and the genuineness of signatures, no notice of defenses against transferor	
		transferor is liable to the immediate transferee only while endorser is liable to all	
	presentment warranty	warranty good title, no knowledge of fraudulent signatures, and no knowledge of material alterations	

유통증권에 관여한 자들은 계약책임(contractual liability)과 담보책임(warranty liability)의 두 가지 책임을 진다. 계약책임은 유통증권에 서명한 자만이 지는 책임인 반면, 담보책임은 서명한 자를 포함하여 negotiation에 관여한 모두가 져야하는 책임이다.

1) contractual liability [계약책임]

발행인, 인수인, 배서인 등과 같이 유통증권에 서명을 한 자가 부담 하에 지는 책임으로 primary liability와 secondary liability의 두 가지가 있다.

A. Primary liability

(1) **Note의 발행인(maker)은 지급기일에 약속한 금액을 지급하겠다는 primary liability를 지게 된다.**

(2) Draft 나 check의 경우에는 발행시점에서 primary liability를 부담하는 자가 없고, 환어음에 대한 accept가 되는 시점부터 accepter가 primary liability를 지게 된다.

B. Secondary liability

(1) Draft의 drawer(발행인)는 secondary liability를 지게 된다. 즉 drawee(인수인)가 지급 또는 인수를 거절하는 경우에 발행인이 책임을 지게 되는 것이다.

(2) Endorser(배서인)는 secondary liability를 지게 된다. 즉, 지불약속을 한 자가 primary liability를 지지 않으면 그다음에 지불책임을 지게 되는 것이다.

(3) **Secondary liability**를 묻기 위해서는

① Holder must **demand payment or acceptance** in timely manner 적시에 지급의 인수나 지불을 요구해야 한다.

② Holder must give endorsers **timely notice of dishonor**
지급 또는 거절 사실(dishonor)을 secondary liability를 부담하는 사람에게 적시에 알려주어야 한다.

2) warranty liability **담보책임**

A. Transfer warranty 양도한 자의 담보책임

다음의 경우 transferor는 transfer warranty를 지게 된다.

(1) Transferor has good title 양도인이 유통증권에 대한 유효한 소유권을 갖고 있는 경우

(2) All signatures are genuine or authorized. 모든 서명의 진정성

(3) Instrument has not been materially altered. 중대한 변조가 없었음

(4) No defense of any party is good against transferor 양도인에게 유효한 defense가 없음

(5) Transferor has no notice of insolvency of maker, drawer, or accepter. 발행인이나 인수인의 지급불능을 알지 못함

배서인[endorser]은 이후의 양수인 전부에게 이러한 담보책임을 지지만 배서 없이 양도를 한자[transferor]는 자기가 직접 양도하여 준 자[immediate transferee]에게만 warranty liability를 지게 된다.

B. presentment warranty 제시한 자의 담보책임

지급제시나 인수제시(presenting negotiable instrument for payment or acceptance)를 하여 부담하는 담보책임으로 다음과 같은 사항을 담보하는 것이다.

(1) Good title[지급제시/인수제시를 한 자가 유통증권의 소유권을 갖고 있음]

(2) No knowledge of unauthorized signature. 발행인의 서명이 위조된 사실을 알지 못함

(3) No material alteration 중대한 변조가 없음

4) Accommodation Party

definition : One who signs a Commercial Paper for the purpose of lending his or her name and credit to another party to the document to help that party obtain a loan or an extension of credit.

EX A person wanting to obtain a car loan may offer a finance company a promissory note for the amount of the requested loan, promising to repay the amount over a number of years. If the company does not consider the person a good credit risk (one who will be able to repay the loan), it will request that someone else sign the note to ensure that the company will be repaid. Such a person may be an accommodation endorser, because he or she endorses the note after it has been completed, or an accommodation maker, because he or she must sign the note with the accommodation party.

An accommodation party is liable to the person or business that extended credit to the accommodation party, but not to the accommodated party. The accommodation party is liable for the amount specified on the accommodation paper. If an accommodation party repays the debt, he or she can seek reimbursement from the accommodated party.

Accommodation party란 실제로는 그 유통증권에 대한 이해관계가 없으면서 증권의 신용도를 높이기 위해 발행인 또는 배서인으로서 서명하는 자로 다른 사람을 위해 자신의 이름을 빌려준 것으로 간주된다. 여기서 발행인으로 서명하게 되면 accommodation maker가 되고 배서인으로 서명을 하게 되면 accommodation endorser가 된다.

5) Signature by authorized agents 대리인의 서명

A. 유통증권 상에 본인[principal]의 이름이 나타난 경우에만 본인이 책임을 부담하고 대리인은 책임이 없다.

EX Oprah Winfrey, signed by Jane Doe[authorized agent]

이 경우 Jane Doe는 책임 없고, Oprah Winfrey만 책임

B. 유통증권에 본인의 이름이 나타나지 않고 대리인의 이름만 나타난 경우에는 대리인만 책임진다.

EX Jane Doe, as agent Oprah Winfrey는 책임안진다.

14 Discharge of Parties

• Mneumonic : NI DRI - MAC - PC - AS - → discharge

Discharge of parties in a negotiable instrument is possible when there is

- negotiable instrument
- intentional destruction
- reacquisition
- impairment of recourse right and collateral
- material alteration,
- cancellation
- payment
- certification
- accord and satisfaction

1) Material Alteration of Instrument by Holder

소지인이 증권에 중요한 변조를 가한 경우 현재의 소지인은 이전소지인(prior party)에게 책임을 묻지 못한다.

2) Cancellation

A. 소지인이 다른 사람의 배서를 삭제하는 것을 cancellation이라고 하는데 배서가 삭제된 자의 책임은 소멸한다.
B. 단, 구두삭제(oral renunciation)는 cancellation으로서 효력이 없다.

3) Payment

Primary liability를 부담하는 자가 지급(payment)을 하게 되면 모든 배서인의 책임은 소멸하게 된다.

4) Certification of Check 수표의 인증

수표의 소지인이 drawee(은행)에게 수표의 인증(certification)을 요구하면 은행은 수표 상에 표시된 거래가 진정한 것인가의 여부를 확인하고서 인증을 해줄 수 있게 된다. 은행은 고객(drawer)의 계좌에서 인증한 금액만큼 은행자신의 계좌로 이체시킨다. 인증이 되면 발행인(drawer)과 모든 배서인은 책임을 면하게 된다.

5) Accord and Satisfaction

Primary liability를 부담하는 자가 지급대신에 accord and satisfaction을 하게 되면 모든 배서인의 책임은 소멸한다.

6) Reacquisition(재취득)

예를 들어 A가 B에게 어음을 지급하고, B가 이를 C에게 배서 교부하고, 순차적으로 D, E, F에게 교부되었는데 이를 다시 C가 취득할 경우, D, E, F의 책임은 면제된다.

7) Impairment of recourse right and impairment of collateral

소구권의 손상과 담보물의 손상

A. Impairment of recourse right
Cancellation이 되면 배서가 삭제된 자의 책임은 소멸하므로 이후 배서인은 그 자에게 소구권(recourse right)을 행사할 수 없게 된다. 따라서 이후 배서인의 입장에서 보면 cancellation은 자신의 소구권을 고의적으로 손상시킨 것이고, 이후 배서인은 책임을 면하게 된다.

B. Impairment of collateral
Note에 제공된 담보물을 없애는 것. 즉, 소지인의 동의 없이 담보물에 대한 담보권을 포기하거나 담보물의 가치를 해치게 되면, 소구의무를 부담하는 자(secondary party)는 책임을 면제받게 된다.

8) Intentional destruction of instrument by holder discharges prior party

소지인이 고의로 증권을 훼손한 경우 소지인은 이전 소지자(prior party)에게 책임을 물을 수 없게 된다.

15 Liability on Instrument with Forged Signatures

위조서명 증권에 대한 책임문제

1) 발행인의 서명이 위조된 경우 [signature of forger]

A. 발행인의 서명이 위조된 경우, 증권의 good title에는 영향을 미치지 않아 유통될 수 있고, 소지인(holder)은 증권의 소유권을 취득할 수 있다.

B. 그러나 forgery는 real defense의 일종이므로 발행인은 HDC에게도 지급을 거절할 수 있다.

2) 배서가 위조된 경우(forged endorsement)

A. A forged endorsement does not transfer title.
배서인의 서명이 위조된 경우, 즉 배서가 위조된 경우에는 소우권이 이전되지 않으므로 소지인은 증권의 소유권(good title)을 취득할 수 없다. 따라서 돈도 받지 못한다(forged endorsement has no good title and no collection)

3) Negligence Rule

Anyone negligent in creating or paying an unauthorized instrument is liable to an innocent third party. Anyone careless in paying an unauthorized instrument is liable. Anyone careless in allowing a forged or altered instrument to be created is also liable.

자신의 서명이 위조되는데 이에 대한 관리감독을 소홀히 하는 등의 과실이 있는 자는 위조의 항변을 할 수 없다.

16 Additional Issue

참고

Draft	**Trade acceptance**	Seller가 자신을 수취인(payee)으로 하고, buyer를 지급인(drawee)으로 하여 draft(환어음)를 발행하면서 buyer의 acceptance를 받는 환어음
	Banker's acceptance	동일한 은행이 drawer겸 drawee인 경우
	Sight draft	**Payable upon presentation**
	Time draft	일정한 지급일자에 지급하기로 되어있는 draft
	Money order	현금우송의 위험을 줄이면서 지불의 확실성을 보장하기 위해 우체국이나 금융회사로부터 구입하여 상대방에게 발송. 구입하는 자는 drawer가 되고, 판매한 자는 drawee, 수취인은 payee가 된다.
Check	Traveller's check	
	Cashier's check	Drawer = drawee = the same bank이고 제3자가 수취인
	Certified check	지급은행이 지급하기로 인증한 수표. 이 경우 은행은 primary liability를 지게 된다.

Banks' Liabilities 은행의 책임

1) Wrongful dishonor of checks

고객계좌에 잔액이 있는데도 불구하고 부도처리한 경우 이를 잘못된 부도(wrongful dishonor)라고 하며 은행은 이에 대한 책임을 져야 한다.

2) Payment of bad checks

발행인의 서명이 위조되어 발행된 수표나 금액이 위조되어 발행된 수표에 대해 은행이 지급을 하였다면 발행인이 과실이 있지 않은 한 은행 책임.

3) Bank Statement–30day Rule

발행인이 bank statement를 받은 후 30일 이내에 위조 또는 변조 사실을 은행에 통지하지 않으면 동일인이 동일수법으로 위변조 한 수표를 지급한 것에 대하여 은행이 책임부담을 할 필요가 없다.

4) Stop Payment Order

Revocation of a check; a notice made by a depositor to his or her bank directing the bank to refuse payment on a specific check drawn by the depositor. An individual who writes a check can revoke it unless it has been certified, accepted, or paid. If a bank pays a check after a timely stop payment order by the depositor, the bank is usually liable to the depositor for the amount paid.

〈개념정리〉

oral stop payment order	for 14 days of an oral notification
written stop payment order	A stop-payment order is a cancellation of the authority to pay and is valid for six months. It should be left on the bank's books for that full six-month period, even if the check is bounced a couple of times. (Yes, even if you punched holes in the account number, routing number, and signature line!) You should only "lift" the stop early if the customer releases the stop

A. 구두로 지급중단 명령한 경우 14일 간 효력 발휘

B. 서면으로 지급중단 명령한 경우 6개월간 효력발휘

C. 지급중단명령이 있는데도 불구하고 은행이 지불했다면 손해배상 책임을 져야 한다.

D. **단, 발행인(drawer)이 소지인(holder)에게 유효한 항변(valid defense)이 없는 경우에는 은행은 지급정지명령을 따르지 않아도 된다.**

18 Transfer of Negotiable Document of Title

1) Types

A. Bill of Lading 선하증권

운송업자(carrier)가 운송할 상품을 받았다는 것을 증명하기 위해 매도인에게 발행하는 증서

B. Warehouse receipt 창고증권

창고업자(warehouseman)가 보관할 상품을 받았다는 것을 증명하기 위해 seller에게 발행해주는 증서로서 창고의 위치에 대한 기재가 있어야 한다.

2) Forms

A. document of title은 증서의 앞면(face)에 "order of the named person" 나 "bearer" 의 기재[즉 특정인의 성명기재나 소지인이라는 문구] 가 있으면 negotiable.

3) Due Negotiation

HDC대신 holder by due negotiation 이라는 용어를 사용하며 HDC의 경우와 요건이 같다.

4) Transferor for value warrants that

대가를 받고 document of title을 양도한 양도인(transferor)은 양수인(transferee)에게 다음사항에 대하여 담보책임을 부담한다.

A. Document is **genuine 진정성**
B. No **knowledge** of any fact that would **impair** its validity or worth 가치나 유효성을 헤치는 사실을 알지 못함
C. **Rightful and fully effective negotiation** with regard to document of title and goods it represents. 진정한 양도

Chapter 4

Insurance

| 용어정리 |

Insurance contract(보험계약) :
The most common type of unilateral contract. The insurance company promises to pay the insured a stated amount of money on the happening of an event if the insured pays premiums.

Insurance policy(보험증서) :
A contract of insurance, describing the term, coverage, premiums and deductibles. also called policy.
"보험에 가입하다"라고 할 때 흔히 buy(purchase, or take out) insurance policy라고 한다.

Insurance premium(보험료) :
The periodic payment made on an insurance policy. also called premium. An insurance premium is the actual amount of money charged by insurance companies for active coverage. An insurance premium for the same service can vary widely among insurance providers.

Insurance proceeds(보험금) :
The returns to be paid to the insured according to the insurance contract.

Insurable interest(피보험 이익) :
An insurance term referring to the relationship between a policy's insured person or property and the potential beneficiary. The beneficiary must have an insurable interest in the insured person or property to receive payment of the policy if the insured died while the policy was in force. Insurable interest exists if there are legal interest and the possibility of pecuniary loss.

Subrogation(대위) : A taking on of the legal rights of someone whose debts or expenses have been paid.

보험은 다수인이 일정한 금액(보험료 premium)을 내어 일정한 공동기금을 만들고, 현실적으로 보험사고를 입은 사람에게 일정금액(sum insured 보험금)을 지급하여 경제생활의 불안에 대비하는 제도인데 보험을 통해 다수인이 위험을 분산하게 하는 제도.

 보험계약(insurance K)

1) 피보험자(insured)가 보험료(premium)를 지급하고 보험자(the insurer)는 특정위험에 의해 보험사고(insured incident)가 발생한 경우 보험금(sum insured)을 수익자(beneficiary)에게 지급하기로 약속하는 것으로 보험계약은 일반적으로 unilateral K이다.

2) 여기서 위험이란 보험증서(insurance policy)에 특별히 정한 위험이다.

3) 피보험자가 보험가입신청을 하는 것(application)이 offer가 되고, 보험회사(보험자)가 보험증서(policy)를 발행하는 것이 acceptance가 된다. 보험증권의 교부(delivery of insurance policy)는 계약의 성립요건이 아니다.

 보험증서(Insurance Policy)

보험증서를 발부한 뒤에 다음과 같은 사유가 발생하면 보험계약이 취소될 수 있다(voidable).

1) Concealment

A. 피보험자(insured)가 보험가입신청(application)을 하면서 보험자에게 중요한 사실(material facts)을 알리지 않은 경우 보험자(insurer)는 보험계약을 취소할 수 있다.

B. 중요한 사실(material fact)란 보험자(insurer)의 위험에 중대한 영향을 미치는 사실을 의미하는데 보험자가 보험가입신청을 받으면서 피보험자에게 질문한 사항들은 중요한(material)한 것으로 인정된다. 따라서 이러한 질문에 올바른 답을 하지 않을 경우 고지의무 위반이 된다.

2) Misrepresentation

피보험자가 계약에 있어 중요한 사실에 대해 부실기재[Ex. Nonexistent subject matter]를 한 경우

3) Breach of Warranty in the Policy

보험에 가입하면서 피보험자가 보험자에게 담보한 사항(warranty incorporated in the policy)을 지키지 않은 경우

 Insurable Interest 보험이익

1) 피보험자(insured)와 보험사고(insured event)사이에 일정한 상관관계가 있어서 보험사고가 발생하면 피보험자가 상당한 손실을 입어야 하는데 이러한 상관관계를 피보험이익 (insurable interst)이라고 한다.

2) 재산과 관련된 보험

A. 피보험이익(insurable interest)이 존재하기 위해서는 그 재산에 대한 법률상의 이익(legal interest)과 금전적 손실을 입을 가능성(possibility of pecuniary loss)이 같이 존재해야 한다.

B. Legal interest = ownership or security interest, judgment lien, etc.

C. 피보험이익(insurable interest)은 보험계약을 체결하는 시점에 있을 필요는 없지만 손실이 발생하는 시점에는 반드시 있어야 한다(must be present at the time of loss).

3) Life Insurance 생명보험

피보험자(insured)는 자신의 생명이나 제3자의 생명에 대해 피보험이익을 가질 수 있는데, 제3자와 밀접한 가족관계 또는 제3자의 사망으로 인해 재산상 손실(pecuniary loss)을 입게 되는 관계 등이 있으면 제3자의 생명에 대해 피보험이익이 있다.

 Liability Insurance 책임보험

1) 피보험자가 제 3자에게 과실에 의한 불법행위(negligence)를 하여 손해(accidental damages)를 입힌 경우 보험자가 피보험자의 책임을 대신하여 부담하는 것을 책임보험이라 한다.

2) 고의에 의한 불법행위(intentional tort, Ex. fraud)의 경우에는 보험자의 배상책임이 인정되지 않는다.

 Malpractice Insurance

1) 책임보험의 한 종류(a form of liability insurance)로서 의사, 회계사, 변호사, 등이 업무상의 과실로 제3자에게 손해를 입힌 경우의 손해를 배상하는 것이다.

2) 다만 업무상의 과실로 인한 손해(harm caused by errors or negligence in work)에 한정하고 고의적인 과실에 의한 손해에 대해서는 배상하지 않는다.

 E&O insurance

 Fire Insurance화재보험

1) 손해보험의 일종으로서 화재로 인한 손실은 물론, 화재를 진압하는 과정에서 사용된 물, 화학물질 등으로 인한 손실도 보상되는데 별도의 약정이 없는 한 화

재로 인한 영업상의 손실은 보상되지 않는다.

2) 일반적으로 손해보험에는 특정재산을 대상으로 하는 "specific policy"와 계속 변동하지만 특정할 수 있는 재산(예. 재고자산)을 대상으로 하는 "blanket policy"의 두 가지가 있다.

7 Subrogation 대위(代位)

A taking on of the legal rights of someone whose debts or expenses have been paid. For example, subrogation occurs when an insurance company that has paid off its injured claimant takes the legal rights the claimant has against a third party that caused the injury, and sues that third party.

The typical insurance subrogation claims arises from an automobile accident or other loss caused by a wrongdoer. The insured has a claim for damages against the wrongdoer. Pursuant to its policy with the insured, the insurance company pays its insured some or all of these damages. The insurance company then seeks to collect from the wrongdoer or his or her insurance company reimbursement for the monies it paid its insured.

1) 피보험인(insured)이 제3자로부터 입은 손해를 보험사(insurer)가 보상해준 경우, 보험자는 피보험자의 제3자에 대한 권리(불법행위를 한 제3자에 대한 손해배상 청구권)를 피보험자를 대신하여 행사하여 그 3자에 대하여 책임을 물을 수 있는데 이를 subrogation이라고 한다.

2) 피보험자가 손해를 야기한 제3자의 책임을 release해주었다면 보험자의 대위권을 행사할 수 없도록 한 것이 되어 보험자의 책임도 없다.

 내가 운전을 하며 가던 중 다른 사람으로부터 부딪힘. 상대방의 잘못에 따라 상대방의 보험사로부터 보상을 받아야 하나 그러한 권리를 나 자신의 보험사에 맡기는 경우 나의 보험사는 상대방의 보험사를 상대로 subrogation right을 행사할 수 있다.

8 Coinsurance Clause 배상비율

1) 보험금액(the amount of insurance)을 보험가액[보험목적물의 경제적 가치]으로 정할 필요는 없고, 보험가액의 일정한 비율(이를 coinsurance %라고 한다)까지만 보험에 가입하면 손실을 모두 보상받을 수 있는데 이를 coinsurance clause라고 한다.

2) 따라서 보험가액에 coinsurance %를 곱한 금액이하로 보험에 가입하지 않게 되면 손실을 모두 보상받을 수는 없고 보상받지 못한 손해는 피보험자(insured)가 부담하여야 한다. 통상 대부분의 coinsurance %는 80%이다.

9 보험가액의 산정

1) 보험가액은 때와 장소, 또는 여러 가지 상황에 따라 변화하므로 그 구체적인 가치는 손해가 발생하였을 때의 공정한 시장가치(FMV)에 의해 정해지는 것이 바람직하다.

2) $\text{total recovery} = \text{actual loss} \times \dfrac{(\text{amount of insurance})}{(\text{coinsurance\%} \times \text{FMV of property at the time of loss})}$

 A는 화재보험을 가입했고, 보험한도(즉, 보험금액)은 $300,000이고, 80%의 coinsurance clause가 있다. 화재에 의해 $200,000의 손실이 발생했고, 화재당시 집의 FMV는 $500,000이었다. 보험회사가 지불해야 하는 보험금은 200,000 ×

(300,000 / 0.8 × 500,000) = $150,000이다.

3) 보험의 목적물이 완전히 멸실(totally destroyed)된 경우에는 위 공식이 적용되지 않고 보험금액의 범위 내에서 손실액 전액을 보상받을 수 있다.

10 Pro Rata Clause

피보험인이 여러 개의 보험을 들었을 경우 각 보험계약에서 정해진 비율에 따라 보상을 받는다.

11 주의할 점

1) FMV 〈 insurance amount

When an insurance claim is made as a result of an accident, the insurance company's coverage for the damage will usually cover the damages up to the FMV of the property.

2) FMV 〉 insurance amount

up to the insurance amount only.

〈개념정리〉

case1	case 2
삼성화재(주)에 제일모직이 500억 원 규모의 화재보험에 가입한 상태인데 1,000억 원의 화재손실이 발생한 경우	삼성화재(주)에 제일모직이 1,000억 원 규모의 화재보험에 가입한 상태인데 500억 원의 화재손실이 발생한 경우
➡ 삼성화재는 500억 원만 보상	➡ 삼성화재는 500억 원만 보상

Chapter 5

AGENCY

〈개념정리〉

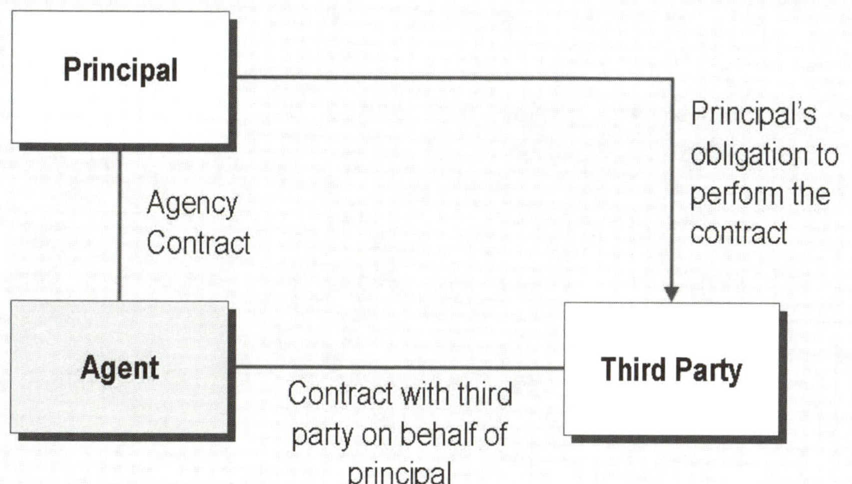

1 Characteristics

1) The Principal/Agent relationship requires

Agency관계가 성립하기 위해서는 다음 다섯 가지 요소가 존재하는지 보아야 한다

Control Agent is subject to the control of principal

Authority of the agent to bind the principal contractually with 3rd Parties

Benefit : agent is working for the benefit of principal

Agreement of the agent to act on behalf of principal

(i.e. meeting of the minds and consent to act)

Fiduciary Relationship between the principal and the agent

2) 대리인 관계의 예

A. Power of attorney위임장

Principal in writing gives(grants) authority to the agent in a specific transaction. 특정거래에만 제한. 위임장에는 **principal의 서명이 필요하다**. 그러나 agent의 서명은 필요하지 않다.

B. Broker

특정상거래에서 매수인이나 매도인을 대리하는 특별대리인(special agent)으로 예를 들면 real estate broker.

C. Exclusive

계약기간동안 특정한 거래에 대하여 배타적인 권리를 가진 agent를 의미한다 (only agent the principal may deal with for a certain purpose during life of the contract). 즉 특정거래에 있어서 다른 사람은 대리권을 갖지 못한다.

EX Real estate broker who has sole right to sell property except for personal sale by principal

2 대리인 관계와 유사한 관계(relationship resembling agency)

1) Agency coupled with interest or agency coupled with an interest (ACWI)

It is an agency relationship in which the agent is given an estate or interest in the property that is the subject of the agency of the principal.

Generally, the ownership of the principal's property does not pass to the agent, whereas in a full trust agreement, ownership does pass to the trustee.

If the agency is coupled with an interest, the agency usually cannot be revoked by the principal before the expiration of the interest and is not terminated by the death or insanity of either the principal or the agent.

소유권자가 그 담보물을 매각할 수 있는 권한을 담보권 자에게 수여한 경우 ACWI라 하는데 담보권자는 그 담보물을 매각한 후 매각대금을 받아 변제 받을 수 있다(agent has an interest in subject matter through a security interest).

EX Mortgagee with right to sell property on default of mortgage

2) ACWI is irrevocable.

ACWI는 취소를 시킬 수 없다.

EX 담보권을 설정하면서 mortgagor가 채무불이행을 할 경우 담보물을 매각할 수 있는 권한을 mortgagee에게 주었다면, 이 경우 mortgagor가 사망했더라도 ACWI는 종료되지 않는다.

〈개념정리 : Agency와 ACWI의 비교〉

	agency	ACWI
Principal's power	Principal이 agent에게 대리권을 수여하여 특정한 법률행위를 하게 해도 principal이 직접 그 법률행위를 할 수 있다	Principal does not have the power to terminate ACWI. Principal이 법률행위를 할 권한을 포기하여 직접 법률행위를 할 수 없다
Example	bouncer in a night club authorized by the nightclub owner.	A(mortgagor)는 자신의 토지에 mortgage를 설정해 B(mortgagee)에게 주었는데 부채상환이 곤란해지자 A가 B에게 자신의 토지를 매각하여 채무를 변제받으라고 한 경우

3 Methods of Creation of Authority

Creation of Authority is done by
Necessity by public policy
Appointment
Representation
Ratification and
By **E**stoppel

1) Necessity(필요성)

특정한 상황에서 대리관계가 존재한다고 보아야 할 공익상의 필요(as a matter of **public policy**)가 있는데 이러한 상황에 의해 대리관계가 형성되는 것이다.

EX In an emergency to contract for medical aid.

2) appointment 대리권의 수여

Principal과 agent사이의 의사표시에 의해 대리관계가 형성되는 것을 의미하는데 대리권에 대한 명시적인 언급이 있는 express appointment와 명시적인 언급이 없는 implied appointment가 있다.

〈개념정리〉

Express appointment	Agreement between the principal and agent express authority 탄생 Ex. 대한 항공에서 탑여행사에 대한항공의 티켓을 싸게 팔 수 있도록 계약을 맺고 허용함
Implied appointment	Reasonably implied authority that is present because of the way based on customs and industry practices implied authority 탄생 Ex. Chili's business manager has the authority to insure Chili's property against fire.

Agency contract이 1년 이내에 완성되지 못할 경우 SOF(1 year rule)가 적용된다.

3) Representation 대리권의 표시

A. Principal이 제3자에게 대리관계에 대하여 표시를 함으로써 대리관계가 형성되는 것을 의미한다.

EX A가 C에게 B가 자신의 agent라고 말한 경우(A가 이러한 대리관계를 형성할 의사를 갖고 있는 상태에서 C에게 이런 표시를 했어야 한다)

B. Principal이 대리관계를 형성할 의사를 갖고 있는 상태에서 제 3자에게 대리권의 표시(representation)를 하게 되면 actual authority(실질적 대리권)이 만들어지는데 이 경우 대리권의 표시(representation)에 대한 제3자의 신뢰는 필요하지 않다(does not require reliance by 3P)

C. 만일 A가 B와 대리관계를 형성할 의향도 없이 이러한 표시를 C에게 했다면 apparent authority라고 한다.

〈개념정리〉

Actual authority	Express authority granted through words. It is a clear expression of authority to act on behalf of the principal. Does not need 3P's reliance
Apparent authority	2-Part Test : ① holding someone out as an agent and, ② 3P's reasonable Reliance [대리관계를 형성할 의도를 실제로는 갖고 있지 않지만 대리인인 것처럼 내세워서 제3자가 믿게 되는 경우]

4) Undisclosed, Partially disclosed, and fully disclosed principal

〈개념정리〉

	identity	Relationship between principal and agent
Fully disclosed	Known to 3rd parties	Known to 3rd parties
<u>Partially disclosed</u>	<u>Not known to 3rd parties</u>	<u>Known to 3rd parties</u>
undisclosed	Not known to 3rd parties	Not known to 3rd parties

A. Fully disclosed agency

◆ An agency that results if the third party entering into the contract knows :

That the agent is acting as an agent for a principal, and

The actual identity of the principal

The principal is liable to the third party.

The agent is not liable.

B. Partially Disclosed Agency

◆ An agency that occurs if :

The agent discloses his or her agency status but does not reveal the principal's identity, and

The third party does not know the principal's identity from another source

Both the principal and the agent are liable to the third party if the principal fails to perform the contract.

C. Undisclosed Agency

◆ An agency that occurs when the third party is unaware of either :

The existence of an agency, or The principal's identity

◆ **Undisclosed principal cannot ratify the unauthorized acts of the agent.**

EX 강남 복부인(Undisclosed principal)은 자신의 신분을 비밀로 하도록 부탁하며 복덕방아저씨들(agents)을 대거 모아 행정복합도시로 개발될 충남지역 일대의 토지를 사재기하도록 지시함. 이에 복덕방 아저씨들은 대량으로 토지를 사재기하였음(authorized act). 나중에 이 사실이 관계당국에 의해 적발됨 이 경우 undisclosed principal의 authorized acts를 한 것이며 이는 undisclosed principal의 benefit을 위한 것이나 나중에는 결국 복부인들의 신분이 밝혀지면서 principal에게 책임을 물을 수 있음. 결국 복부인은 부동산투기로 구속됨

5) Ratification

A. 어떤 자가 대리권이 없이 법률행위(unauthorized act)를 하였는데 이를 principal이 사후에 인정함으로써 그 법률행위의 효과가 principal에 미치도록 하는 것을 의미한다.

B. 추인이 되려면 lawful and delegable, principal is legally competent, awareness, **entire ratification, not partial** 등이 필요하다.

C. Undisclosed principal cannot ratify unauthorized acts of agent-**undisclosed principal 은 추인할 수 없다.** 그러나 fully disclosed principal and partially disclosed principal can ratify.

6) By estoppel(禁反言의 원칙)

Principal이 묵인 또는 다른 방법으로 제3자가 대리관계가 존재한다고 믿게 될 경우 principal은 나중에 대리관계가 존재하지 않는다고 부인하지 못하게 됨으로써 대리관계가 형성된다(Principal is not allowed to deny agency relationship when s/he caused 3P to believe it exists and it is imposed by law not by agreement).

Desert Fox, who is not an agent of Little Prince, bargained for hungry Little Prince to buy foods for Little Prince while in Little Prince's presence. If Little Prince remains silent, he will not be able to deny the agency.

4 Apparent Authority(표현대리,表見代理)

Agent가 principal을 대리하여 제3자와 법률행위를 하였는데, agent에게 그 법률행위를 대리할 수 있는 대리권이 존재하지 않는 경우, 제3자는 principal에게 그 법률행위의 책임을 물을 수 없다. 그런데 principal이 제3자로 하여금 agent가 대리권이 있다고 믿을 만한 원인을 제공해 제3자가 agent에게 대리권이 있다고 믿을 만한 합리적인 믿음과 신뢰(reasonable belief and reasonable reliance)가 있다면, 그 믿음과 신뢰는 보호되어야 한다. 이 경우, 제3자는 표현대리권(apparent authority)을 근거로 principal에게 법률행위의 책임을 물을 수 있다. Apparent authority에는 다음과 같은 것들이 있다.

• Mneumonic : AAA by TRAPS

- AA is **apparent authority**
- AT is **After Termination**
- R is **Representation**
- A' : **apparent authority**
- P is **position**
- S is **secret Limitation**

1) After termination 대리관계의 종료이후의 대리관계

대리관계(agency)가 종료된 이후에도 제3자가 그 사실(즉 종료된 사실)을 모를 경우 이전의 agent와 법률행위를 할 수 있다. 즉, 대리관계가 종료된 이후 표현대리권이 생기는 경우는 대리관계가 principal이나 agent의 행위에 의하여 종료된 경우이다 (Agent has apparent authority after termination of agency until those with whom the agent has dealt are given actual notice).

EX 삼성전자의 김 과장이 티벳에 파견되었다가 현지거점 폐쇄 및 본국귀환 명령을 받았는데 삼성전자는 이 사실을 비밀에 부치도록 조속히 귀국하도록 김 과장에게 지시함. 본사의 지시에도 불구하고 김 과장은 귀국하지 않고 현지에서 사표를 낸 뒤 티벳 사람들에게 자신이 삼성맨임을 자랑하며 현지인들과 삼성의 제품을 파는 계약을 맺음. 이 경우 삼성전자(principal)는 김 과장(agent)의 행위에 대해 책임을 질 수도 없고(not liable), 또한 이 같은 행위를 허락해줄 수도 없음 (cannot ratify). 그러나 티벳 사람들은 김 과장과 일정한 apparent authority가 있다고 보고 나중에 삼성측에 소송을 제기할 수 있음 ➡ 소송만 가능한 것인지 반드시 승소한다는 의미는 아님.

2) Representation 대리관계의 표시

Principal이 대리관계를 형성할 의사를 갖고 있는 상태에서 제3자에게 대리관계에 대하여 표시하면 대리관계가 형성되는데 만약 principal이 대리관계를 형성할 의사를 갖고 있지 않은 상태에서 제3자에게 대리관계에 대하여 표시(representation)하였다면 actual authority는 만들어지지 않는다. 만일 이 경우 제3자가 principal의 대리관계의표시를 믿고 신뢰하였다면 표현대리권이 생겨나게 된다(apparent authority exists only for those who know of principal's representations whether directly or indirectly).

3) Position(지위)

Agent가 principal과의 관계에서 특정한 지위를 갖고 있는 경우 제 3자가 그 지위로 인하여 대리권이 있다고 믿고 신뢰할 수 있으며 만약 agent에게 actual authority가 없다면 제3자는 자신의 신뢰를 근거로 agent의 apparent authority를 주장할 수 있다(an agent insofar as third persons are concerned can do what the predecessor did or what agents in similar positions in the general business world are deemed authorized to do for their principles)

EX Mr. Principal, owner of Best Buy Shop, appoints Mr. Baker to be agent manager of his(Principal's) shop, but tells him not to buy goods on hs own. Mr. Baker has apparent authority to purchase as similar managers would.

특히 agent를 통하여 과거의 비즈니스관계(old business relationship) 로 인하여 principal이 혜택(benefits)을 입은 경우가 있을 경우 이를 근거로 principal은 agency 관계를 부인하지 못한다.

4) Secret limitation

Principal과 agent간 대리권의 제한(limitation)이 비밀리에 설정되어있다면 그 사실에 대해 제3자가 알지 못하는 한, principal은 이를 제3자에 대한 항변사유로 내세울 수 없다.

EX Principal, owner of the Costco, authorizes Agent to go to Yangjae, Seoul to buy a piece of property to open up another outlet of the Costco. Principal tells Agent not to pay more than $1,000,000. Agent makes a contract with Thomas to buy some property for Principal, but he agrees to pay Thomas $1,000,100. Thomas was not was of the limitation on the purchase price. Principal is bound to the contract with Thomas for the full price of $1,000,100.

5 Estoppel

True authority는 아니지만 detrimental reliance가 있었을 경우 인정되는 금반언에 의한 authority로 때로는 apparent authority와 ratification과 구분이 어려울 경우도 있다.

 Cpacity to be agent or principal

〈Principal〉

1) Principal이 되기 위해서는 대리인을 선임할 수 있는 법적인 행위능력을 갖고 있어야 한다(principal must be able to give legal consent)

2) 미성년자의 경우 대리인을 선임할 수 있지만, 대리관계를 취소하는 것도 가능하다(minors can appoint an agent, but minors may disaffirm the agency)

3) 법인격이 없는 단체(unincorporated association)는 legal entities가 되지 못하므로 대리인 선임자격이 없다.

〈Agent〉

1) Agent가 되기 위해서는 단지 principal 본인의 지시를 수행할 수 있을 정도의 정신적, 육체적 능력만 갖추면 된다.

2) legal entities는 물론이고 unincorporated associations도 가능하다.

3) 정신지체아(mental incompetent) 혹은 어린아이(an infant of tender years)는 agent가 될 수 없다.

〈개념정리〉

자격요건	Principal	Agent
Infant	Principal이 되어 대리인 선임가능하며 대리인관계를 취소하는 것도 가능하다(Yes)	너무 어린아이는 Agent가 될 수 없다(No in the case of an infant of tender years)
Unincorporated associations	Principal이 될 수 없다(No)	Agent가 될 수 있다(Yes).

7 Obligations and Rights

〈Principal's obligation to agents〉

1) Compensation(보상)

Principal은 계약에 따른 보수를 지급해야하며, 만일 reasonable amount for the agent's service를 지급해야 한다.

2) Indemnification(배상)

Principal의 합법적인 지시에 따라 업무를 수행한 경우, agent에게 발생한 liability and loss에 대해서는 배상해주어야 한다.

3) Reimbursement(비용상환)

Agent가 업무수행을 하면서 지출한 합리적 비용을 상환해주어야 한다.

〈Agent's obligations to principal〉

4) Duty of loyalty(충성의무)

대리인은 reasonable care and skill을 다해 principal의 합리적인 지시를 따라야 할 의무가 있다.

5) FBI(충실의무) = fiduciary duty for the best interest of principal

Agent는 principal에 대해 fiduciary duty를 갖고 있으며 principal의 best interest를 위해 행동하여야 한다.

6) Reporting duty(보고의무)

Principal이 원하는 정보를 보고할 의무를 갖는다.

7) Must stop acting as agent upon termination 해고당하는 즉시 agent로서 행동해서는 안된다.

8) Not to Mingle funds

Agent는 이익을 포함하여 principal에게 귀속된 것들을 모두 상환해야 하며 자신의 재산과 principal의 재산을 뒤섞지 말아야 한다.

9) Not to compete and not to act adversely (경쟁금지 및 반이익적인 행위금지)

Agent는 Principal과 경쟁해서도 안되고, principal의 이익에 반하는 행동을 해서도 안된다.

• Mneumonic : **a loyal FBI agent must STRep, but no MC**

An **agent** has
Duty of **loyalty**
Fiduciary ducty for **the best interest** of the principal
Stop behaving as agent upon **termination**
Reporting duty
Not to **mingle** his funds with Principal's
Not to **compete** with Principal

〈Subagent(복대리)〉

10) 원칙적으로 agent는 subagent를 선임할 수 없고, principal만이 subagent를 선임할 수 있다.

11) 단, principal이 그 권한을 agent에게 수여했거나 agent가 복대리인을 선임하는 것이 불가피한 경우(i.e. 만일 선임하지 않으면 principal에게 손해가 발생하는 경우) 에는 agent가 직접 subagent를 선임하는 것이 가능하다.

12) Subagent는 principal과 agent모두에게 fiduciary duty를 부담한다.

13) Subtenancy(= sublease)와 subagency는 다르다.

〈개념정리〉

Subagency			Subtenancy	
principal	←		LL	
	↑			
↑	↑		↑	
agent	↑	subagent는 agent와 principal모두에게 fiduciary duty	tenant	subtenant는 tenant에게만 충성의무가 있고 LL에게는 없다.
	↑			
↑	↑		↑	
subagent	→		subtenant	

8 Principal's Liability to 3rd Parties(principal의 제3자에 대한 책임)

1) Agent가 대리권한 혹은 표현대리권한을 갖고 principal을 대신하여 제3자와 계약을 체결한 경우 principal이 disclose되었는지 여부가 중요하다.

A. Disclosed principal은 계약상의 책임을 져야 한다. 즉 일단 principal의 정체가 공개되면 책임이 있다.

B. Undisclosed principal은 책임을 져야하는 것이 대원칙이나 다음의 경우에는 책

임을 지지 않는다.

(1) 공개되지 않은 principal은 agent의 승인되지 않은 행위에 대하여 추인할 수 없다(Undisclosed principal cannot ratify unauthorized acts of the agent).

(2) 제3자가 principal의 정체를 알고 난 뒤에 agent에게만 책임을 지라고 요구할 경우

(3P holds agent responsible(3P has a choice to hold principal or agent liable once the identity of principal becomes known))

(3) Agent가 계약을 완전히 이행하고 난 뒤

(4) 계약서에 undisclosed principal은 분명하게 배제된다고 명시되었을 경우

C. <negotiable instrument의 예외>agent가 제3자에게 negotiable instrument를 교부한 경우 principal이 fully disclosed된 경우에 한해서만 principal이 책임을 진다 (Only fully disclosed principal is liable on a negotiable instrument) .

1) Agent가 principal을 대리하여 계약을 체결하였는데 agent가 대리권(표현대리권)을 갖고 있지 못할 경우

〈개념정리〉

a) principal이 적법하게 계약을 추인(ratification)한 경우	principal은 계약상의 책임을 부담한다.
b) principal계약을 추인하지 않았다면	principal은 계약상의 책임을 부담하지 않는다.

9 Termination of Principal-Agent Relationship

1) by **agreement** of parties

당사자 간의 합의에 의하여 시간의 경과(Ex. 1년 유효 대리인계약), 임무의 완성(Ex. 부동산 구매 대리인계약), 혹은 상호합의에 의하여 대리인 계약이 종료될 수 있다.

2) 일방적인 termination에 의해 종료될 수 있다.

기간이 정해져 있더라도 일방적인 종료가 가능하지만, 계약위반에 따른 책임을 져야 한다.

3) 법률의 규정(by operation of law)에 의하여 계약이 종료될 수 있다.

A. Agency contract의 목적이 불법이 된 경우(Ex. Agent에게 필요한 사업면허취득의 실패)

B. Principal이나 agent가 bankruptcy, death, insanity 등의 사유가 발생했을 경우

4) 그러나 ACWI는 취소되지 않는다(irrevocable)

5) 일반적으로 principal-agent간의 행위에 의하여 대리관계가 종료된 경우에는 표현대리가 생겨나지만, 법률의 규정에 의하여 대리관계가 생겨난 경우에는 표현대리권이 생겨나지 않는다. 이 경우, 표현대리권을 소멸시키기 위한 Notice조차 필요 없게 된다.

10 Liability of Principal for TORTS of Agent : (Master-Servant Rule)

1) P will be liable for torts committed by Agent if a P/A relationship exists & the tort was committed by A within scope of that relation .

EX Bouncer and nightclub owner for the negligence behaviors

2) master-servant rule은 employee에게는 적용되지만 independent contractor에게는 일반적으로 적용되지 않는다.

〈개념정리〉

	Employee	Independent contractor(IC)
Controlled by the Employer in	Time spent and results	Results only
Employer(principal) cares only	Both process and results	Results only
Employer(principal) is liable for the wrongdoing of	When done within the work scope and legality(detour), but not when done outside the work scope and legality(frolic)	Generally a principal is not vicariously liable for the negligence of IC, since the principal is not in a position to control the manner in which the IC performs the works.
Exceptionally, even the employer (principal) can be held liable		When involved with ultrahazardous activity, inherently dangerous, or legally specified activities, For example, 1) Where K requires the intrinsically dangerous work 2) Where the principal is charged by law for the duty breached 3) Where the work will create a nuisance 4) Where the work will involve a peculiar risks of harm unless proper preparations are taken 5) Where the act is illegal Rationale for the exceptions 1) Non-delegable duty 2) Public policy

참고 frolic v.s. detour

1. frolic-occurs when the employee departs from the course and scope of employment to a significant degree in pursuit of the employee's own interests

2. detour- less serious deviation from the course and scope of employment

3. the employer is vicariously liable for torts committed during detours, but not those committed during frolics.

3) 일반적으로 **independent contractor**의 행위에 대하여 employer에게는 책임을 물을 수 없지만 다음의 경우에는 employer에게도 책임이 있다.

A. **land occupier** liable for injuries arising from independent contractors work on the land. 여기에서 contractor는 unforeseeability를 주장하면 책임에서 벗어날 수 있다.

EX 볼링장 주인이 샹델리어 전문가(independent contractor)를 초빙하여 샹델리어를 새로 설치하는 데, 샹델리어가 잘못 부착되어 볼링 치러 온 고객이 그 샹델리어에 머리를 맞아 다치게 될 경우 볼링장 주인은 샹델리어 전문가와 더불어 처벌받는다.

B. Under the public policy of non-delegable duty:

The principal is vicariously liable for the agent's N despite the principal's own exercise of due care.

EX1 Vehicle owner to keep it in safe working order; the duty of the business to keep it's premises and instrumentalities safe for its customers; taxi company giving a repair service to other agents.

EX2 DRAM SHOP DUTY OF CARE:

A bar owner [or other commercial vendor that sells liquor for on-the-premises consumption] has a duty to use ordinary care not to serve alcohol to a person that the bar owner [or other commercial vendor] knows or reasonably should know from the circumstances is already intoxicated. The policy of holding a tavern owner, or other purveyor of alcoholic beverages, liable for injuries in certain circumstances was first announced in Oklahoma in the landmark 1986 case of Brigance v. Velvet (Dove, 725 P.2d 300).

C. **ultrahazardous activity(inherently dangerous activity)**의 경우 설령 independent contractor가 한 일일지라도 owner에게 책임을 물을 수 있다.

EX A지역의 토지를 소유하고 있던 John Doe는 해당토지에 있는 돌산을 제거하기 위해 다이너마이트 전문취급업자인 Boy를 불러 돌산제거 작업을 의뢰함. 돌산은 무사히 제거되었으나 이웃에서 밍크를 키우던 Farmer 자신의 밍크가 다이너마이트 폭발음에 의해 모두 사망한 것을 알게 되었음. 이 경우 Farmer는 Boy뿐만 아니라 John Doe를 상대로 해서 소송을 제기하는 것이 가능함

Chapter 6

Employment Law

1 Federal Social Securities Act

〈개념정리〉

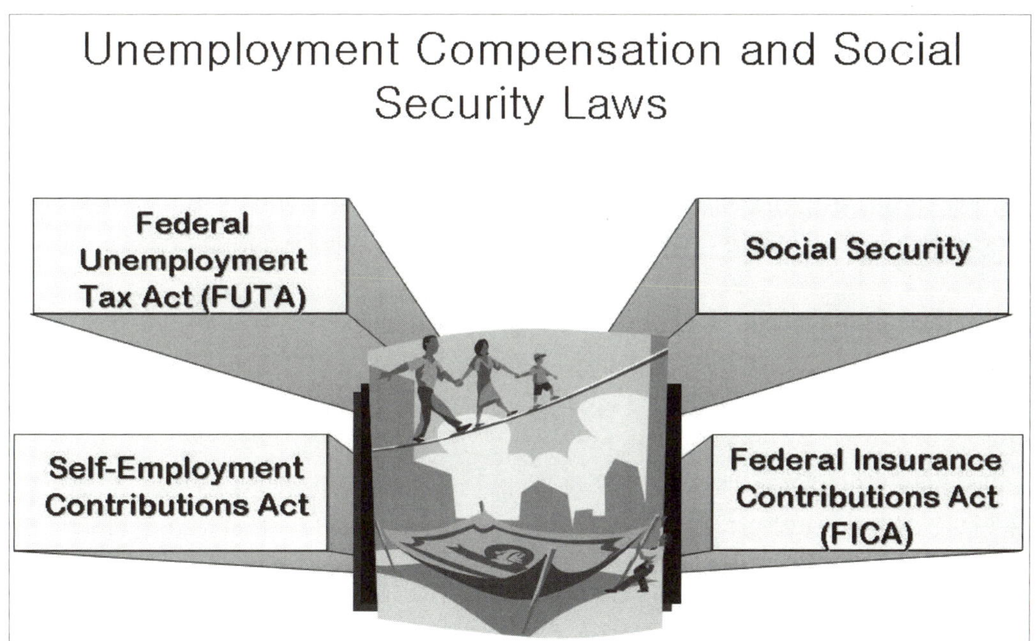

참고 미국서 사업할땐 노동법 모르면 낭패

LA진출 국내 프랜차이즈 소송당해 곤욕

북미지역에 진출한 국내 프랜차이즈 업체들이 미국 노동법을 제대로 알지 못해 소송에 휘말리거나 손해를 보는 사례가 늘고 있다. 국내 프랜차이즈 업체는 최근 5년 사이 50여 개에 이르고 있다. 여기에 치킨 브랜드인 BBQ를 비롯해 10여 개 업체가 올 가을 북미지역 진출을 추진하고 있다.

LA에는 작년부터 미스터피자와 교촌치킨, 파리바게뜨와 윈, 빵굼터, 칠보면옥, 명동교자 등 수십개 업체가 이미 점포를 개설했다. 그러나 이들 업체 중 상당수가 현지 노동법을 정확히 이해하지 못해 노동법에 정통한 종업원들과 마찰을 빚고 있는 것으로 나타났다. 성차별이나 인종차별, 성희롱으로 인한 소송도 발생하고 있다. 현재 LA 한인타운에만 노동법 관련 소송을 진행 중인 프랜차이즈 업체가 2~3곳에 이르는 것으로 알려졌다. 국내 업체에서 가장 빈번하게 문제가 되는 노동법 위반 사례는 시간외수당을 잘못 계산하거나 아예 주지 않은 것.

시간외수당은 일주일당 40시간이상을 근무하면 초과 근무시간에 대해 1.5배를 줘야 한다. 40시간 미만이라 하더라도 하루8시간을 넘기면 1.5배를 줘야 하며, 12시간 이상일 때는 두 배를 줘야 한다. 특히 주급으로 일정액을 주기로 계약했을 때도 해당 금액을 40시간으로 나눠 시간당 급여를 계산하고 초과 근무 시 1.5배 급여를 지급해야 한다.

국내 프랜차이즈 업체들은 이런 규정을 가볍게 생각하는 사례가 많다. 한국식으로 생각해 근무시간을 철저히 관리하지 않는 사례도 허다하다. 일부 업체는 종업원들의 근무시간을 재는 '타임카드'를 구비하지 않았다가 낭패를 보는 일도 많다.

어떤 업체들은 현금으로 지급하면서 증거를 남기지 않았다가 급여 미지급으로 소송을 당하는 일도 있다. 종업원 주장에 감정적으로 대응하는 바람에 법정 싸움으로 비화하면서 엄청난 변호사 비를 감당해야 하는 사례도 생기고 있다.

C업체 미국법인 대표는 "미국에 진출한 지 3년 만에 노동법 위반과 관련해 두 번이나 종업원들과 마찰을 빚었다"며 "소송이 진행될 경우 많은 비용과 시간을 할애해야 한다는 주위 권고에 따라 사전협의를 통해 보상금을 지급했다"고 말했다. [로스앤젤레스 김경도특파원] 9/18/07 매일경제

1) 다음과 같은 기본사항을 보장하기위한 것이다.

Hospital Insurance [의료보장]

Old Age Insurance [노령자보장]

Unemployment Insurance [실직자 보장]

Survivorship and Disability Insurance[재해자 보장]

주의 : 위의 hospital insurance에는medicare 는 포함되지만, 저소득층과 신체장애자를 위한 의료보조금인 medicaid는 포함되지 않으므로 주의할 필요가 있다.

Medicare is a federal health insurance program for people aged 65 and older, certain people under 65 with disabilities and certain people with kidney disease. Medicaid, which is administered by the states, is a program of health coverage for certain people with low incomes. Eligibility for Medicare depends on age or disability only; eligibility for Medicaid depends on age, disability or family status and on an individual (or family) income and resources.

2) 재원(sources of financing)

A. 근로자의 노령화, 재해, 의료보험 등을 위해서 Fed Insurance Contributions Act에 근거하여 근로자와 사용자에게 세금(FICA tax) 을 부과하고 있다.

B. 자영업자의 경우 노령화, 재해, 의료보험 등을 위해 Self-Employment Contributions Act에 의해 그들에게 세금을 부과하고 있다.

C. 근로자의 실업자 보험수당을 위해 Fed Unemployment Tax Act에 의해 사용자에게 세금(FUTA tax)을 부과하고 있다.

〈개념정리〉

FICA(원천징수 원칙)	SECA	FUTA
근로자 부담 사용자 부담	자영업자 부담	사용자만 부담

Fed Inurance Contributions Act(FICA)

1) 사용자와 근로자가 공동으로 납부하며, 사용자는 근로자가 내야할 세금을 임금을 지불하면서 임금으로부터 원천징수(withhold)하여야 한다.

2) **사용자는 원천징수한 근로자 몫과 같은 금액의 사용자 몫을 모두 정부에 납부하여야** 한다.

3) 또한 납세의무자의 tax identification number(TIN)를 국세청(IRS)에 보고해야 한다. 이러한 보고의무를 소홀히 하면 벌금이 부과된다.

4) 사용자는 납부한 FICA tax중 자신의 몫을 소득으로부터 공제할(deductible) 수 있지만, 근로자는 자신의 몫을 소득으로부터 공제받을 수 없다.

5) **사용자는 근로자 몫의 FICA tax를 자발적으로 대신 납부해줄수 있다.** 이 경우, **사용자는 근로자의 몫을 추가적 인건비로서 소득으로부터 공제받을 수 (deductible) 있는 반면, 근로자는 추가적 소득으로서 이에 대한 소득세를 부담 (taxable)**하게 된다.

6) **강제성** : 다른 연기금에 가입했다고 해서 FICA tax를 납부하지 않을 수 없다. 또한 fed social security act에 의해 보장되는 program을 받지 않겠다고 하면서 FICA tax를 납부하지 않을 수도 없다.

 Self-Employment Contributions Act (SECA)

1) 자영업자들의 노령화(old age), 재난재해(survivor's and disability), 입원비(hospital insurance) 등에 대비하기 위해서 self-employed persons의 net income에 social security self-employment tax를 부과하도록 한 법

2) Self-employed persons라고 함은 **자영업자, partnership의 partner, 회사의 이사(corporate director), 등이고 independent contractor도 여기에 포함**된다.

 Fed Unemployment Tax Act(FUTA) 연방실업세법

1) 이법은 일자리창출이 아니라 실업수당 지급(unemployment compensation benefits)을 지급하는데 주목적이 있다. FUTA tax는 근로자임금(wage)에 일정세율을 곱하여 산출된다. 다만 기본 금액(base amount)가 있다.

2) Fed unemployment tax는 **사용자(employer)만이 납부하는 것으로 근로자에게 납세의무가 없다.** 사용자가 납부한 이 세금은 사업경비로서 fed income tax를 계산할 때 소득에서 공제가능하다(deductible as business expenses)

 주 실업세법State Unemloyment Tax Act

1) 주법에 의해 낸 unemployment tax는 FUTA tax에서 세액공제(credit) 가능하다.

2) 사용자의 해고건수 신고내역(the number of claim)에 따라서 주법에 따른 unemployment tax가 변동된다.

Definitions : Wages

1) Wages 임금

임금은 근로의 대가로 받는 모든 보상(all compensations for employment)을 의미한다. 예를 들면 생산성 향상에 따라 자동차를 해당부서 직원들에게 선물했다면 이 또한 포함된다.

2) FICA tax 및 FUTA tax는 사용자가 근로자에게 지급하는 임금(wages)을 기준으로 하여 부과되므로 임금의 정의는 매우중요하다.

3) 임금에 포함되는 것

A. **M**oney Wages 금전성 임금

B. **Base** Pay of those in services 기본급

C. **Contingent** fees 각종 성공불

D. Most **Tips**

E. **Bonuses** and Commissions

F. **Com**pensation not paid in case 현금이외의 보상 EX car

G. **Vacation and dismissal allowances** 휴가 및 해고수당

4) 임금에 포함되지 않는 것

A. **Wages greater**than base amount (base amount를 초과하는 임금)

B. **Reimbursed**expenses 사용자가 부담한 경비를 근로자가 지출하고 나중에 회사로부터 보상받는 것

C. Employee **medical** and hospital expenses paid by employer
사용자부담 근로자 병원비

D. Employee **insurance** premium paid by employer 사용자부담 근로자 보험료

E. Parent to employee **retirement plan** by employer 사용자부담 퇴직연금 납입액

7 Definitions : Employees

1) 근로자(**employees**)란 작업의 결과(**results**)뿐만 아니라 그 방법(**method**)에 있어서도 사용자의 물리적 통제(**physical control**)을 받는 사람이다.

2) Partner[파트너], self-employed person[자영업자], corporate director[이사], independent contractor[독립계약자]는 employee 취급을 받지 않아, 실업자 수당 대상이 되지 못한다(not covered by unemployment compensation). 이들은 SECA 적용을 받는다.

3) Independent contractor는 방법(method)만을 알아서 하면 되고, 사용자는 결과(results)에 대해서만 책임을 따진다는 점에서 근로자(employee)와는 다르다(구분을 잘 해둘 것)

EX A house builder is only responsible about the results to the home owner.

4) 따라서 사외이사(outside director)나 명예이사(honorary director)라 할지라도 그에 따른 수당(Ex. Honorary director fee)를 받았다면 이는 employee로서가 아니라 self-employed persons인 것으로 취급된다.

〈개념정리〉

	Employee(EE)	Independent contractor(IC)
paid by	time	results
controlled both in	process and results	results
principal is liable when	EE did the wrongdoing within work scope and in legality	Generally principal is not liable for IC's wrongdoing. IC only is responsible.

Definitions : Old-age, survivor's and disability insurance benefits 고령 및 장애 보험 benefits

1) 근로기간에 따라 fully insured와 currently insured로 구분되며 여기에는

A. Lump-sum death benefits (사망 시 한꺼번에 지급되는 benefits)

B. Benefits for disabled workers and his/her dependents
장애근로자 및 가족용 benefits

C. Survivor benefits 유가족 benefits 등이 있다.

2) **이혼한 배우자(divorced spouses = divorcee)도 이러한 benefits**을 받을 수 있음에 유의해야 한다.

9 Benefits의 감액

1) 조기퇴직(**early retirement**)하면 benefits이 감액된다.

2) Benefits을 받고 있으면서도 일정한도 이상의 **earned income**이 있으면 benefits이 감액된다.

3) Earned income이란 일을 함으로써 얻는 소득을 의미함으로 사적연금(private pension plans)으로부터 받는 연금, 이자소득, 투자소득, 보험금 등은 포함되지 않는다.

4) Limited partner가 limited partnership으로부터 받는 것은 투자소득(investment income)으로 간주되어 self-employment income이 아니다.

10 Unemployment Benfits 실업수당

1) 실업수당을 수령할 수 있는 자격과 금액은 **주법(stae law)으로 정한다.**

2) 자신의 아무런 잘못 없이 **[no fault of their own] 해고된 근로자만 이러한 실업수당을 받을 수 있다.**

3) 정당한 사유 없이 자발적으로 직장을 그만두거나 정당한 사유로 해고된 경우 그 근로자는 실업수당을 받지 못한다.

4) 자영업자(self-employed person)도 실업수당을 받지 못한다.

11 Workers' Compensation Act [worker' s compensation]

EE는 common law상의 권리를 포기하는 대신 자동적으로 보상을 받을 수 있도록 하여 맞교환을 하는 성격의 법이다.

1) Statutory insurance scheme designed as exclusive remedy for aggrieved **employees <u>hurt on the job</u>**. 근로자가 작업 중에 재해를 입었을 경우 그 재해로 인한 손해배상을 받는 것을 의미한다.

2) 사용자(Employers = ER)가 의무적으로 부담(**compulsory <u>statutory coverage</u>**)하게 되는데 그 책임의 성격은 엄격책임(ER **strict liabity**)이므로 사용자의 과실이나(negligence or faults of employers)에 관계없이 발생한다.

3) 사용자는 assumption of risk, negligence of fellow employees, contributory negligence, comparative negligence 등의 common law 상의 defense 사용이 불가능하다. (no defense for employers)

4) 근로자는 일반적으로 workers' compensation에 의해 손해배상 받을 수 있는 권리를 포기할 수 없다. 이러한 권리를 포기하는 고용계약서는 무효이다.

5) 사용자가 부담하는 workers' compensation 이나 이를 위한 보험료는 사용자의 **비용처리(혹은 제조원가)**할 수 있다. 사용자가 지급하도록 주법에 되어 있으므로 이를 근로자 자신의 소득에서 공제(deduct)할 수 없다.

6) 사용자는 workers'compensation에 대비한 보험에 가입해야 하는데 보험 없이도 이를 지급할 능력이 있다는 것을 입증하면 보험에 가입하지 않아도 된다.

7) EE Get - all med, partial salary, disability benefits, death benefits, but no pain & suffering, no punitive. 업무상 다치거나 사망한 근로자에게는 의료비, 급여(2/3) 장례비용, 노동력상실로 인한 disability benefits, 근로자가 사망한 경우에는death benefits이 지급된다.

8) 근로자가 법에 따라 workers' compensation을 받은 경우, 사용자를 상대로 소송을 제기할 수 없다.
an agrrieved EE cannot sue his fellow EE for their N arising out of and during the course of employment, nor can he hold his ER vicariously liable for its N because of the workers' compensation statute. 피해입은 EE는 피해준 동료 EE의 업무상과실이나 ER에게 책임을 물을 수 없고, Vicarious Liability책임도 물을 수 없다.

9) 다만 사용자가 고의로(intentionally) 근로자를 다치게 한 경우에는 workers'compensation benefits 이외에 intentional torts(불법행위)로 사용자에게 책임을 물을 수 있다.

10) 업무외의 재해를 입은자(hurt off duty), 농업에 종사하는 근로자(farming workers)와 임시사무직 근로자(temporary office workers)는 적용되지 않는다.

11) 근로자는 업무상 재해를 제기한 제 3자를 상대로 직접 또는 보험사를 통해서 소송을 제기할 수 있다(subrogation)

12) 통지의무 : 업무상 재해를 입은 근로자는 업무상 재해가 발생하면 그 사실을 신속하게[사고발생일로부터 30일내] 사용자에게 통지하여야 한다.

13) 업무상의 재해(**occupational disease**) 뿐만 아니라 기존의 질병이 더욱 악화된 경우(**aggravated preexisting disease**)도 이에 해당한다.

12 Occupational Safety and Health Act[OSHA}

1) 작업장의 안전기준(safety standards)를 수립하여 근로자의 안전도모(job safety)를 위한 법이다.

2) OSHA는 연방정부, 주정부, 그리고 일부산업의 근로자를 제외하고는 거의 모든 근로자(almost all employees)에게 적용된다.

3) Occupational Safety and Health Adminsitration이 OSHA를 집행하는데 사용자 또는 근로자의 요청에 의해 조사를 할 수 있으며, 사용자에게 통지를 하지 않고 불시에 작업시간에 조사가 이루어질 수도 있다.

4) OSHA의 위반자에게는 작업장개선명령(order to correct unsafe conditions)등을 내릴 수도 있고, 고의적인 위반(willful violations)자에게는 벌금(civil penalities) 또는 징역에 처하도록 법무부 검찰 측에 요청할 수 있다.

13 Title VII of the Civil Rights Act of 1964

1) 사용자가 고용인을 채용(hiring), 승진(promotion), 이동(transfer), 해고(firing), 또는 보상(compensation)을 하는데 있어서 종교(religion), 인종(race), 국적(nationality), 성별(sex)등을 이유로 차별하지 못하도록 하는 법이다.

2) 주간통상(interstate commerce)에 종사하는 사업을 하는 15인 이상의 근로자를 가진 사용자나 노동조합에 적용된다.

3) 사용자는 다음과 같은 이유로 항변을 할 수 있다.

A. 직업상의 자격요건(외국어, 컴퓨터, 자격증 등 bona fide qualification)

B. 연공제 및 실적제(seniority or merit system)

C. 전문적 능력시험(professionally developed ability)

D. 국가안보(national security)

14 Age Discrimination in Employment Act(ADEA)

1) 직장에서 연령에 의한 차별을 금지하기 위한 법으로 40세 이상의 근로자에게 연령을 이유로 HPCF(채용, 승진, 보상, 해고) 상의 차별을 못하도록 하며, 70세 미만의 근로자에 대한 강제퇴직(mandatory retirement)를 금지시키는 법이다.

2) 차별을 당한 근로자는 금전적 손해배상(monetary damages-체불임금 요구), 복직(reinstatement), 승진(promotion)등의 구제수단(remedities)를 가질 수 있다.

3) 단 연령 때문에 차별을 당했다는 이유로 조기퇴직(early retirement)를 요구할 수는 없다.

15 Equal Pay Act(EPA)

1) 임금지불에서 남녀차별을 금지하는 것으로 EEOC에서 규율된다.

2) 사용자(ER)는 동일노동(equal work)에 대해 동일임금(equal pay)을 지급하여야 한다.

3) 동일노동에 대한 차별적 임금(differential wages)은 연공제(seniority system), 실적제(merit system), 작업의 질(quality of work) 등에 따라 정당화될 수도 있다.

4) 이법은 임신을 이유로 차별을 못하게 하는 **Pregnancy Discrimination Act** 및 **Family and Medical Leave Act**와 연관성이 있으므로 함께 알아두어야 한다.

16 Family and Medical Leave Act (FMLA)

1) **50인이상** 근무하는 직장에서 **1년이상(1,250시간)** 근무한 직원에게는 가정상의 문제, 질병으로 인한 휴직 등을 보장해주기 위해 사용자가 **12주일간**의 무급휴가(**without pay**)를 보내줄 수 있도록 한 법이다.

2) **휴직사유**

A. 근로자의 중병(EE's serious **health problem**)

B. 부모, 배우자, 자녀의 병간호(care for serious health problem of parents, spouses, or child)

C. 자녀의 출산육아(**birth and care of baby**)

D. 양자입양(**adoption** or foster care)

17 Amercians with Disabilities Act (ADA)

1) 이법은 근로현장에서 장애인을 차별하지 못하도록 하며, **장애인에게 reasonable accommodation and public service을 제공하여 장애인이 큰 어려움 없이 일을 할 수 있도록** 하기 위한 것이다.

2) 단, 이 법은 장애인을 강제로 고용하도록 하는 것은 아니어서(not to force the manatory employment of the disabled) 사용자는 장애인을 고용하기 위한 계획을 별도로 수립할 필요는 없다.

3) 사용자가 일을 할 수 있는 장애인(qualified person with a disability)에게 HPCF에 있어서 장애인을 이유로 차별하는 것을 금지하고 있다.

4) Reasonable accomodation

장애를 가진 근로자에게 합리적인 범위 내에서의 편의를 제공한다면 그 근로자가 중요한 일을 수행할 경우, 사용자는 적절한 편의를 제공해주어야 한다. reasonable accommodation[합리적인 편의제공]이란 새로운 장비구입(acquiring new equipment), 탄력적 작업시간 설정(establishing flexible working hour), 작업계획수정(modifying work schedules)등을 포함한다.

5) No Undue Hardship

사용자가 장애를 가진 근로자에게 합리적인 편의를 제공해주는 것이 undue hardship (지나치게 부담)이 된다는 것을 입증하면 편의를 제공하지 않아도 된다. Undue hardship 이란 매우 어렵거나 비용이 많이 드는 것(significant difficulty or expense)을 의미한다.

6) Public Service/Private service

대중교통(public transportation) 및 대중용 편의시설(public accommodations)등을 의미하는데 민간기관(private entities)에서 운영하는 public services도 여기에 포함된다.

ADA에 따라 이러한 public service의 이용가능성(access)를 높여주어야 한다.

18 Consolidated Budget Reconciliation Act(COBRA)

1) 근로자가 직장을 그만둔 후 자신의 선택에 따라 이전에 가입한 **직장의료보험(group health coverage)을 18개월 동안 그대로 유지**할 수 있도록 한 법.

2) 근로자가 중대한 잘못(gross misconduct)로 인해 해고된 경우에는 COBRA의 혜택을 받을 수 없다.

19 Fair Labor Standards & Union

1) Fed Fair Labor Standards Act

A. 연방법으로 법정최저임금(minimum wages)및 주당근로시간(maximum weekly hours)등에 관해 규율하고 있다.

B. 주당 40시간을 초과하는 노동에 대해서는 **통상임금의 1.5배의 초과근무수당(time-and-a-half provision)**을 지급해주어야 한다.

C. 최저임금과 초과근무수당은 전문직종사자(professionals), 외판원(outside salesperson) 등은 적용되지 않는다.

D. 택시운전사, 철도종업원 등은 최저임금의 적용은 받지만, 초과근무수당의 적용은 받지 않는다.

E. 근로자의 임금을 계산할 때 **시간, 주, 월 단위를 기준으로 계산할 수 있다.**

F. 미국노동부(Department of Labor)에서 이 법을 집행하며, 이 법을 위반한 사용자에게는 벌금이나 감옥 형을 내릴 수 있다.

2) National Labor Relations Act(NLRA, Wagnor Act)

A. 근로자에게 노동조합(labor union)을 만들 수 있도록 허용하고, 지원하는 법이다.

B. 사용자는 노동관련 사항(work-related issues), 예를 들어 해고(firing practices), 작업시간(working hours), 퇴직규정(retirement rules), 안전조항(safety conditions), 임금(여기에는sick pay, vacation pay등도 포함된다) 등에 대해서는 노조와 협의하여야 한다.

3) Taft-Hartly Act[THA]

A. secondary boycotts, featherbedding(필요이상으로 근로자를 고용하도록 사용자에게 강요하는 것) 등을 금지하는 법으로 노동조합의 불공정관행(unfair labor practices)을 금지하기 위한 것이다.
B. 파업이전의 냉각기간(cooling-off period)에 관해 규정되어있다.

4) Landrum-Griffin Act [LGA **노조법**]

A. 노동조합 내부의 민주화를 위한 법으로 노조의 재무상황 보고(financial reporting), 노조간부의 부정행위(misdeed)에 대한 민형사소송(civil and criminal action)등을 규정하고 있다.
B. 노조집행부의 선출, 조합 총회 등에 있어서 조합원에게 권리를 부여하고 있어서 노조원들의 권리장전 (bill of rights for union members)라고 할 수 있다.

20 Employee Retirement Income Security Act of 1974(ERISA)

1) 사용자가 pension plan을 갖고 있을 경우 ERISA에 따라 일정기준을 맞추어야 한다.

2) 근로자가 pension plan에 납입한 금액(**EE contributions** to pension pan)에 대해서는 근로자의 퇴직이후 pension benefits을 받을 수 있는 권리를 즉시 부여(**vest immediately**)해야 한다.

3) 사용자가pension plan에 납입한 금액(**ER contributions** to pension plan)에 대해서는 pension benefit을 받을 수 있는 권리를 해당근로자가 고용된 시점으로부터 **5년~7년 이후부터** 부여해야 한다.

4) Pension plan에 의해 적립된 자금은 사용자가 관리하되, **ERISA규정에 따라** 오용(avoid mismanagement)을 막기 위해 상세한 기록 및 보고의무(annual reports)에 따라야 한다.

5) 사용자는 근로자가 pension plan에 가입하는 것을 지연시킬 수 없다.

6) Pension plan은 contributory pension plan과 noncontributory pension plan으로 구별할 수 있는데 **noncontributory pension plan에 있어서는 ER만이 pension plan에 납입**하고, 근로자는 납입할 필요 없다.

Chapter 7

Environmental Law

1) CL approach

환경에 관한 법률이 제정되기 이전에는 CL상의doctrine of nuisance(安穩妨害 nuisance if substantial and unreasonable interference with one's use and enjoyment of private land)에 의거하여 불법행위의 한 유형으로 보아 손해배상과 금지명령 (injunction) 을 내렸다.

2) Liability for Negligence

사용자(피고)가 공해물질 배출을 통해 예측 가능한 피해(foreseeable harm)를 주지 않도록 하기 위하여, 합리적인 주의(reasonable care)를 하지 못하여 원고가 피해를 입었다는 것을 원고가 입증하게 되면 피고는 원고에게 과실에 의한 손해배상책임을 지게 된다.

3) SL

공해관련 책임입증이 쉽지 않으므로 엄격책임(무과실책임, strict liability)개념을 도입하여 피해자의 입증의 어려움을 완화해주었다.

1 연방법에 의한 규제

1) 미국 환경청(Environmental Protection Agency, EPA)

A. 행정명령(administrative orders)과 과징금(civil penalties)을 통해서 환경에 관한 연방법들이 잘 준수되도록 하고, 위반자들을 상대로 민·형사소송을 제기되도록 법무부에 통보하는 역할을 한다.

B. 환경관련 규제조치 권고안을 발의하고, 환경관련 법규를 연구한다.

C. **일반 민간인이 환경법 위반자를 상대로 직접 소송을 제기할 수도 있고**, 환경청(EPA)을 상대로 환경법을 위반한 자에 대해 법을 집행하도록 소송을 할 수도 있다.

D. 환경법 위반자에 대해서는 주정부도 소송을 제기할 수 있다.

E. 그러나 일반인(private citizens)이 환경법위반자를 상대로 제기한 소송에서 **미국환경청(EPA)은 원고를 도와줄 수는 없다.**

2) National Environmental Policy Act[NEPA]

A. 모든 연방기관들(all fed agencies)이 법을 제정할 때 환경영향평가보고서(environmental impact statement, EIS)를 작성하도록 하여 환경적인 요소를 고려하도록 의무화 한 것이다.

B. EIS의 "환경"이란 문화적(cultural and national heritage interest), 미적(aesthetic)환경 뿐만 아니라,자연환경(natural environment) 등도 포함된다.

C. EIS에는 다음과 같은 내용이 들어가야 한다.

(1) 피할 수 없는 부작용(unavoidable adverse consequences of action, **U**AC)

(2) 목적달성을 위한 다른 대안의 존재여부(alternative to achieve goals, **A**AG)

(3) 예상되는 환경에 대한 영향(expected impact on environment, **EI**)

D. NEPA의 enforcement는 주로 환경법을 위반한 사람들에 대한 소송을 통해서 이루어진다.

 Clean Air Act[CAA]

1) 미국환경청은 자동차와 같이 움직이는 공해원(**mobile** sources)와 공장과 같이 움직이지 않는 공해원(**stationary** sources)에 대한 배출기준(air quality standards)을 설정할 수 있다.

2) 산성비(acid rain)나 오존층(ozone layer)에 영향을 미치는 여러 가지 오염물질(toxic pollutants)에 대한 규제 및 원자력 발전소의 방사능물질(radioactive particle)의 배출(emissions)에 대한 규제가 이루어지고 있다.
자동차들의 배출기준을 위반한 차량들의 리콜(recall)도 이 법에 따라 이루어지고 있다.

3) 민간단체(civic group)나 일반인은 이 법에 따라 위반자에게 소송을 제기할 수 있는데 **일반인이 승소할 경우, 변호사비용(attorney fees)을 포함한 소송비용(court costs)도 받을 수 있다.**

4) **EPA는 위반자가 법을 위반함으로써 얻은 효익(benefits)에 해당하는 금액만큼 과징금(civil penalties)을 부과할 수 있다.**

5) 고의성이 있는 위반자에게는 법무부에 통보하여 벌금(criminal fines)이나 징역형(imprisonment)에 처하도록 할 수 있다.

Clean Water Act(CWA)

1) rivers, seas, ponds, wetlands, streams 등의 오염을 제거하거나 방지하기 위한 기준(standards)을 설정할 수 있다.

2) 이법에 의해 핵발전소(nuclar power planst)등에서 배출되는 온수(heated water) 도 규제되고 있다.

Safe Drinking Water Act[SDWA]

1) 상수도(public water systems)에 의해 가정에 공급되는 수돗물의 안전성(safety of water)을 규제하기 위한 법이다.

2) 마실 수 있는 우물(wells for drinking water)에 쓰레기(waste)를 버리는 것도 이법의 규제대상이 된다.

〈개념정리〉

water refinery	controlled by FDA			
	bottled water		consumers	
	controlled by EPA under safe drinking water act			
	tab water		consumers	

 Federal Insecticide, Fungicide, and Rodenticide Act(FIFRA)

1) 살충제(insecticide), 살균제(fungicide), 쥐약(rodenticide), 제초제(herbicide) 등의 판매 및 사용을 규제하기 위한 법이다.

2) 살충제, 제초제 등을 판매하기 위해서는 EPA에 등록(registration)을 반드시 해야 한다.

3) 이법은 각종 곡물사료(food crops)의 제초제의 잔존량(**amount** or **quantities** of pesticide residue)을 제한하고, 각종 표시(**labeling**)에 대해 관여한다.

4) 이법에 따라 EPA는
A. 사용법의 승인(**certify** them for general or restricted use),
B. 등록거부(**deny** registration),
C. 조건부 등록허용(grant conditional registration when useful until effects known)
D. 등록의 중지(**suspend** registration), 등의 조치를 취할 수 있다.

5) 일반인은 EPA에 등록의 중지 및 취소청원(petition)을 할 수 있다

 Comprehensive Environmental Response, Compensation, and Liability Act(CERCLA)

1) **superfund** legislation이라고도 알려져 있으며 위험한 화학물지 제조업자(manufacturers of damgerous chemicals)에게 세금을 매기도록 한 법이다.

2) 위험물질(hazardous substances)의 생성과 운송에 관해 규제하고 있는데 이 때 위

험물질에는 석유(petroleum)와 천연가스(natural gas)는 포함되지 않는다.

3) 이법에 따라 정화(cleanup)가 필요한 오염된 지역(hazardous waste site)을 파악하고, 이를 정화하는데 필요한 비용에 대해 누가 책임을 부담할지에 대해 결정하고 있다.

4) 정화비용(**cleanup cost**)과 환경파괴에 의한 손해배상 (hazardous waste sites)을 파악하고 이를 정화하는데 필요한 비용에 대해 누가 책임을 부담할지에 대해서는 다음과 같은 자들이 **joint and several liability**를 부담하게 된다.

joint and several liability[연대책임]
the plaintiff can choose to collect all of his damages from one defendant or some of the damages from each defendant, regardless of how the court apportioned liability. The defendant or defendants that pay the plaintiff, will then have to demand reimbursement from the other defendants that were held liable, in proportion to the amount that the court found those other defendants at fault.

EX If the roof of a building caves in causing you personal injury, and the court finds that the architect was 10% at fault for design error, the project manager was 20% at fault for failing to properly supervise, and the roofing contractor was 70% at fault for construction error, you can choose to collect all of your damages from the architect even though he was only 10% at fault.

A. 현재 오염지역을 소유하거나 관리하는 자(current **o**wners or operators of site)
B. 과거에 오염지역을 소유하거나 관리한 자(**past** **o**wners or operators of site)
C. 오염지역에 오염물질을 운송한자(persons who **transported** wastes to site = transporter)
D. 오염지역에 오염물질을 운송하도록 arrange한 자(persons who **arranged** to have waste transported = arranger)

5) 이경우 정화비용에 관한 책임은 엄격책임(SL)에 근거하고 있으며 피고에게 가능한 항변은 acts of God (천재지변), 전쟁(act of war), 제3자의 행위(act of unrelated 3 P) 등이다.

6) 정화비용에 대한 책임은 **joint and several liability**이기 때문에 오염에 대해 일부 책임이 있는 사람에게도 정화비용전체에 대한 책임을 물릴 수 있다.

7) 오염을 야기한 일반인(private parties)의 법적책임은 CERCLA에서 다루고 있지 않으므로 일반인은 CL에 의한 소송을 통해 손해를 배상받을 수밖에 없다.

7 환경법의 준수여부에 관한 감사(environmental compliance audits)

1) 환경에 관한 연방법 및 주법을 준수하고 있는지를 체계적이고 객관적으로 검토하기 위한 감사이다.

2) 감사의 목적

A. 환경법 위반사실 및 환경법위반이 될수 있는 관행을 미리 발견하여 회사는 환경문제로 인한 소송위험을 회피(**avoid litigation**)할 수 있다.

B. 자발적으로 위반사실을 발견함으로써 형벌(avoid **criminal sanctions**)을 피할 수 있다.

C. 증권관련법의 공시의무(comply with **disclosure requirements**)을 이행할 수 있다.

Chapter 8 Antitrust Law

연방법으로서 상품과 서비스를 가장 경제적이고 효율적으로 분배 및 생산되도록 하여 자유롭고 경쟁적인 시장을 유지하고 공정성과 소비자들에게 보다 폭넓은 선택을 해주도록 하는데 그 목적을 두고 있다(to promote the production and distribution of goods and services in the most economical and efficient manner by preserving free, competitive markets. Also promotes fairness and give consumer a wider choice).

1) 만일 불법적인 제한내용이 담긴 계약일 경우

계약이행을 할 수 없고(unenforceable), 민・형사상의 책임과 injunctions도 가할 수 있다.

A. vertical restraint 수직적 제한

경쟁관계에 있는 두 제조업자가 가격과 서비스 면에서 경쟁하는 소매업자와 제각기 관찰 이 불가능한 관계를 맺는 것을 말한다.

EX 삼성전자와 E-mart간 TV를 놓고 제휴하는 경우

B. Horizontal Restraint(수평적 제한)

동일한 업종이나 동일한 수준의 배포단계에 있는 업체

EX HDTV 생산 분야의 삼성전자와 LG전자

2) 위와 같은 제한이 있게 될 경우 합리성 기준(standards of reasonableness)이 적용된다.

3) exceptions to the antitrust laws [반독과점법의 예외]

注意|

Labor Unions(노조)	단, nonlabor group과 결합하거나 불법행동을 할 경우에는 적용대상이 된다
Patents(특허권)	20-year monopoly허용, Design patent는 14년 허용
Copyrights(저작권)	Author's life + 70년 Publisher의 경우 95 years after publication or 120 years after creation
Trademarks(상표권)	Monopoly with an indefinite number of renewals if still used 계속 사용하는 한 무한정으로 갱신가능
Insurance	주법으로 관할하며 주 당국에서 관리감독
US exporters	외국사와 경쟁하는 경우 최대한 협력허용
States' Oil Quota	주간통상을 통해서 판매되는 석유에 대해서는 주별로 quota를 정할 수 있다.

Sherman Act of 1890

1) 거래를 제한하는 모든 계약, 결합, 그리고 공모는 불법이다(제1조) Contracts, combinations, and conspiracies in restraint of trade are illegal.

A. 보통 rules of reason을 사용하여 unreasonable restraints만 불법으로 규정

B. 불법인 경우 제한 자체가 위반인 경우도 있음(perse violations)

(1) 경쟁사간의 가격담합(**price fixing**)은 그 자체만으로 위반임.

(2) joint **boycott**(group agreement not to deal with another)도 그 자체만으로 위반임.

(3) **Horizontal** territorial limitation은 그 자체만으로 위반

EX1 Two companies agree not to sell at each other's section of the city.

EX2 무학소주, 선양소주, 보배소주, 한라소주가 지역을 나누어 판매하기로 한 경우.

(4) verticial terrioritaI limitation(Ex. Franchise)는 지나칠 경우에만 위반임

2) 독점을 하거나 하려고 시도하는 것은 불법이다(formation of, or the attempt to form a monopoly, is illegal)

A. percentage share of the market is a determining factor. 시장점유율이 기준이 된다.
B. product market and geographic market을 참조로 하여 시장점유율을 판정한다.

2 Clayton Act of 1914

셔먼 법이 독점을 위법한 것으로 규정한 반면, 클레이턴 법은 독점형성을 촉진하거나 독점으로 인한 위법거래관행을 유형별로 다소 자세히 규정하고 있다. 즉 클레이턴 법은 일정한 유형의 지주회사와 중역 겸임 등을 금지하고 자연 경쟁자간의 차별적 운송계약과 시장의 경쟁력을 현저하게 약화시키거나 독점을 할 의도를 가진 시장분할과 합병도 마찬가지로 금지하고 있다.

A. Prohibit a corporation from acquiring the stock of a competing company(merger) where theeffect might substantially lessen competition or tend to create a monopoly.
B. Fair company doctrine a merger that is anticompetitive may be allowed if the acquired company is failing and there is no other willing purchasers whose acquisition of the

company would reduce competition less.
피인수회사가 경영상태가 부실해 망해가거나 경쟁을 약화시킬만한 구매자가 없는 회사를 사들이는 경우 합병이 반경쟁적이 아니므로 허용한다.

C. 금지된 행위(prohibits)
  (1) **Interlocking** directorates 여러 회사 혹은 상호 경쟁회사의 이사진을 겸하는 것
  (2) **Price discrimination** between different purchasers
  (3) 구매자별로 다른 가격적용
  (4) **Exclusive**dealing agreements 독점취급 계약

Samsung requires Costco not to sell any other competitor manufacturers' TV sets such as LG's and Haier's.

  (5) **Tying** arrangements 끼워 팔기

3 Robinson_Patman Act of 1936

1) amended the Clayton Act to expand control in the area of price discrimination and makes buyers liable for price discrimination.

2) Robinson-Patman act **prohibits discrimination** as to price between purchasers of goods of **like quality and grade 유사품질과 등급의 상품을 가격이외의 다른 이유로 차별하는 것을 금지한다.**
A. if its effect is to <u>substantially lessen competition</u> or tend to create a monopoly
B. if the effect is to injure or prevent competition by competitor's or customers' competitors.
C. includes price discrimination between different geographical areas unless based on

Chapter 9

Property Law

〈개념정리〉

<table>
<tr><td colspan="2"></td><td>property</td><td></td></tr>
<tr><td colspan="2">real property</td><td></td><td>personal property = chattel</td></tr>
<tr><td rowspan="4">land,
building,
house,
apartment,
etc.</td><td rowspan="4">easement,
profit(= mining right, mineral right, timber right, etc.),
license,etc.</td><td>fixture</td><td>trade fixture</td></tr>
<tr><td rowspan="2">growing crops</td><td>movable and tangible property(goods)</td></tr>
<tr><td>harvested crops</td></tr>
<tr><td>inalienable property(bodily parts)</td><td>intangible personal property (intellectual property(trademark, copyright, patent), stock,etc.)</td></tr>
</table>

미국부동산법의 특징은 여러 가지지만 대표적으로

1) possessory right(점유권)을 소유권(ownership right = title)의 의미로 혼용해서 사용하는 경우도 있으므로 혼동하지 않아야 한다.

2) 한국처럼 지나치게 세입자를 보호하는 것이 아니고 오히려 집주인이나 임대인이 유리하게 되어있는 경우가 많다.

3) 계약서는 일종의 약속이므로 약속을 '무조건 준수'가 대원칙이다.

Distinction between real and personal property

1) Real Property

A. 부동산은 토지와 토지의 정착물(예 빌딩), 그리고 광물채굴권(mining right), 지상권(air right)등을 의미한다.

B. 재배되고 있는 곡식(growing crops)은 동산 또는 부동산으로 본다. 그러나 수확된 곡식(harvested crops)은 토지와 분리되어 곡식은 부동산이 아닌 동산으로 본다.

2) Personal Property[= chattel]

A. 자동차, 시계, 책 등과 같이 형태를 가진 유형동산(tangible personal property)와 형태를 갖지 않은 무형동산(intangible personal property)로 구분된다.

B. 주식, 상표권(trademark), 특허권(patent), 저작권(copyright), 어음 등은 종이에 권리가 표창되어 나타나지만 무형동산이다.

Law of fixtures - For an article of personal property to become a fixture on land,

1) **An**nexation of the article to the land constructively or actually[manner of affixatioin 부착된 정도]

2) **Ada**ptability of the article for the use in the land[적합성],

3) **Int**ention of the annexor that the article will become a fixture[의도] ➡ annexor의 intent를 볼 수 있는 가장 좋은 방법은 다음 사항을 고려하여 판단한다.

A. The relationship between the annexor and the premises

B. The degree of annexation

C. The nature and use of the chattel

Trade Fixture

임차인(tenant)이 임대인(Landlord)의 건물에 상업적 목적으로 설치한 동산은 부동산의 일부가 되는 것이 아니라 여전히 임차인의 동산으로 보게 되는데 이를 trade fixture라고 한다.

Finding Personal Property

A finder of property acquires no rights in mislaid property, is entitled to possession of lost property against everyone except the true owner, and is entitled to keep abandoned property.

〈개념정리〉

Mislaid property	Lost property	Abandoned property
no rights at all	entitled to possession against everyone but the true owner	entitled to keep the abandoned property

1) Mislaid property

소유자가 일정장소에 두고 가져오는 것을 잊은 물건으로서 이를 발견한 자는 소유권을 취할 수 없다(no ownership).

2) Lost Property

소유자가 잃어버린 경우로서 이를 발견한 자는 진짜 소유자(except true owner)를 제외한 다른 모든 사람에게 대항할 수 있는 소유권(title)을 갖게 된다.

3) Abandoned Property(= abandoned property)

소유자가 누가 그 물건을 취득할 것인지를 정하지 않은 채 물건의 소유권을 자발적으로 포기하는 것으로 이를 발견한 자는 원래 소유자를 포함한 모든 사람에게 대항할 소유권을 갖게 된다.

5 Bailments(동산의 위탁)

위탁자(bailor)가 수탁인(bailee)에게 동산의 소유권(title)을 이전함이 없이 점유(possession)만을 넘겨주는 것을 의미함. 이 경우 수탁자는 위탁자에게 반환 또는 위탁자의 지시에 따라 처분할 의무를 갖게 됨.

요건 (In order to have a bailmor-bailee relationship, we need)

① delivery of personal property to bailee 점유의 이전

② possession by bailee 수탁자의 점유

③ bailee has duty to return property or dispose of property as directed by owner. 수탁자의 의무발생

6 Common carrier bailment

만일 common carrier[Ex. 기차, 버스, 등 공공성 교통기관]가 bailee가 되었을 경우 strict liability를 지게 된다.

Intellectual Property {IP}지적재산권법

1) To create products and services by granting property rights and incentives. 권리와 인센티브 제공
2) To provide public access to IP 대중의 접근성향상이 목적

〈개념정리〉

		effective period	**remarks**
intellectual property	copyright	70~120 years	Even the unpublished copyright or unregistered trademarks can be protected before registration. Softwares are proctected under copyright law and patent law.
	patent	20 years (14 years for design patent)	
	trademark	indefinitely	

 Copyrights 저작권법

1) 유형의 창작물[original work in any tangible form]을 보호하는 것이 목적이고 표현된 것만 저작권에 의해 보호될 수 있고(copyrightable), 표현되지 않은 idea는 보호받지 못함.

2) 1998년 3월1일 이후 만들어진 창작물은 copyright notice가 필요없게 됨.

3) 1978년 1월1일 이후 만들어진 copyright는 life of author + 70년간 유효하다.

4) 출판사(publishing house)가 소유권을 갖고 있는 경우에는 95년간, 혹은 저작권이 생겨난 경우에는 120년간이며 둘 중에서 먼저 짧은 쪽이 우선 적용된다.

5) 저작권법에 의해 보호받기 위해 저작권의 등록(registration of copyright)이 필요한 것은 아니지만, 등록을 한 경우에는 법정손해배상(statutory damages)및 변호사비용(attorney fee)등을 받을 수 있는 권리를 가질 수 있음.

Fair Use Doctrine

Fair use is a doctrine in United States copyright law that allows limited use of copyrighted material without requiring permission from the rights holders, such as use for scholarship or review. It provides for the legal, non-licensed citation or incorporation of copyrighted material in another author's work under a four-factor balancing test.

a) The purpose and character of the use, including whether such use is of a commercial nature or is for nonprofit educational purposes;
b) The nature of the copyrighted work;
c) The amount and substantiality of the portion used in relation to the copyrighted work as a whole; and
d) The effect of the use upon the potential market for or value of the copyrighted work.

a) Fair use doctrine의 적용을 받는 경우 copyright을 침해하지 않는 범위내에서 저작물(또는 소프트웨어)을 copyright owner의 허락 없이 사용할 수 없다.

b) 이 원칙의 적용을 받을 수 있는 경우로는 보도(news reporting), 연구(research), 강의(teaching), 논평(comment)등이다.

교수가 강의목적상 특정작품의 복사본을 학생들에게 나누어주는 경우 fair use doctrine이 적용되고 일일이 저작자의 동의를 받아야 하는 것은 아니다.

c) 그러나 access to digital work 등은 fair use doctrine의 목적이 아니다.
Folsom v. Marsh, 9 F.Cas. 342 ;Time Inc. v. Bernard Geis Associates; Campbell v. Acuff-Rose Music 등 주요 판례 참고

9 Computer software copyright

1) 소프트웨어는 저작권보호를 받는다(copyrightable).

2) Human readable source code와 machine language object code의 저작권도 보호받는다.

3) Software라고 할 때 computer program과 database도 포함된다.

4) 소프트웨어를 구입한자는 back up copies를 만들 수 있으며, 개인적 용도로 이를 복사(duplicate)가능하다. software의 fair use rule

5) 기업체가 copyright을 갖고 있을 경우, 제품탄생 후 100년 또는 공표이후 75년 중에서 더 짧은 쪽이 적용된다.

10 Patent Law(특허법)

1) 특허법은 기계(machine), 공정(process), 기술(art), 방법(method), 물질의 배합(composition of matter), 유전공학에 의한 식물이나 동물 등에 대한 발명으로 new and useful improvement가 되도록 하여야 한다.

2) 단순한 아이디어나 너무 뻔한 것은 보호받지 못한다.

3) 일반적으로 특허(patents)는 특허신청일로부터 20년간 유효하며, 디자인특허(design patent)는 특허발행일로부터 14년간 유효

4) 이전에는 software와 인터넷을 통한 비즈니스 모델은 idea로 보아 특허법에 의해 보호되지 않는다고 하였으나, 최근에는 이를 발명(invention)으로 보아 특허법으로도 보호한다. ➡ 즉, software는 copyright과 patent law 모두의 보호를 받는다.

5) 특허법 보호를 위한 규제수단

- 금지명령(injunctions)
- 특허침해로 입은 특허권자의 lost profit에 대한 손해배상
- 합리적 금액의 royalty 부과

 상표법(trademarks under Lanham Act)

1) 상표법은 상표로서 식별력이 있는 기호, 문자, 도형, 포장, 소리(distinctive graphs, words, shapes, packaging, or sounds) 등을 보호하기 위한 것이다.

EX Coca-cola, Kodak, Dunkin' Doughnut

2) 상표로 보호되기 위해서는 식별력(distinctive)여부가 가장 중요하다.

3) 일반적으로 쓰는 말(generic word, ex. Software) 등은 식별력을 갖지 못하기 때문에 상표로 보호받을 수 없다

4) 과거에는 상표로 보호받았지만, 그 용어가 일반화되어 쓰는 말이 되면 보호받지 못한다.

EX Escalator, Dry Ice, etc.

5) 상표는 최초로 상업적으로 사용함으로써(by its use in commerce) 상표를 취득할 수 있다.

6) 상표는 꼭 등록할 필요는 없지만, 등록하게 되면 상표권에 대한 constructive notice를 하게 되는 것이고, 등록을 하지 않은 경우에 비해 보호를 더 많이 받게 된다.

7) 상표권은 상실되지 않는다면 무한히 보호받을 수 있다(valid indefinitely). 단, 포기(actual abandonment)와 추정적 포기(constructive abandonment, 즉 상표권자의 방치)의 경우에는 상표권이 상실된다.

12 Interests in Real Property

Possessory interest와 non-posessory interest로 나누고, 다시 possessory interest는 present interest와 future interest로 구분된다. Non-possessory interest에는 easement(사용권), profit(채굴권) 등이 있다.

참고

real property	**possessory interest**	present interest	fee simple absolute
			fee simple defeasible
			fee tail
		future interest	reversion
			remainder
	non-possessory interest		easement
			profit
			license

13 Present interest

현재 점유할 수 있는 권리로 fee simple absolute, fee simple defeasible, fee tail, life estate 등으로 나눌 수 있다.

1) Fee simple absolute[FS Absolute] - absolute ownership of potentially infinite duration, freely devisable, descendable & alienable. 법률상 인정되는 부동산의 모든 권리를 포함하고 있는 재산권

2) Fee Tail - To A & heirs of his body

직계자손에게만 유산상속 되는 부동산

3) FS defeasible

A. FS determinable : 현재점유하고 있는 권리가 일정한 사실의 발생에 의하여 자동적으로 종료(automatic termination)되고 점유할 수 있는 권리가 권리수여자(grantor)에게 돌아가는 재산권 So long as, while, until, during, while, until 등의 문구가 따른다.

EX As long as the building is used for church purpose

B. FS subject to condition subsequent : 현재 점유하고 있는 권리가 일정한 사건의 발생 후 권리수여자가 그 권리를 종료시키는 적극적인 행위(affirmative action)를 한 경우에만 권리수여자에게 돌아가는 재산권으로 But if; however if; provided, however; on condition that; upon the condition 등의 문구가 따라온다.

EX To John Doe, but if liquor is ever served on the premises, the grantor has the right to enter the premises.

C. Life Estate 한사람동안의 생애기간동안 점유할 수 있는 부동산

EX Conveyance of land to John Doe so long as he shall live.

14 Future interest

1) Reversion : future interest reverts back to transferor at the end of transferee's esteate.
현재 점유하고 있는 부동산이 일정기간/조건을 경과하면 grantor에게 되돌아가는 권리

EX John Doe conveys his land to "Jane Doe for life." John Doe has reversion.

2) Remainder : 제 3자에게 이전되는 권리

EX John Doe conveys his land, "to Jane Doe for life, remainder to Timothy Kane and his heirs."

Nonpossessory Interest in Land

1) Easement(사용권)

Definition : A right to use another person's real estate lawfully for a specific purpose. The most common type of easement is the right to travel over another person's land, known as a right of way. In addition, property owners commonly grant easements for the placement of utility poles, utility trenches, water lines or sewer lines. The owner of property that is subject to an easement is said to be "burdened" with the easement, because he or she is not allowed to interfere with its use.
다른 사람의 토지를 제한된 방법으로 사용할 수 있는 권리

EX If John permits Sue to travel across his main road to reach her own home, John cannot do anything to block the road. On the other hand, Sue cannot do anything that exceeds the scope of her easement, such as widening the roadway.

참고

Creation of easement	Termination of easement
Prescription[사용권에서의 prescription은adverse possession과 구성요건이 유사], implication(암묵적인 합의), necessity(필요성), grant(허용), reservation(문건에 의한 포함) 등에 의해 생겨난다.	Dream Cars : **D**estruction, release, estoppel, abandonment, **m**erger, condemnation, adverse use against the express easement, relinquishment(= abandonment), prescription, severance

2) Profit채굴권/벌목권/채취권

The produce of the soil, whether it arises above or below the surface as herbs, wood, turf, coals, minerals, stones, also fish in a pond or running water.

3) license : the right to be in another's premises lawfully.

우체부나 경찰 등이 공익목적상 잠시 합법적으로 남의 토지에 들어갈 수 있는 권리

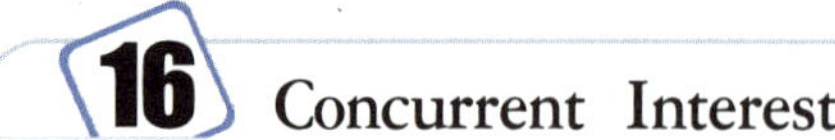

16 Concurrent Interest

〈개념정리〉

	Form of ownership	Right of survivorship	Transfer without the consent of the others
Tenancy in common	Each owner has an undivided interest in the subject property which passes to that person's respective heirs (or devisees if the owner dies with a valid will). 각 소유자는 분할되지 않는 지분을 각각 갖는다.	none. Deceased tenant's interest passes to his or her heirs. 공동으로 소유하던 다른 사람이 죽으면 그의 지분은 그의 유가족에게 간다. 그의 지분은 다른 남은 공동 소유자에게 가지 않는다.	Tenant may unilaterally transfer his or her interest without the consent of co-tenants. Transfer does not sever TIC. 다른 사람 동의 없이 일방적으로 자신의 지분을 넘길 수 있다 우리나라의 부동산공동소유와 유사
Joint Tenancy	Unity of possession, interest, time and title is necessary to form a joint tenancy. PITT의 일치가 있어야만 형성이 가능하다.	If a joint tenant dies, his or her interest is immediately extinguished and ownership of the property rests with the remaining joint tenant(s). 공동으로 소유하던 사람 중의 하나가 죽으면 그의 지분은 자동으로 살아남은 사람들에게 넘어간다. 유언장도 소용없다.	Tenant may transfer his or her interest without the consent of co-tenant. Transfer severs joint tenancy. 다른 co-tenant의 동의 없이 일방적으로 자신의 지분을 타인에게 넘길 수 있다. corporation은 joint tenancy 설립불가능
Tenancy by the entirety	a statutory form of ownership created by a conveyance to a husband and wife. Unity of possession, interest, time, title, and legal marriage is required to form a TBE.	right of survivorship	In tenancy by the entirety, neither can deal with the property independently of the other. 상대방의 동의 없이 다른 사람에게 함부로 넘기면 무효이다.

1) Tenancy in Common [TIC공유권]

Under a tenancy in common form of ownership, each owner has an undivided interest in the subject property which passes to that person's respective heirs (or devisees if the owner dies with a valid will).

A. 공동소유자(tenants in common) 가운데 한사람이 사망하면 그의 지분은 상속인에게 이전된다(혹은 유언장으로 남겨도 된다).
B. 공동소유자는 자신의 지분(interest)을 이전할 수 있지만, 재산의 특정부분(specific portion of property)만 골라서 이전할 수는 없다.
C. "each owns the whole"이라는 원칙이 적용되며 굳이 재산의 특정부분을 골라서 이전하려면 우선 법원의 분할명령(judicial participation)을 받아서 분할한 후 이전하여야 한다.

우리나라의 부동산 공동소유와 비슷하다.

2) Joint Tenancy(JT합유) : "joint tenancy with a right of survivorship" or JTROS. If a joint tenant dies, his or her interest is immediately extinguished and ownership of the property rests with the remaining joint tenant(s). Unity of possession, interest, time and title is necessary to form a joint tenancy.

A. 공동소유자(joint tenants)가운데 한사람이 사망하면 그의 지분이 다른 사람에게 넘어가게 된다. 이를 right of survivorship이라고 한다.
B. To create a joint tenancy with the right of survivorship, the PITT(possession, interest, title, and time) must be present, i.e, a TIC cannot be converted into JT by agreement 말로만 합의한다고 해서 TIC가 JT가 되는 게 아니고 PITT가 갖춰지고 명시적으로 표시가 되어야 한다.
C. a joint tenant may convert his JT into TIC.
JT는 공동소유자간의 유대관계가 강하고, 소위 공동목적이 되는 경우가 많기 때문에 특별한 약정이 없으면 지분을 양도받은 자는 **JT**가 될 수 없고, **TIC**가 된다.

D. A joint tenant may transfer his or her interest without the consent of co-tenant. Transfer severs joint tenancy. 다른 co-tenant의 동의 없이 일방적으로 자신의 지분을 타인에게 넘길 수 있다.

3) Tenancy by the Entirety[TBE] 부부합유

Tenancy by the entirety is a statutory form of ownership created by a conveyance to a husband and wife. Unity of possession, interest, time, title, and legal marriage is required to form a TBE.

The primary difference between tenancy by the entirety and joint tenancy is that joint tenants may deal with the property as they wish. If one joint tenant decides to convey her interest in the property, that interest is conveyed, and the joint tenancy is destroyed. **In tenancy by the entirety, neither can deal with the property independently of the other.** The judgment creditors of one party cannot enforce their liens against the property. If the debtor spouse dies first, the lien can never be enforced against the property. Of course, if the non-debtor spouse dies first, the lien could be enforced.

A. 합법적인 부부간에만 인정되는 합유로서 만일 이혼 등의 사유가 발생하면 TIC로 바뀐다.

B. 특정 주(Ex. California, Massachusetts 등)에서 동성 간의 결합을 허용하더라도 결혼(marriage)으로는 인정받지 못한다(under Federal Defense of Marriage Act)

C. 동성 간 결합, 혹은 사실혼 관계에는 성립되지 못한다.

〈개념정리〉

legally married husband and wife	➡ spouses	in marriages	**TBE can be formed**
gay and lesbian (homosexual) couples	➡ (life) partners	in civil unions	TBE **cannot** be formed
those cohabitating couples	➡ living together, they may hold themselves out as husband and wife	in common law marriages	TBE **cannot** be formed
How about transsexual's marriage?			

 Ks for the sale of land

〈개념정리〉

Marketable title-no encumbrances	**Unmarketable title** - encumbrances
zoning restrictions, public easement, recorded easement etc.	unrecorded easement, unrecorded lien, etc.

1) **Marketable title** is one that is free from unreasonable doubt in fact or in law. Ownership and possession of real property that is readily transferable since it is free from valid claims by outside parties. The title must be free from an unreasonable risk of litigation related with mortgages, easements, liens, defects in the chain of title. Marketable title이라 함은 담보권(mortgage, lien) 또는 지역권 등을 포함한 아무런 부담이 없는 소유권.

2) Title is considered marketable even if the property is subject to zoning restrictions, public easement[public right of way], or recorded easement.

18 Types of Deed

(주의) 미국에는contract와 deed가 따로 있고 분쟁이 발생할 경우 deed가 우선한다.

부동산에 관한 interest를 양도(conveyance)하는 경우, grantor가 grantee에게 교부하는 문서를 deed라고 하며 다음과 같은 종류가 있다.

1) General warranty deed

A. Grantor는 자신이 title을 갖고 있고, 이를 이전할 권리[right to convey title]를 갖고 있다는 것을 담보하는 title이다.

B. Covenant for quiet enjoyment
Grantor나 유효한 권리를 가진 제3자에 의해 양수인이 점유[possession]를 방해받지 않을 것이라는 점을 담보한다.

C. Covenant free from encumbrances
Deed에 명시되지 않은 부담(encumbrances : 지역권 등)에 의해 grantee가 방해받지 않으며 이런 방해를 받을 경우 grantor에게 책임을 물을 수있다.

2) Bargain and sale deed

Covenants that grantor has done nothing to impair title.

3) Quitclaim deed : no warranty of title.

The Grantor makes no guarantee or promises that the property is free of debt. the Grantor makes no promises that no one else claims to own the property.

Does not even guarantee that the Grantor has any ownership interest at all.

〈개념정리〉

Quitclaim Deed	General Warranty Deed (Express)
일단 transfer 하고 나면 Grantor는 책임면제 contains no covenants ☞ Conveyances under a quitclaim deed give the buyer only that which the seller owns.	다음내용을 보장한다. i) Present Covenant(SEC) : **Only to original Grantee** (No run with the land) 1세대만 넘어가고 그 다음에는 running with the land하지 않는다. ii) Future Covenant (**FEW**) : To all Grantee, Grantor는 자신의 Grantee에게만 책임 부담 ☞ warranty deed를 convey했다는 것은 이미 defective하지 않은 deed를 넘겼다는 의미이다.

QUIT CLAIM DEED **SAMPLE**

THIS SPACE PROVIDED FOR RECORDER'S USE

FILED FOR RECORD AT REQUEST OF John Smith

WHEN RECORDED RETURN TO:

NAME John Smith

ADDRESS P.O. Box XXX

CITY, STATE, ZIP Las Vegas, NV 89108

QUIT CLAIM DEED

THE GRANTOR(S), John Smith ________ for and in consideration of: One dollar and love and affection ________ conveys and quit claims to the GRANTEE(S), John Smith, Jr. and Mary Smith, husband and wife, the following described real estate, situated in the County of Clark, State of Nevada, together with all after acquired title of the grantor(s) therein (legal description): The Southerly 90 feet of lots 8 and 9, Block 12, Stewart's first addition to Highland home, an addition to the City of Las Vegas, as per plat recorded in Volume 2 of plats, page 85, Records of Clark County
situated in the County of Clark, State of Nevada.

DATED ____________________ DATED: ____________________

____________________ ____________________

Grantor Grantor

State of Nevada }
} ss
County of Clark }

On this day personally appeared before me ____________ and ____________, Grantor(s), to me known to be the individual(s) described in and who executed the foregoing instrument, and acknowledged that s/he signed the same as his/her free and voluntary act and deed for the uses and purposes therein mentioned.

GIVEN under my hand and official seal this _____ day of _________, 199_.

____

NOTARY PUBLIC in and for the State of Nevada,
Residing at ____________________
My commission expires ____________________

QUIT CLAIM DEED

THIS SPACE PROVIDED FOR RECORDER'S USE

FILED FOR RECORD AT REQUEST OF

WHEN RECORDED RETURN TO:

NAME______________________________

ADDRESS___________________________

CITY, STATE, ZIP____________________

QUIT CLAIM DEED

THE GRANTOR(S), _______________________ for and in consideration of: ____________________ conveys and quit claims to the GRANTEE(S), ___________________________ the following described real estate, situated in the County of __________State of Nevada, together with all after acquired title of the grantor(s) therein (legal description):

DATED ____________________ DATED:____________________

____________________ ____________________

Grantor Grantor

State of Nevada }
} ss
County of Clark }

On this day personally appeared before me ______________ and ________________, Grantor(s), to me known to be the individual(s) described in and who executed the foregoing instrument, and acknowledged that s/he signed the same as his/her free and voluntary act and deed for the uses and purposes therein mentioned.

GIVEN under my hand and official seal this _____ day of _________, 199_.

____

NOTARY PUBLIC in and for the State of Nevada,
Residing at______________________________
My commission expires ____________________

NORTH CAROLINA GENERAL WARRANTY DEED

Mail after recording to ____________________

This instrument prepared by ____________________

Brief description for the index ____________________

THIS DEED made this the, __________ day of ____________________, 20 _____, by and between

GRANTOR		**GRANTEE**
	+	
	+	
	+	
	+	
	+	
	+	
	+	
	+	
	+	
	+	

The designation Grantor and Grantee as used herein shall include said parties, their heirs, successors, and assigns, and shall include singular, plural, masculine, feminine, or neuter as required by context.

WITNESSETH, that the Grantor, for a valuable consideration paid by the Grantee, the receipt of which is hereby acknowledged, has and by these presents does grant, bargain, sell and convey unto the Grantee in fee simple, that certain lot or parcel of land situated I the City of ____________________.
____________________ Township, Brunswick County, North Carolina, and more particularly described as follows:

The property hereinabove described was acquired by Grantor by instrument recorded in ____________________. A map showing the above-described property is recorded in Map Book __________
at Page __________.

TO HAVE AND TO HOLD the aforesaid lot or parcel of land and all privileges and appurtenances thereto belonging to the Grantee in fee simple.

And the Grantor covenants with the Grantee, that Grantor is seized of the premises in fee simple, has the right to convey the same in fee simple, that title is marketable and free and clear of all encumbrances, and that Grantor will warrant and defend the title against the lawful claims of all persons whomsoever, except for the exceptions stated. Title to the property hereinabove described is subject to the following exceptions:

IN WITNESS WHEREOF, the Grantor has hereunto set his hand and seal, or if corporate, has caused this instrument to be signed in its corporate name by its duly authorized officers and its seal to be affixed by authority of its Board of Directors, the day and year first above written.

________________________ ________________________(Seal)
(Corporate Name)
BY: ________________________ ________________________ (Seal)
________________President

ATTEST: ________________________ ________________________(Seal)
________________ Secretary (Corporate Seal)

NORTH CAROLINA ________________COUNTY

This the___day of ____________ , 20___, I certify that the following person(s)________________________
_______ Personally appeared before me this day, and (I have personal knowledge of the identity of the principal(s)) (I have seen satisfactory evidence of the principal's identity, by a current state or federal identification with the principal's photograph in the form of a ________) (a credible witness has sworn to the identity of the principal(s)); each acknowledging to me that he or she voluntarily signed the foregoing document for the purpose stated therein and in the capacity indicated: ____________
________________ .

My Commission Expires: ________ Notary Public:________________ (Seal)

Notary printed or typed name ________________________

NORTH CAROLINA ________________COUNTY

This the___day of ____________ , 20___, personally came before me ____________________,
who, being by me duly sworn and properly identified by state or federal photograph identification
(____________________) says that he or she is a duly authorized officer of said corporation
and that ____________________ signed the foregoing or annexed instrument on behalf of
said corporation, and that I, ____________________, acknowledge the said writing to be the
act and deed of said corporation.

My Commission Expires: ________ Notary Public:________________ (Seal)

Notary printed or typed name ________________________

19 Executing a deed

1) Deed must have description of the real estate. Deed의 작성

A. Deed에는 소유권을 이전하려는 부동산의 명세(description)는 나와야 하지만, 구매가격(purchase price)은 포함되지 않아도 된다.

B. Grantor의 서명은 반드시 필요하나 grantee의 서명은 반드시 필요하지는 않다.

C. Delivery of deed가 반드시 있어야 한다.

There is an effective delivery when there are

(1) Conduct, wording, recording evidencing
부동산을 취득할 때 보통의 경우 recording을 하는 것이 바람직하지만, wording 만으로 충분할 수 있다. 만약 subsequent buyer가 unrecorded deed에 대해서도 충분히 인지(actual notice)하고 있다면.

(2) The grantor's intent that the deed has some

(3) Present operative effective that title passes immediately and irrevocably, even though the right of possession may be postponed until the future.

D. Grantor's intent to convey the title to the grantee가 필요하다.

20 Recording a Deed

1) 소유권 취득사실을 등기하여 세상에 알리는 constructive notice행위이다(= recording gives constructive notice이다.

만일 recording을 하는 것이 actual notice[recording gives actual notice]라고 하면 틀린 답이므로 주의할 것.

2) 각 주(州) 마다 다음과 같은 deed-recording 법이 있으므로 매우 주의해서 구분해야 한다.

〈개념정리〉

Pure Race statute(BFP와 무관) 使用用語 : … **first recorded** "A conveyance of an estate in land shall not be valid against a subsequent purchaser for value unless the conveyance is first recorded."	notice는 상관없음. 무조건 먼저 record하는 자가 취득함 BFP아닌 자도 보호받을 수 있다 ☞ the most accurate reflection of title of property in the jurisdiction.
Pure notice statute 使用用語 : **notice- … recorded** " without notice there of, unless it is recorded"	BFP wins regardless of whether or not he records first. BFP는 prior grantee와의 관계에서 자기가 **record하느냐에 상관없이** 보호 받는다. [즉 BFP에게 가장 유리하다]
Race-notice statute 使用用語 : **notice- … first recorded** In race-notice jurisdiction, such as NY, when BFP purchases for value and without notice, the BFP will prevail over those who make a claim to the party.	Unrecorded conveyance or other instrument is invalid as against BFP for value without notice, who records "first." 즉, ☞ **먼저 record하는 자가 보호됨.** 둘 다 record안한 상태에서는 먼저 취득한 자가 보호됨first-in-time rule ☞ without notice라는 말이 없어도BFP + first record일 경우에는 보호된다.

 Title Insurance

Title insurance in the United States is indemnity insurance against financial loss from defects in title to real property and from the invalidity or unenforceability of mortgage liens. Title insurance is principally a product developed and sold in the United States as a result of the comparative deficiency of the US land records laws. It is meant to protect an owner's or a lender's financial interest in real property against loss due to title defects, liens or other matters. **It will defend against a lawsuit attacking the title**

as it is insured, or reimburse the insured for the actual monetary loss incurred, up to the dollar amount of insurance provided by the policy. -D.B. Burke, Jr., Law of Title Insurance, Little Brown & Company (1986) § 1.1, p. 2.).-

1) Grantee가 취득한 소유권에 우선하는 소유권, 저당권(mortgage), 지역권(easement) 등으로 인해 소유권이 상실되거나 소유권을 제대로 행사할 수 없는 경우에 대비하여 grantee가 가입하는 보험.

2) Grantee는 보험에 가입하면서 보험료를 낮추기 위해 일정한 흠결(defect)에 대해서는 보험으로 보장되지 않도록 할 수 있는데, 이러한 예외(exception)는 보험증서에 기재해야 한다.

3) The title insurance회사는 나중에 title에 대해 통상적인 합리적 주의(exercise of reasonable care)를 했는데도 문제(defects)가 발견되면 책임을 안진다.

22 Adverse Possession(AP, 점유취득시효)

1) 토지의 점유자[possessor]가 일정한 법정기간(statutory period)동안 점유를 하였고, 그 점유가 일정한 요건을 충족하게 되면 점유자가 소유권(title)을 취득하는 것

2) 요건(Necessary elements)

• Mneumonic : OCEAN AP

- **O**pen and Notorious Possession
- **C**ontinuous Possession
- **E**xclusive Possession
- **A**ctual Possession
- **N**on-Permissive[Hostile] Possession

A. Open and Notorious Possession 공개적인 점유

Reasonable notice to owner

B. Continuous Possession 지속적인 점유

need not be constant, but possession as normally used.

C. Exclusive Possession 배타적인 점유

possession to exclusion of all others 다른 사람들의 점유를 최대한 배제한 점유

D. Actual Possession 실질적인 점유

possession of land consistent with its normal use[farming on farm land]

E. Non-Permissive[Hostile] Possession 적대적인 점유

does not occur when possession started permissively. 소유자가 허락해서 점유를 한 것은 해당하지 않음

not satisfied if possessor aknowleges other's ownership. 점유자가 소유자의 소유권을 인정하는 경우에는 적대적 점유가 아니다.

23 Easement by Prescription

Easement를 AP와 유사한 방법[OCEAN]으로 취득하는 것

24 Mortgages[저당권]

| 용어정리 |

Mortgage = an interest in land as security for a loan or other obligation.

Mortgagor = the party transferring the interest in land.

Mortgagee = the provider of the loan or other interest given in exchange for the security interest.

Foreclosure = a process that allows the mortgagee to declare that the entire mortgage debt is due and must be paid immediately.

Acceleration (on Default) = on default the principal and interest of the underlying debt will both become due and payable forthwith at the option of the mortgagee.

Redemption = When the mortgagor fulfills his obligations under the contract, the mortgage will be void and the mortgagee will be bound to reconvey the legal interest to the mortgagor.

Bona fide purchaser(BFP) = one who has purchased an asset (including a promissory note, bond or other negotiable instrument) for stated value, innocent of any fact which would cast doubt on the right of the seller to have sold it in good faith.

1) Mortgage란 부동산에 대한 담보권으로 채무자(debetor)는 채권자(creditor)에 대한 자신의 채무지급을 담보하기 위해 채권자에게 mortgage를 주게 된다. 이 경우 채무자는 mortgagor이고, 채권자는 mortgagee가 되므로 용어를 혼동하지 않도록 주의

2) 집과 관련하여 mortgage를 설정하고 돈을 빌려주는 사람(mortgage lender)은Real Estate Settlment Procedures Act[RESPA]의 적용을 받는다.

3) First mortgage가 당연히 secondary mortgage보다 우선권(priority)를 갖는다. 특히 나중에 공개경매를 통해 부동산을 처분 하고 난 뒤에 secondary mortgage는 first mortgage이후에 자신의 지분을 주장할 수 있다.

25 Mortgage의 성립요건

1) Mortgagor가 mortgage를 만들어 여기에 서명을 해야 한다.

2) Mortgage는 부동산에 대한 권리(interest in real property)이므로 Land K로 보아 SOF의 적용을 받는다.
따라서Must be in writing and signed by party to be charged가 되며 여기서 'party to be charged'는 mortgagor가 된다.

3) Mortgage는 real property와 부채(debt)에 관해 기술되어있으면 되며, 부채금액과 이자율 등은 기재할 필요 없다.

4) Mortgagor는 mortgage를 mortgagee에게 전달하여야 한다.(mortgage must be delivered to mortgagee)

26 Recording of Mortgage

1) 등기를 하는 목적은 mortgagee(저당권자)가 mortgage를 취득했다는 사실에 대해 세상에 알리기 위한 것, 즉 constructive notice를 위한 것이다.

2) Mortgage를 등기하게 되면, 그 이후에 해당부동산의 소유권을 취득한 사람(subsequent purchaser)및 그 부동산에 대한 mortgage를 취득한 자(subsequent mortgagee)로부터 mortagee가 보호가 되는 효과

3) <u>거래당사자(immediate parties)끼리는 등기(recording)이 없더라도 mortgage는 유효(enforceable)</u>

27 Types of Mortgage Statutes

1) Race Statute

Subsequent mortgagee가 previous mortgagee보다 먼저 reocrding을 한 경우에만 priority주장가능

2) Notice Type Statute

Subsequent mortgagee가 previous mortgagee에 대해 알지 못한 경우, subsequent mortgagee가 previous mortgagee에 대해 priorty[우선권] 주장가능

3) Race-Notice Statute[Notice-Race Statute]

Subsequent mortgagee가 previous mortgagee에 대해 알지 못한 상태에서 먼저 recording을 한 경우, subsequent mortgagee가 previous mortgagee에 대해 우선권(priority)을 주장할 수 있다.

28 Mortgage가 설정된 부동산 처분시 buyer의 대응

1) **Assuming the mortgage** : a person, usually the buyer of the property, takes it upon himself to pay the mortgage loan either with just the consent and agreement of the original mortgagor (usually the seller of the house) or with the consent of the both the mortgagor and the mortgagee(the lender).

a) The assuming grantee becomes primarily liable for the mortgage debts, mortgage를 떠안은 사람이 1차 책임을 지게 되고,

b) The mortgagor's liability is secondary or similar to that of a surety.

2) Taking title subject to the mortgage :

A. The mortgage continues to encumber the property but you, as a buyer, are not personally liable to pay the mortgage. subject to mortgage라는 말이 나오면 구매자의 개인책임은 없는 것이다

B. Mortgage가 설정되어있다는 것을 알면서(aware)하면서 구매를 한 경우이므로 Mortgage가 recording되어있는 경우에만 적용될 수 있다.

C. 매수자는 mortgage가 있다는 것을 알면서 구매한 경우이므로 mortgagee에 대해 대항하지 못한다. 따라서 mortgagor가 채무를 불이행하게 되면 mortgagee는 그 부동산에 설정된 mortgage를 실행하여 그 부동산이 매각되도록 할 수 있다 (Mortgagee may still foreclose on the property even in the hands of the buyer).

D. subject to mortgage라고 말로 하면서도 payment of mortgage obligation을 assume한 경우는 결국 assumption이 이루어진 경우이다. 이런 종류의 속임수 문제에 주의할 것

3) Bona Fide Purchaser(BFP)

One who has purchased an asset (including a promissory note, bond or other negotiable instrument) for stated value, innocent of any fact which would cast doubt on the right of the seller to have sold it in good faith. This is vital if the true owner shows up to claim title, since the BFP will be able to keep the asset, and the real owner will have to look to the fraudulent seller for recompensation.

A. Buyer가 mortgage에 대해 모르고(without notice), 그 부동산을 구입한 경우

B. 위의 "without notice"라는 말은 "실제 통보도 없었고(without actal notice)" + "상황상으로 알수도 없었던(without constructive notice)"를 의미한다.

C. 매수자가 BFP의 요건을 갖춘 경우에, mortgagee는 그 부동산에 설정된 mortgage를 foreclose(경매처분) 할 수 없게 되므로 매수자는 mortgage가 없는 상태(free of the mortgage)로 부동산을 취득하게 된다.

29 Rights of Parties

1) Mortgagor[debtor]는 mortgage가 설정된 부동산을 점유(possession)하며 이를 사용할 권리를 갖게 된다.

2) Mortgagee[creditor]는 mortgage가 설정된 부동산에 대한 담보권(lien)을 갖는다.

30 담보권의 실행(foreclosure)

definition : a judgment by a court in favor of foreclosure of a mortgage or deed of trust, which orders that the real property which secured the debt be sold under foreclosure proceedings to pay the debt. Usually this move is made to get a "deficiency judgment" for any amount still owed after the foreclosure sale.

1) Mortgagor가 채무를 불이행(default)하게 되면 mortgagee는 채무자에 대한 권리를 mortgage와 함께 제3자에게 양도(assign) 하거나 mortgage를 foreclosure해버릴 수 있다.

2) Foreclosure란 법원에 대한 신청행위로 이를 통해 담보권을 매각할 수 있다. Foreclosure sale은 법원의 감독관리 하에 하는 것이 특징이다.

3)

〈개념정리〉

The equity of redemption right	Borrower has a right to redeem before the foreclosure sale to redeem the land. Mortgagor는 자신의 부동산에 대한 foreclosure세일이 완료되기전 채무원금(principal), 이자(interest), foreclosure와 관련한 비용을 지급하고 foreclosure sale을 중단시킨 후에 자신의 부동산을 찾아올 수 있다 = **즉, foreclosure 이전에 빚을 갚겠다면 받아주어야 한다.**
The statutory power [= statutory right] of redemption	The borrower has a right to redeem for some fixed period of time after the foreclosure. Foreclosure sale에서 넘어간 금액을 지급하기만 하면 **foreclosure가 끝났더라도 일정기간 내에 부동산을 되찾아올 수 있는 법적으로 인정되는 권리**

4) Surplus and Deficiency after Foreclosure

A. Foreclosure sale에서 제반 관련비용을 제하고 남은 매각대금(proceeds from sale)에서 mortgagor에게 채무를 상환하게 되는데 이러한 상환이후에도 매각대금이 남을 경우 이를 surplus라고 한다.

B. Mortgagee는 surplus를 mortgagor에게 반환(return)하여야 할 의무가 있다.

C. Mortagor는 surplus를 반환받지 못했다고 해서 해당부동산을 계속해서 점유할 수 없다.

D. 만일 foreclosure sale후에도 deficiency가 발생한다면 mortgagor가 책임을 져야 한다.

E. 만일 buyer가 assuming the mortgage를 한 경우에는 Deficiency도 책임을 져야하지만, subject to mortgage를 한 경우에는 buyer는 deficiency책임은 없다.

 Lessor-Lessee (Landlord Tenant Law)

1) Lease란 임대인(lessor, landlord = LL)와 임차인(lessee, tenant)간에 맺어지는 <u>임대차계약(contract)이자 점유의 이전(conveyance)</u>로 구성된다.

2) 임대차계약(contract)에는 임대차 대상목적물에 대한 설명(description of leased premises)과 기본적 조건을 반드시 포함하여야 한다. 단, 임대료(rent)의 지급기일(due date)은 포함하지 않아도 무방하다.

3) 만일 1년 미만의 임대계약(contract)은 SOF의 적용을 받지 않으므로 구두(oral)로 체결이 가능하다

 Types of Tenancy

〈용어정리〉

tenancy	= leasehold
landlord(landlady)	= lessor
tenant	= lessee
sub-tenant	= sub-lessee

1) Tenancy for years(a term of years) : fixed, determined period of time. You must know the termination date. No notice to bring this leasehold to an end. 일정기간(Ex. 6개월, 1년)단위로 계약해가면서 사는 경우로 임차인에게 점유권(possession)을 부여하고, 그 기간이 종료되면 통고 없이 임대차계약관계가 종료된다.

1년이 넘을 경우 SOF의 적용을 받는다.

2) Periodic Tenancy : continues for successive intervals until LL or T give proper notice for indefinite duration. 별도의 임대계약을 종료하겠다는 의사표시가 없는 한 임대차가 자동으로 갱신.

3) Tenancy at will : a tenancy for no fixed duration, may be terminated at any time. However, a reas. demand to Quit (vacate) is required. 임대차기간의 제한은 없고, 당사자들이 언제든지 임대차를 종료시킬 수 있는 임대차

4) Tenancy at sufferance (with reluctant tolerance) : wrongful holdover. Lasts until LL evicts(treating T as a trespasser) or elects to hold tenant to a new term of periodic tenancy. ➡ T가 만기를 지나 뭉개고 있으면 주인은 이를 불법침입자로 간주하여 쫓아 내든지 아니면 기존조건을 재갱신해서 밀어붙일 수 있다.

A. T breaches duty while in possession - LL may (a) evict (b) sue for rent due - No self-help

B. T breaches but is out of possession - Surrender, Ignore & hold T responsible for unpaid rent; Re-let & hold T liable for any deficiency .

33 Duties of tenants

1) T's Duty to Pay Rent 계약에 명시하지 않은 이상, T는 임대료 납부의무 무조건 준수. 예컨대, 장마, 화재, 천재지변(acts of God)의 경우는 물론 고속도로 건설 등 공용수용(condemnation), 혹은 LL가 계약내용을 일부 위반하거나, T가 사망해도 임대료 납부의무가 있다

2) Duty to repair - if lease is silent required to keep property in reasonably good repair. 임대부동산의 일상적인 수리에 대한 책임이 있다.

EX 전구교체

3) 그러나 일상적인 수리(ordinary repair)가 아니고, 구조적 수리(structural repair)는 임대인(LL)의 의무이다.

34 LL' s Duties (The Duty of the Landlord) 임대인의 책임

1) LL duty to deliver possession - LL must put T in actual physical possession at commencement or be in breach.
임대인은 임차인이 임대부동산을 점유하여 사용할 수 있도록 해야 한다

2) Implied covenant of quiet enjoyment - Neither lessor nor a 3P with a validclaim will evict T unless T has breached lease K. 임대인이나 3자에 의하여 추방되지 않고 임대부동산을 점유할 권리가 임차인에게 있다.

3) Implied warranty of habitability - applies only to residential leases. This is non-waivable warranty. Standard - premises must be fit for basic human habitation. 거주가능성에 대한 담보책임

35 Assignment & Sublease(Subletting)

Assignment & Sublease(Subletting) - in the absence of a provision in the lease, a T may freely transfer his interest in whole (assignment) or in part (sublease). 임대차의 양도(assignment)와 전대(sublease)는 계약에서 특별히 제한하는 문구가 없는 한 임차인(T)는 자유롭게 할 수 있다.

〈개념정리〉 assignment와 sublease의 차이

Assignment		Sublease	
landlord ↓ Tenant 1 ↓ Tenant 2 (Tenant 2 → landlord 직접 연결)	landlord와 Tenant2가 직접 privity를 갖게 되고 Tenant1은 빠지게 됨	landlord ↓ tenant 1 ↓ Tenant 2	landlord와 Tenant 2(sub-tenant)는 직접 연락할 일이 없다. Tenant1과 Tenant2 간의 privity는 지속됨

1) Assignment : an assignment occurs if the T transfers the entire estate, or the balance thereof, to the 3P. Places the transferee/assignee into a direct contractual relationship with the owner/LL. LL과 양수자간 직접적인 관계를 갖게 되고 모든 권리와 의무가 함께 양수도 된다.

2) sublease(sublet)

If a lesser estate is conveyed so that the T retains an interest in the leasehold, the transfer is properly classified as a sublease. Contractual relationship remains between the original LL and T, remains between Tand sub-T, but not between the original LL and the sub-T (LL와 T 사이, T와 sub-T간에 계약관계가 유지되며, LL- sub-T간은 아무런 관계가 없다)

Chapter 10

SECURED TRANSACTION

| 용어정리 |

Attachment(담보권의 설정) : A seizing of a person's property to secure a judgment or to be sold in satisfaction of a judgment.

Collateral(담보물) : Property that is pledged as security against a debt. Property that is subject to a security interest.

Consumer goods(소비제품) : goods that are used or bought for use primarily for personal, family, or household purposes.

Creditor(채권자) : One who gives credit for money or goods

Debtor(채무자) : One who owes an obligation to another, especially an obligation to pay money

Equipment(장비) : goods other than inventory, farm products, or consumer goods

Foreclosure(경매처분) : a correlative right in the mortgagee to extinguish the right of redemption, which might otherwise exist persistently.

General creditor(무담보부 채권자) : = unsecured creditor

Inventory(재고) : goods, other than farm products, which (A) are leased by a person as lessor, (B) are held by a person for sale or lease or to be furnished under a contract of service; (C) are furnished by a person under a contract of service

Lien : A legal right or interest that a creditor has in another's property, lasting usually until a debt or a duty that it secures is satisfied.

Mortgage : A conveyance of title to property that is given as security for the payment of debt or the performance of a duty.

Mortgagee : One to whom property is mortgaged. also termed mortgage holder

Mortgagor : One who mortgages property. the mortgage-debtor or borrower

Obligor(채무자) : One who has undertaken an obligation; a promisor or debtor

Obligee(채권자) : One to whom an obligation is owed. a promisee or creditor

Perfection(담보권의 완성) : validation of a security interest as against other cerditors, usually by filing a statement with some public office or by taking possession of the collateral.

Redemption : The right of redemption is the right to pay the debt and regain title to the land or other estate, even after default.

Secured creditor(담보부 채권자) : A creditor who has the right, on the debtor's default, to proceed against collateral and apply it to the payment of the debt.

Secured transaction(담보부 거래) : A business arrangement by which a buyer or borrower gives collateral to the seller to guarantee payment of an obligation. Article 9 of the UCC deals with secured transaction.

Security interest(담보권) : a property interest created by agreement or by operation of law to secure performance of an obligation. UCC limits the creation of a security interest to personal property.

Unsecured creditor(무담보부 채권자) : A creditor who, upon giving credit, takes no rights against specific property of the debtor. also termed general creditor

<Black's Law Dictionary, Abridged 7th Ed.>; Randal C. Picker.

채권자(creditor)와 채무자(debtor)간의 개인적인 채무변제약속이외에 다른 보장수단을 얻고자 하는 경우, 담보물(collateral)을 확보함으로써 담보부거래(secured transaction)를 하게 된다. 이때 부동산이 담보일 경우에는 mortgage라고 불리우며 property law의 적용을 받게 되는 반면 **동산(personal property)나 가구(fixture)의 경우 UCC article 9의 적용을** 받게 된다.

UCC article 9의 담보물(collateral)의 종류

Personal property

1) Commercial paper

A. Negotiable instrument 유가증권
(bonds, stock, document of title, chattel paper, promissory note, commercial tort claims)

B. Commodities, and commodities accounts

2) Intangible property

A. Accounts receivable

B. General intangibles(copyrights, patents, good will)

3) Goods

A. Inventory [판매 및 대여영업을 위해 보유하는 물건]

B. Consumer goods [personal, family or household purpose개인용이나 가족용 또는 가정집용으로 구매한 경우]

C. Equipment[사업에 사용하는 물건]

D. Raw materials

E. Farm products[농업용 가축livestock, 농작물crops 및 농기구]

〈개념정리〉

동산 (personal property)의 경우, 유형동산(tangible personal property)과 무형동산(intangible personal property)으로 구분이 가능하다. 그중에서도 특히 유형동산은 사용용도에 따라서 명칭이 달라진다. 예를 들어 냉장고의 경우 채무자(debtor)가 채권자(creditor)에게 담보물(collateral)로 제공했다면,	
집에서 사용하던 냉장고였다면	☞ consumer goods
냉장고가게를 운영하던 주인이 가게에서 판매하던 제품이었다면	☞ inventory
식당을 운영하는 사람이 고기보관을 위해 사용하던 대형냉장고였다면	☞ equipment

The determination as to whether goods are "consumer goods", "inventory" or "equipment" is made at the time the security interest attaches.

4) **Fixtures** : Fixtures on realty - if a screw driver is needed to remove it, consider it a fixture. If it can be unplugged from the wall and removed, it is not a fixture.

3 UCC Article 9 not applicable for

1) **real** property. **부동산**

(Section 9-109(d)(11) of Revised Article 9 : Article 9 does not apply to "the creation or transfer of an interest in or lien on real property.)

2) **Assignment of wage claims** 담보목적으로 급료나 임금, 또는 다른 고용의 대가로 받은 보상을 양도하는 것

3) **Statutory liens** (주법상의 수리공 artisan's lien 과 건축업자 mechanic's lien)

4) **Checks, drafts,** or **certificate of deposits**

4 담보권의 설정(attachment of security interest)

1) **definition** : A seizing of a person's property to secure a judgment or to be sold in satisfaction of a judgment

정의 : 판결에 따라 특정인의 자산에 대해 압류하는 등의 방법을 통해 빚을 갚도록 하려는 행위로 담보권의 설정이라고 한다.

2) 담보권이 설정되면 담보권자(secured party)는 채무자(debtor)에게 담보권의 효력을 주장할 수 있다.

3) 담보권이 설정되면 해당담보권에 대해 알고 있는 제3자(third parties actually aware of security interest)에 대항해 우선권(priorities)이 생기게 된다.

4) Attachment의 설정요건

• Mneumonic : attach VCR by SPC

- Value given by the creditor
- Contract or security agreement
- Rights of the debtor in the property at issue
- Sign
- Possession
- Control

A security interest **attaches** to collateral when it becomes enforceable against the debtor with respect to the collateral. Attachment makes security interest "enforceable" and there are three basic requirements for a security interest to attach

A. The debtor agrees to grant a security interest in the specific property to the creditor for the value the secured party gave.담보권자가 value를 지불하여 채무자는 특정부동산에 대해 security interest담보권을 제공하기로 동의한 경우

여기에서 value란 consideration [약인]을 제공하겠다는 약속을 포함해서 금전거래 관계나 preexisting claims가 있는 경우이다.

B. **Contract**, or security agreement, must evidence the secured transaction unless the secured party has taken possession of the collateral.

C. The debtor must have **rights in collateral**
채무자가 담보물에 대한 ownership이나 점유권(possessory right)의 일부가 있어서 담보권을 설정할 수 있는 권리를 갖고 있어야 한다.
[can be expressed by **signing** the security interest, **possessing** and **conrolling** the collaterals]

EX Suzie Wong이 HSBC에서 돈을 대출받아 소파를 구입한다고 가정할 경우, HSBC는 12월 1일 대출신청을 받아 12월 3일 대출하기로 승낙하면서 구입할 소파에 대한 담보권(security interest)를 요구하였고 Suzie는 이에 동의하였다. Suzie가 HSBC에게서 12월 4일 돈을 받아 소파를 12월5일 구입하였다. 이를 날짜별로 정리해보면

〈개념정리〉

12월 3일	담보권을 설정(attachment)한다는 합의(contract = secrutiy agreement)
12월 4일	대가의 지급(value paid)
12월 5일	세 가지 요건이 모두 충족되는 시점은 Suzie가 소파를 실제 점유하여 rights in collateral 이 생겨나게 되는 12월5일이며 이날 담보권이 attachment 된다.

5 담보권의 완성Perfection of the Security Interest

• Mneumonic : A-F-P for perfection

- Automatic perfection for most consumer goods
- File financing statement
- Possession of collaterals

1) The signed security agreement must be "perfected" **to cut off the interest of a subsequent purchaser, subsequent creditor, or by the debtor's subsequent trustee in bankruptcy.** A security interest may be perfected by the creditor : **The key is notice - notice to other potential creditors of the debtor that a security interest might exist with respect to the collateral. 완성이란 후순위 구매자, 후순위 채권자, 혹은 채무자의 후순위 trustee 등과 같은 사람들의 권리를 잘라주는 효과.**

2) 동일 담보물에 대해 여러 개의 담보권(security interest or lien)이 설정될 수 있는데 담보권 완성이란 담보권자(secured party)가 다른 담보권 자에 우선하여 자신의 채권(claim)을 확보하기 위해 필요한 절차, 즉 우선권(priorities)을 확보하기 위한 절차라고 할 수 있다.

3) 담보권의 완성은 동일 담보물에 대해 이해관계를 갖고 있는 제3자에게 담보권자의 담보권을 통지(notice)하여 다른 후순위 담보권자를 끊어주는 효과를 갖고 있다.

4) 3가지 담보권 완성방법

이미 attachment가 된 담보권만 perfection이 될 수 있다.

A. Automaticperfection of most consumer goods

일정요건이 충족되면 perfection을 위한 추가절차 없이 자동적으로 담보권이 perfection되는 것

B. Filing financing statements

일정사항이 기재된 financing statements를 record office등에 제출하여 담보권을 perfection하는 것

C. Possession of collateral

담보권자가 담보물을 점유 또는 통제함으로써 담보권을 perfection하는 것

6 Filing Financing statements

A security interest in chattel paper, negotiable documents, instruments, or investment property may be perfected by filing.

참고 "Chattel paper" means a record or records that evidence both a monetary obligation and a security interest in specific goods, a security interest in specific goods and software used in the goods, or a lease of specific goods.

1) Financing statements에는 다음내용이 기재되어야 한다.

A. Debter's **name** 채무자 성명

B. Secured party's **name** 담보권자 성명

C. **Indication(identification)** of collateral covered 대상담보물의 명세(A financing statement sufficiently indicates the collateral that it covers if the financing statement provides :

(1) A description of the collateral and

(2) An indication that the financing statement covers all assets or all personal property.

Description such as all assets are sufficient.

2) 담보권 설정계약서(security agreement)가 있어서 financing statements의 요건을 충족하는 경우 담보권 설정계약서를 filing할 수 있다.

3) Filing은 state law(주법)에 따라서 규율되는데, 담보물의 종류에 따라 county recorder's office (군등기소)나 Secretary of state 등에 filing되며 전자적 방법도 가능하다.

4) 담보권의 설정(attachment)과 filing이 모두 이루어지는 시기에 담보권(security interest)은 완성된다. 따라서 filing에 의한 perfection의 요건은 attachmetn와 filing이라고 할 수 있다.

참고 1

UCC FINANCING STATEMENT

FOLLOW INSTRUCTIONS (front and back) CAREFULLY

A. NAME & PHONE OF CONTACT OF FILER [optional]

B. SEND ACKNOWLEDGMENT TO: (Name and Address)

THE ABOVE SPACE IS FOR FILING OFFICE USE ONLY

1. DEBTOR'S EXACT FULL LEGAL NAME - insert only one debtor name (1a or 1b) - do not abbreviate or combine names

1a. ORGANIZATION'S NAME			
OR 1b. INDIVIDUAL'S LAST NAME	FIRST NAME	MIDDLE NAME	SUFFIX
1c. MAILING ADDRESS	CITY	STATE / POSTAL CODE	COUNTRY
1d. TAX ID #: SSN OR EIN / ADD'L INFO RE ORGANIZATION DEBTOR / 1e. TYPE OF ORGANIZATION	1f. JURISDICTION OF ORGANIZATION	1g. ORGANIZATIONAL ID #, if any	NONE

2. ADDITIONAL DEBTOR'S EXACT FULL LEGAL NAME - insert only one debtor name (2a or 2b) - do not abbreviate or combine names

2a. ORGANIZATION'S NAME			
OR 2b. INDIVIDUAL'S LAST NAME	FIRST NAME	MIDDLE NAME	SUFFIX
2c. MAILING ADDRESS	CITY	STATE / POSTAL CODE	COUNTRY
2d. TAX ID #: SSN OR EIN / ADD'L INFO RE ORGANIZATION DEBTOR / 2e. TYPE OF ORGANIZATION	2f. JURISDICTION OF ORGANIZATION	2g. ORGANIZATIONAL ID #, if any	NONE

3. SECURED PARTY'S NAME (or NAME of TOTAL ASSIGNEE of ASSIGNOR S/P) - insert only one secured party name (3a or 3b)

3a. ORGANIZATION'S NAME			
OR 3b. INDIVIDUAL'S LAST NAME	FIRST NAME	MIDDLE NAME	SUFFIX
3c. MAILING ADDRESS	CITY	STATE / POSTAL CODE	COUNTRY

4. This FINANCING STATEMENT covers the following collateral:

5. ALTERNATIVE DESIGNATION [if applicable]: ☐ LESSEE/LESSOR ☐ CONSIGNEE/CONSIGNOR ☐ BAILEE/BAILOR ☐ SELLER/BUYER ☐ AG. LIEN ☐ NON-UCC FILING

6. ☐ This FINANCING STATEMENT is to be filed [for record] (or recorded) in the REAL ESTATE RECORDS. Attach Addendum [if applicable] 7. Check to REQUEST SEARCH REPORT(S) on Debtor(s) [ADDITIONAL FEE] [optional] ☐ All Debtors ☐ Debtor 1 ☐ Debtor 2

8. OPTIONAL FILER REFERENCE DATA

FILING OFFICE COPY — NATIONAL UCC FINANCING STATEMENT (FORM UCC1) (REV. 07/29/98)

참고 2

UCC FINANCING STATEMENT AMENDMENT

FOLLOW INSTRUCTIONS (front and back) CAREFULLY

A. NAME & PHONE OF CONTACT AT FILER [optional]
Alice Willison (304) 232-3232

B. SEND ACKNOWLEDGMENT TO: (Name and Address)

Loan Department
First National State County Bank
1 Bank Plaza, Suite 2000
Charleston, WV 25301

THE ABOVE SPACE IS FOR FILING OFFICE USE ONLY

1a. INITIAL FINANCING STATEMENT FILE #
0237899

1b. ☐ This FINANCING STATEMENT AMENDMENT is to be filed [for record] (or recorded) in the REAL ESTATE RECORDS.

2. ☐ TERMINATION: Effectiveness of the Financing Statement identified above is terminated with respect to security interest(s) of the Secured Party authorizing this Termination Statement.

3. ☐ CONTINUATION: Effectiveness of the Financing Statement identified above with respect to security interest(s) of the Secured Party authorizing this Continuation Statement is continued for the additional period provided by applicable law.

4. ☐ ASSIGNMENT (full or partial): Give name of assignee in item 7a or 7b and address of assignee in item 7c; and also give name of assignor in item 9.

5. AMENDMENT (PARTY INFORMATION): This Amendment affects ☐ Debtor or ☐ Secured Party of record. Check only one of these two boxes.
Also check one of the following three boxes and provide appropriate information in items 6 and/or 7.
☐ CHANGE name and/or address: Give current record name in item 6a or 6b; also give new name (if name change) in item 7a or 7b and/or new address (if address change) in item 7c. ☐ DELETE name: Give record name to be deleted in item 6a or 6b. ☐ ADD name: Complete item 7a or 7b, and also item 7c; also complete items 7d-7g (if applicable).

6. CURRENT RECORD INFORMATION:

6a. ORGANIZATION'S NAME			
Wiley's Wizard and Party Shop, Inc.			
OR 6b. INDIVIDUAL'S LAST NAME	FIRST NAME	MIDDLE NAME	SUFFIX

7. CHANGED (NEW) OR ADDED INFORMATION:

7a. ORGANIZATION'S NAME					
Wiley's Wonderful Wizard Works, Inc.					
OR 7b. INDIVIDUAL'S LAST NAME		FIRST NAME	MIDDLE NAME		SUFFIX
7c. MAILING ADDRESS		CITY	STATE	POSTAL CODE	COUNTRY
888 Magic Drive		Charleston	WV	25301	USA
7d. TAX ID #: SSN OR EIN	ADD'L INFO RE ORGANIZATION DEBTOR	7e. TYPE OF ORGANIZATION	7f. JURISDICTION OF ORGANIZATION	7g. ORGANIZATIONAL ID #, if any	☐ NONE

8. AMENDMENT (COLLATERAL CHANGE): check only one box.
Describe collateral ☐ deleted or ☐ added, or give entire ☐ restated collateral description, or describe collateral ☐ assigned.

10,000 wands, Merlin Industries Item # 03948
10,000 robes, Merlin Industries Item #20203
10,000 hats, Merlin Industries Item # 490588
100 boxes, eyes of newt, Merlin Industries Item #34567
100 boxes, toes of frog, Merlin Industries Item #45678

9. NAME OF SECURED PARTY OF RECORD AUTHORIZING THIS AMENDMENT (name of assignor, if this is an Assignment). If this is an Amendment authorized by a Debtor which adds collateral or adds the authorizing Debtor, or if this is a Termination authorized by a Debtor, check here ☐ and enter name of DEBTOR authorizing this Amendment.

9a. ORGANIZATION'S NAME			
First National State County Bank			
OR 9b. INDIVIDUAL'S LAST NAME	FIRST NAME	MIDDLE NAME	SUFFIX

10. OPTIONAL FILER REFERENCE DATA

FILING OFFICE COPY — NATIONAL UCC FINANCING STATEMENT AMENDMENT (FORM UCC3) (REV. 07/29/98)

 Perfection by secured party's control(possession) of collateral

A security interest in investment property, deposit accounts, money, letter of-credit rights, chattel paper, etc. may be perfected by control of the collateral.

> **참고** Deposit Account : a demand, time, savings, passbook, or similar account maintained with a bank

1) 돈(**m**oney), 유통증권(negotiable **i**nstruments), 유가증권(certified **s**ecurities), 유형동산 증명서(tangible chattel **p**aper) 등은 실제 점유(possession)을 해야지만 담보권이 완성된다.

EX Jack wishes to borrow money from Kookmin bank by using several shares of stock he owns. In addition to completing the three steps needed for attachment, the bank must possess the shares in order to perfect. Filing is not effective in this case.

2) 그 외의 경우, 담보권은 filing 이나 control 에 의해서 perfection 될 수 있는데 일반적으로 채무자는 담보물의 점유를 담보권 자에게 이전하는 것을 원하지 않는다.

담보권 자에게 담보물의 점유를 이전하는 대표적인 경우로서 전당포업자(pawn broker)이다.

3) possession 보다 control에 의하여 perfection이 이루어지는 경우는 신용장(letter of credits)등을 예로 들 수 있다.

8 Automatic Perfection

담보권이 perfection을 위한 추가적인 절차 없이 자동으로 perfection이 되는 경우로 담보권 자를 보호하는데 목적이 있다. 대표적인 예가 PMSI(purchase money in security interest in consumer goods), 약속어음의 판매(sale of promissory notes), proceeds of sale of perfected security interest 등이다.

1) Automatic Perfection

A. PMSI in **consumer goods**

B. PMSI is (1) money lent to the debtor to buy the actual collateral or (2) seller financing

C. Consumer goods : personal, family, home, or household use

Purchase Money Security Interest in Consumer Goods

[소비자용품 담보부 할부금융]

Purchase money security interests : lien rights that the seller retains in the goods purchased when the seller finances the purchase. The lien can be created by a specific written agreement or may arise when the item is financed on the seller's revolving credit plan or store credit card. This kind of lien does not have to be perfected by the usual filing of a UCC financing statement.

1) 외상으로 물건을 판매한 매도인이 그 물건에 대해 담보권을 갖는 경우(seller retains security interest in the same item sold on credit to secure payment)와 물건을

구입하도록 돈을 빌려준 사람이 빌려준 돈으로 구입한 물건에 대해 담보권을 갖게되는 경우(a person or a bank provides loan for and retain security interest in the same item purchased by debtor)를 의미한다.

2) consumer goods란 채무자가 담보물을 주로 개인용 또는 가정용으로 구입하기 위해 구입한 것을 의미한다.

3) 소비자용품(consumer goods)에 PMSI가 설정(attachment)된 경우 자동적으로 완성(automatic perfection)이 된다. 반면, 재고제품(inventory)나 장비(equipment)의 경우 등록[filing of financing statements]등의 절차를 반드시 거쳐야만 PMSI가 될 수 있다.

4) 담보물이 자동차(motor vehicles)나 트레일러(trailer)인 경우에는 PMSI in consumer goods라고 할지라도 automatic perfection이나 perfection by attachment가 안된다.

자동차의 경우, PMSI에 대한 perfection은 소유권 증명서(certificate of title)에 담보권을 기재하고, 이를 주정부에 filing함으로써 이루어진다.

5) PMSI in consumer goods가 automatic perfection이 된 경우 **담보권자(secured party)는 이 소비제품(consumer goods)이 담보권의 대상인 것을 모르는 다른 소비자(BFP for value who buys goods from consumer for consumer use)에게 판매되면 자신의 담보권을 주장할 수 없게 된다.** 즉 PMSI in consumer goods를 가진 자는 이 사람에게 우선권을 갖게 되지 못하므로 이러한 경우를 막기 위해서는 PMSI in consumer goods라도 등록을 하는 것이 안전하다.

여기서 다른 소비자는

A. 담보권의 존재사실을 모르고 (bona fide)

(1) 대가를 지불했으며(value)

(2) 소비자로부터(from consumers)

(3) 가정용 또는 개인용으로 사용할 목적으로(for consumer use)

(4) 담보물을 구입한자(Purchser)를 의미한다.

6) 다음의 경우에는 담보권자의 권리가 담보물을 구입한 자에게 우선권을 갖게 된다.

A. 담보권자(secured party)가 담보물이 매각되기 전에 PMSI in consumer goods를 filing한 경우

B. 담보물을 구입한 자가 담보물을 구입하기 전에 담보권이 타인에게 설정되어 있다는 것을 알고 있었던 경우

〈개념정리〉

Ex.1	Mr. Baker purchases a refrigerator on credit from E-Mart for use in his home giving E-Mart a security interest, then sellers the refrigerator to Miss Charles for a fair price for her household use. Miss Charles was not aware of the security interest that E-Mart has in the refrigerator.	➡ Miss Charles wins since she is a BFP.
Ex.2	If E-Mart had filed a financing statement on the refrigerator before Miss Charles purchases the refrigerator from Mr. Baker.	➡ E-Mart wins because the filing is effective even against BFP such as Miss Charles for consumer use.
Ex.3	If Miss Charles had purchased the refrigerator from Mr. Baker not for her household use, but for her buiness purpose to use it in her Outback restraurants.	➡ Miss Charles is not free from E-Mart's security interest.
Ex.4	If Miss Charles had been already aware of the security interest owned by E-Mart in the refrigerator when she purchased the consumer goods from Mr. Baker.	➡ E-Mart wins, since E-Mart perfected its right by filing the financing statement and Miss Charles cannot become a BFP.

After-Acquired Property Provision[AAPP]

After-acquired Property : personal or real property acquired by a debtor after he/she has agreed that all his/her property secures a debt. Thus, the new property also becomes security for the debt.

1) 담보권 설정계약에서 현재의 재산을 포함하여 **미래에 취득하게 될 재산 (after-acquired property)**도 담보권 자에게 담보로 제공한다고 합의할 수 있는데, 이러한 내용의 조항을 After-acquired Property Provision이라고 한다.

EX The Secured party lends $10,000,000 to the Best Buy Stores taking security interest in "all of Best Buy's inventory, whether now held or hereinafter acquired." This sort of clause is called an after-acquired property provision and it is enforceable.

2) 취득할 재산(**after-acquired property**)에 대해서 담보권을 설정한다는 합의는 일반적으로 **재고자산(inventory), 매출채권(accounts receivable), 또는 유형고정자산(equipment)등을 담보물로 하는 경우에** 이루어지는데, 담보물이 변동되므로 이러한 것을 floating lien이라고 한다.

3) 앞으로 취득할 재산에 대해 이미 대가(value)를 지불했으면 채무자가 담보물을 취득(possession)하는 시점에서 담보권이 설정(attachment)이 이루어지게 된다. 이것을 포괄담보(security interest in after-acquired property)라고 한다.

4) Although security interests in tort claim now come under the revised Article 9, this security will not attach to an after-acquired commercial tort claim.

〈개념정리〉

Included in after-acquired property	But **not** inclusive of
- Current consumer goods at inventory - After-acquired consumer goods - Present commercial tort claims.	- After-acquired commercial tort claims

11 Field Warehousing

담보물인 재고자산(inventory)이 채무자의 창고에 있지만, 창고안의 "fenced-off portion(특정구역)"에 두도록 하여 창고업자(warehouseman) 또는 담보권자가 통제를 하고 있어 점유를 하는 것과 같은 효과를 갖는 경우를 의미한다.

12 Consignment위탁판매

definition : a delivery of goods with a value over $,1000 to a merchant for the purpose of sale.

The merchant must be one who is not generally known to be engaged in the sale of goods by others. UCC Section 9-102(a)(20).

Priorities : General Rule

1) 여러 담보권이 모두 perfection되었다면 먼저 filing을 한자 또는 먼저 perfection이 된자가 이긴다.

2) Perfection된 담보권(perfected security interest)은 perfection이 되지 않은 담보권(imperfect security interest)에 우선한다.

3) 두담보권 모두 perfection이 되지 않은 경우에는 먼저설정(attachment)된 담보권이 우선한다.

4) 일반 무담보 채권자(general creditors, general unsecured creditors)는 담보권자(secured creditors, whether perfection is made or not by the secured creditors)에 우선하지 못한다.

14 Priorities : Buyer in Ordinary Course of Business[BIOCOB]

Buyer in the ordinary course of business : a bona fide purchaser who in a normal or regular business procedure buys goods from a seller in the business of selling goods of that kind. Under the Uniform Commercial Code a buyer in ordinary course of business takes the purchased goods free of the property interests of a third party.
[source] : http://dictionary.getlegal.com/buyer-in-ordinary-course-of-business

1) 일상적인 거래를 통해서 구입한 매수인(someone who purchase collateral from **merchant's inventory or equipment**)을 의미하는데 이러한 매수인은 perfection여

부에 상관없이 어떤 담보권에 대해서도 우선권을 갖는다.

2) 여기서 "일상적 거래(ordinary course of business)"라는 것은 매수인이 구입한 것과 같은 종류의 물건을 파는 것을 영업으로 하는 자(a person or company that normally deals in those goods,i.e. merchant)로부터 구입하는 것을 의미하므로 결국, 매수인이 매도인의 재고자산 (inventory)이나 장비(equipment)을 구입하였다면 일상적 거래를 통해 구입한 매수인이 되는 것이다.

3) BIOCOB은 구입하는 물건에 담보권(security interest)이 설정되어있다는 것을 알고 있는 경우에 도그 담보권에 우선한다(Buyer has priority even if s/he knows that security agreement exists). 즉 **BIOCOB = supreme winner**라고 이해할 수 있다.

EX 용산전자상가에서 컴퓨터를 대량으로 취급하는 상인에게서 노트북 한 대를 샀는데 나중에 알고 보니 외환은행이 그 상인의 모든 재고에 대해 담보권을 설정해두었다며 전화를 해서 노트북을 돌려달라고 할 경우

➡ 소비자는 노트북을 돌려줄 필요가 없다. BIOCOB이므로 supreme winner가 되기 때문이다.

4) BIOCOB v.s. BFP in consumer goods for consumer use

〈개념정리〉

	BIOCOB	BFP in CG for CU
요 건	someone who purchase collateral from merchant's inventory or equipment 상인의 재고나 장비로부터 담부물을 산 사람	① bona fide 담보권의 존재사실을 모르고 ② pay value 댓가를 지불하고 ③ from consumers 소비자로부터 ④ purchaser for personal or family use. 개인용 혹은 가정용으로 담보물을 구입한 자
우선할 수 있는 담보권	모든 담보권에 우선할 수 있다.	PMSI in consumer goods라도 filing을 한 담보권에는 우선하지 못한다.
매수인이 담보권의 존재를 알고 구입한 경우	상관없이 prevailing since BIOCOB = supreme winner	위 요건을 충족시키지 못하면 우선권을 갖지 못한다.
구입목적	상관없음	가정용 또는 개인용으로 사용할 목적이어야 함. (for consumer goods, individual use, family use, home use, household use)

15 Priorities : PMSI(Purchase Money Sewrity Interest)

1) PMSI in consumer goods는 별다른 조치 없이 automatic perfection이 된다. 그런데 만약 PMSI를 등록하지 않으면 이를 모르는 선의의 소비자(BFP)에게 담보권을 인정받지 못할 위험이 있다

2) PMSI in non-inventory : 20-day grace period.

담보권이 설정(attachment)된 날로부터 20일간의 유예기간(grace period)이 있는데 PMSI의 담보권자가 이 유예기간 내에 filing을 하게 되면 설정된 시점에서 perfetion된 것으로 인정한다.

EX On Jan.1st, Mr. Baker purchased some equipment from Shop & Save on credit. All elements of attachment are satisfied on this date. On Jan. 3rd, Mr. Baker borrowed money from Citibank using equipment purchased from Shop&Save as collateral. Attachment is accomplished and a financing statement is correctly filed by the bank on Jan.3rd. On Jan.7th, Shop & Save files a financing statement. Because of 20-day grace period, Shop&Save has priority over Citibank

3) PMSI in inventory 의 경우에는 20일간의 유예기간이 주어지지 않지만, 다음의 요건을 충족하면 우선권을 갖게 된다.

A. PMSI의 담보권자가 다른 채무자에게 통보(notice)를 해야 한다.
B. PMSI의 담보권자가 채무자(debtor)가 담보물을 점유하기 전에 자신의 담보권을 perfection해야 한다.

4) Knowledge of preexisting security interest has no effect. 뒤에 설정된 담보권이 perfection이 된 경우라 할지라도 이 담보권자가 먼저 설정된 담보권에 대해서 알고 있었다면 먼저 설정된 담보권의 perfection여부에 관계없이 먼저 설정된 담보권이 우선한다(Security interest, whether perfected or not, wins over subsequent perfected security interest if latter party knew of previous security interest).

 Lien Creditor(repairman or contractor)와의 관계

1) Lien creditor" means :

A. A creditor that has acquired a lien on the property involved by attachment, levy or the like;

B. An assignee for benefit of creditors from the time of assignment;

C. A trustee in bankruptcy from the date of the filing of the petition; or

D. A receiver in equity from the time of appointment.

저당권자란 **attachment** 등의 방법에 의해 부동산에 대하여 저당권(lien)을 취득하게 된 사람으로서 **assignment**에 의해서 된 **assignee**와 **bankruptcy**의 **trustee**, 형평소송의 법정관리인 등을 포함한다.

2) lien creditor는 완성되지 않은 담보권(unperfected security interest)에 대해 우선권을 갖는다.

3) 이 경우 lien creditor가 다른 담보권(security interest)가 설정되어있는지를 알고 있었는가는 우선권결정에 전혀 영향이 없다.

4) PMSI in noninventory + 20일의 grace period이내에 attach 되어security interest가 생겨난 경우에는 PMSI의 담보권자가 lien creditor보다 우선한다.

5) Lien이 생기기 전에 perfection된 다른 담보권(security interest)은 lien에 대해 우선권을 갖는다. 그러나 perfection이 않되었다면 lien에 대해 우선권을 갖지 못한다.

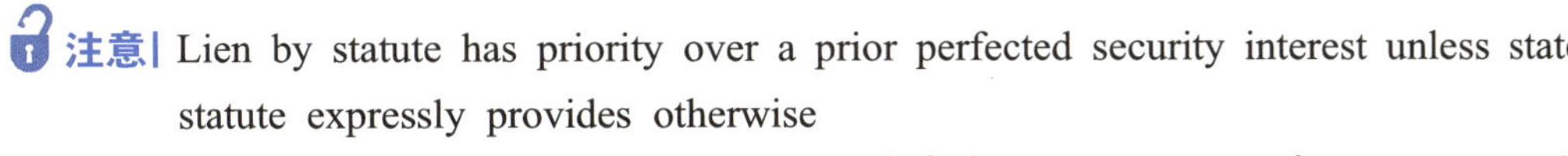

注意| Lien by statute has priority over a prior perfected security interest unless state statute expressly provides otherwise
예외적으로 주법에 별도로 정한바가 없다면 mechanic's lien과 artisan's lien은 이러한 lien이 생기기 이전에 perfection이 된 다른 담보권보다도 우선권을 갖는다.

17 Rights of Parties upon Default

1) 일반적으로 담보권에 대하여 대금지불을 제대로 하지 않으면 breach, 즉 default가 발생하게 된다.

2) **Self-Help Repossession** - permissible so long as the secured creditor does NOT BREACH THE PEACE - meaning that the actions of the secured party MAY NOT BE likely to cause violence

3) Upon default of a debtor, the secured party has a right to take possession of the collateral, either by self-help or by an act for replevin. Self-help may be used only where it will not involve a breach of the peace.

채무자가 채무불이행을 하게 되면 담보권자는 담보물을 점유할 권리가 있다. 만약 담보권자가 담보물을 이미 점유하고 있는 경우에는 repossession의 절차가 필요한 데 이 경우, 평화의 파괴(not breaching the peace)를 않도록 하는지 여부가 중요하다.

A. Repossession이란 담보물을 통하여 변제를 받는 절차인데 담보채권자는 자신의 선택에 따라 담보물(collateral)로부터 변제를 받거나 아니면 담보물을 통하여 일반 채권자(general creditor)로서 변제를 받을 수 있다.

4) **Repossession by Judicial Action** - If the secured party chooses not to resort to self-help, may go to court seeking writ of replevin ordering sheriff to obtain possession of the collateral and deliver it to the secured party

A. 채무자에게 서면통보를 반드시 해야 하는 것이 원칙이다.
B. Consumer goods를 제외하고는 다른 담보권 자에게도 이를 알려야 한다.
C. **60% rule in consumer goods : If the secured party proposes to satisfy obligation by retaining the collateral, s/he can only retain consumer goods if the debtor has paid less than 60% of the purchase price or obligation**
채무자가 담보물인 consumer goods의 구입가격(purchase price) 또는 채무액(obligation)의 60%미만을 지급한 경우, 담보권자는 채무자의 동의가 없이 담보물을 자신의 소유로 함으로써 채무자의 채무에 대한 만족을 얻을 수 있다.
D. **90 day-rule** : 만일 60%이상을 채무자(PMSI in consumer goods)가 이미 지불했다면 담보권자(secured party)는 점유를 한 날로부터 90일 이내에 반드시 담보물을 매각하여야 한다. 예외적으로 채무자가 해당 담보물에 대한 권리를 포기했을 경우, 매각을 하지 않아도 된다.

5) 담보물을 처분하는 경우 Foreclosure

A. public or private sale 둘 다 가능하다.
B. reasonable practices and reasonable time and place를 통해 이루어져야 한다.
C. consumer goods로 이루어진 collateral 인 경우를 제외하고는 관련 당사자 모두에게 통지를 해야 한다.

6) 담보물을 제3자에 대한 청구권(claims)인 경우

A. 담보물이 매출채권과 같이 제3자에 대한 채권인 경우, 채무자가 채무를 불이행하면 담보권자는 제3자로부터 그 채권을 회수할 수 있는 권리(right of recollection from third parties)가 있다.
B. 담보권자는 직접 자신에게 지불하도록 제3자에게 통지(notice)할 권한이 있다.

C. 담보권자는 제3자로부터 회수한 금액이 자신의 채권액보다 적은 경우 차액을 반환하도록 요구하거나(이 경우의 소송을 deficiency action이라고 한다), 남은 금액을 되돌려 주어야 한다(이 경우 채무자가 제기하는 소송을 surplus action이라고 한다).

D. 담보권자는 합리적 채권회수비용(reasonable expenses)을 제3자로부터 회수한 금액에서 공제(deduct)할 수 있다.

E. 매각대금에서 매각비용을 공제한 후, 담보권의 우선순위가 앞선 채권자부터 변제를 받게 된다.

18 Right of redemption (Debtor's limited right of redemption)

Right of redemption : Right of a mortgagor to recover mortgaged property from a judicial sale or foreclosure by paying the lender the outstanding principal and interest due, plus the lender's costs in foreclosure. Also, the right of a debtor in bankruptcy to redeem personal property by paying creditors the fair market value of assets securing their lien.

A. The right of redemption is the right to pay the debt and regain title to the land or other estate, even after default.

B. The right of redemption cannot be waived contractually for consumer protection.

C. To redeem, the debtor must pay all obligations secured by the collateral PLUS the Secured Party's reasonable expenses, including reasonable attorneys fees
채무자는 담보물이 처분되기 이전에 원금과 이자 및 담보권자의 비용을 담보권자에게 지급하고 담보물을 되찾아 올 수 있다.

D. Debtor's right to redeem the collateral is cut-off once the Secured Party has resold the collateral or completed foreclosure.
담보권자가 담보물을 재판매 해버리거나 담보물이 처분된 이후에는 이러한 권리가 인정되지 않는다.

19 Good faith purchaser for value = bona fide purchaser for value

담보물의 매각과정에 흠결이 있다는 사실을 알지 못하고(with no knowlge of defects in sale), 대가를 지불한 매수인을 의미하며 선의의 매수인은채무자의 권리도 없고, 어떤 담보권도 없는 소유권을 취득한다(good faith purchaser for value of collateral takes free of debtor's rights and any secured interest or lien subordinate to it).

Chapter 11

Debtor-Creditor Relationship(DCR)

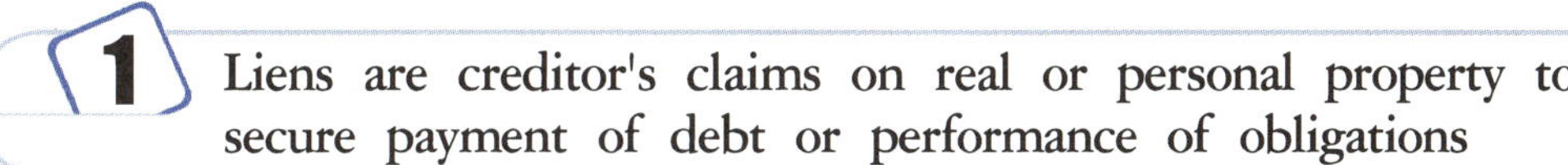

1 Liens are creditor's claims on real or personal property to secure payment of debt or performance of obligations

담보권이란 채권자가 채무자의 부채상환의무 이행을 하도록 담보하기위하여 부동산 또는 동산 등의 특정한 재산에 설치한 채권자의 권리를 의미한다.

취득가능한 담보권의 종류는 다음과 같다.

〈개념정리〉

consensual lien(= imposed by a contract between the creditor and the debtor.)	non-consensual lien(= typically arise by statute or by the operation of the common law. These laws give a creditor the right to impose a lien on an item of real property or a chattel by the existence of the relationship of creditor and debtor)
mortgages	tax lien(imposed to secure payment of a tax)
car loans	weed liens and demolition liens (assessed by the government to rectify a property from being a nuisance and public hazard)
security interests	artisan's lien
chattel mortgage	innkeeper's lien
property improvements	mechanic's lien(which secure payment for work done on property or land)
	judgment lien(imposed to secure payment of a judgment)
	maritime lien(imposed on ships by admiralty law)

1) 저당권(mortgage) under property law

2) 성문법상의 담보권(법정보호 담보권, statutory lien) : Mechanic's lien, artisan's lien, innkeeper's lien 등으로 주법에 따른다.

3) 판결에 의한 담보권(judgment lien) : 채무변제소송에서 채권자가 취득할 수 있는 저당권이나 법원판결에 따른 채무자의 재산과 채무자가 취득할 재산에 설정되는 담보권

4) 연방세무담보권(federal tax lien) : 미국세청(IRS)에서 세금미납에 따라 설정하는 담보권

5) 합의에 의한 담보권(consensual lien) mostly under UCC Article9 (already covered in secured transaction).

3 Mechanic's Lien(materialman's lien, construction lien (건물 공사 등의) 선취 특권)

definition : a security interest in the title to property for the benefit of those who have supplied labor or materials that improve the property. The law of mechanic's liens on real property governs the creation and enforcement of these liens on items of personal property that have been attached to real property in such a way as to be a fixture.

注意| mechanic이란 단어만 보고 부동산과는 상관이 없는 lien이라고 착각하기 쉽다.

1) 건축업자가 타인의 부동산을 건축하거나 수리해준 경우, 부동산 소유자는 건축업자에게 건축비 또는 수리비(debts for services to improve real property)를 지급해야 한다. 이 경우 건축업자는 건축비 혹은 수리비를 지급받을 때까지 그 부동산에 대해 법에 의한 담보권을 갖게 된다.

2) 채무자가 채무를 갚지 않으면 담보권자는 통지(notice)를 하고, 담보권을 실행하여 담보물을 매각하고 자신의 보수를 변제받을 수 있다.

Artisan's Lien(Repairman's Lien)

definition : An artisan's lien arises when a customer brings personal property owned by the customer to an artisan to be serviced (including stored) and does not pay the agreed upon amount at the agreed upon time. The legal basis is contractual between the owner and the lienor. The subject of the contract is the customer's personal property without which the lienor can perform no service. No opportunity for non-payment can arise unless the customer first entrusts personal property to the lienor.-New Jersey Law Revision Commission, Report and Recommendations Relating to Distraint and Artisan's Lien.

1) When one repairs or improves personal property for another and retains possession of that personal property

타인의 동산을 수리하거나 개량한 자가 그 보수를 지급받는 것을 담보하기 위하여 그 동산을 점유함으로써 얻게 되는 담보권이다.

 차 수리공이 수리비를 받을 때까지 차를 점유하고 있는 경우

2) 채무자가 채무를 갚지 않으면 담보권자는 통지(notice)를 하고, 담보권을 실행하여 담보물을 매각하고 자신의 보수를 변제받을 수 있다.

5 Innkeeper's Lien

definition : Whenever the keeper of any hotel, inn, boarding house, lodging house, bed and breakfast, or furnished apartment receives into his or her hotel, inn, boarding house, lodging house, bed and breakfast, or furnished apartment any person, guest, boarder, lodger, or tenant, the keeper shall have a lien upon and right to detain the goods, baggage, and effects of such guest, boarder, lodger, or tenant to secure and compel the payment of customary charges for the food and lodging furnished to the guest, boarder, lodger, or tenant. Michigan Legislature : INNKEEPER'S LIEN TO SECURE PAYMENT OF CHARGES

숙박업자의 담보권으로 숙박요금을 지급받기위하여 숙박업자가 투숙객의 짐(baggage)을 점유함으로써 취득하는 담보권이다.

6 Judgment Lien

definition : A lien on the property of a debtor resulting from a court's judgment. To create a judgment lien against personal property, the judgment creditor typically files a notice of judgment lien with the Secretary of State where the judgment debtor resides. A judgment lien against personal property of the judgment debtor is typically effective against property upon which a security interest may be perfected, such as accounts receivable, chattel paper, equipment, farm products, and negotiable documents of title (although some states exclude certain property such as motor vehicles and inventory of a retail merchant held for sale). As with a real property lien, typically the judgment is satisfied from the sale proceeds when the judgment debtor sells property that is subject to the lien.

1) 채권자가 피고를 상대로 하는 소송에서 승소한 경우, 피고의 재산으로부터 변제받기 위하여 만들어지는 담보권으로 채**권자가 승소한 판결을 가지고 법원으로부터 writ of execution [처분영장]**을 받아 집행관(sheriff)에게 제출하면, 집행관은 피고재산을 압류하여 **매각(seize and sell)하고, 그 매각대금(proceeds)**를 **채권자에게 지급함으로써 채권자는 변제**를 받게 된다.

〈개념정리〉

while waiting for the verdict or judicial forelosure to be completed, both creditor and debtor may take one of the measures against each other		
creditor(provisional remedies)	Judgment lien	**debtor(frauduelnt conveyance)**
Lis pendens Preliminary **I**njunction **A**ttachment **R**eceivership		**E**quitable Interest **P**ossession **S**ecret conveyance

2) 사해행위(fraudulent conveyance)

definition : The illegal transfer of property to another party in order to defer, hinder or defraud creditors.

채무자는 채권자가 judgment lien을 통해 변제를 받는 것을 방해하고자 하는 사해행위(fraudulent conveyance)를 하게 되는데, 이러한 사해행위에는 다음과 같은 것이 있다.

• Mneumonic : Fraudulent conveyance-EPS

- E is Retaining **equitable interest** after conveyance
- P is Retaining **possession** after conveyance
- S is **Secret** conveyance

A. debtor retaining equitable interest after conveyance of property

채무자가 자신의 재산을 제3자에게 이전하여 신탁(trust)을 만든 후 그 재산으로부터의 수익을 받는 것

B. debtor retaining possession after conveyance

채무자가 자신의 재산을 제3자에게 이전하고도 계속 점유하는 것

C. secret conveyances

채무자가 자신의 재산을 몰래 타인에게 이전하는 것

3) Provisional Remedies

definition : a temporary measure generally passed by the judge or any judicial officer to maintain the present status of the case as it is, till he/she finally gives a verdict to the case. This is done so that neither party can cause any damage to each other while awaiting the final verdict

채권자는 채무자를 상대로 소송을 제기하여 판결을 받아 강제집행을 할 수 있는데 소송 진행 중에 재산을 몰래 처분하여 채권자에게 손해를 입힐 수 있다. 이를 방지하기 위하여 채권자가 취할 수 있는 임시대책(provisional remedies)로서 lis pendens, preliminary injunction, attachment, receivership 등이 있다.

• Mneumonic : Provisional Remedies- LIAR

- **L is lis pendens** (a.k.a notice of pendency)
- **I is preliminary injunction** used to maintain status quo during pendency of action.
- **A is attachment**
- **R is receivership**

L is lis pendens (a.k.a notice of pendency) which warns someone of the P's claim that may effect the D's ownership, use, or possession of that real property.

특정부동산에 대해 소송이 진행된다는 사실을 등기를 해둠으로써 해당 부동산을 취득하려는 자에게 통지를 하는 효과를 갖게 된다.

I is preliminary injunction used to maintain status quo during pendency of action. 재판 진행 중에 피고인에게 일정한 행동을 하지 못하도록 하는 것이다.

A is attachment : a court-ordered seizure of property due to lack of payment **prior to** court judgment for past-due debt.

1) 지급일이 지난 채무(past-due debt)에 대하여 법원판결에 앞서 채무자의 재산을 처분하지 못하도록 보전하는 절차로서 법원의 명령에 의한다.

2) 법원의 판결이전에 채무자가 재산을 이전하거나 처분하게 되면 채권자는 판결을 받더라도 변제를 받기 어려울 수 있으므로 채권자는 판결을 받기 전에 미리 채무자의 계산에 대해 attachment를 하는 것이 일반적이다.

3) Writ of attachment

A. Attachment의 요건이 충족된 경우, 법원은 writ of attachment 를 채권자에게 주는데, 채권자는 이를 집행관(sheriff)에게 제출하면 집행관은 채무자의 재산을 가압류(seizure)하게 된다.

B. 채권자는 채무자를 피고로 하는 소송에서 승소한 후 가압류한 재산으로부터 채무를 변제받을 수 있다. 채권자가 병원으로부터writ of attachment를 받게 되면 채권자는 채무자 소유의 personal property 의 점유를 이전받게 되는 경우도 있다

注意| 채무자가 반드시 real property를 소유하는 경우에만 적용되는 것이 아니고 personal property를 소유하는 경우에도 attachment가 가능하다.

R is receivership or court receivership(법정관리) which appoints someone to oversee property involved in an equitable action.

7 Garnishment

definition : Garnishment is the process by which a creditor seizes a person's wages or other financial accounts. Once a creditor sues, and obtains a judgment, it can use various means to collect the judgment. Garnishments and writs of attachments are both prejudgment remedies available to a creditor where the debtor owns no real property.

1) Seizing debtor's property possessed by third parties.

채무자의 재산 중에 제3자에 대한 청구권(claim)이 있을 경우 그러한 청구권에 대하여 취해지는 구제수단(remedy)으로 attachment와 더불어 debotor 가 수중에 부동산을 소유하고 있지 않는 경우 취하기 좋은 수단이다.

EX1 채무자가 소유한 은행예금(debtor's bank account)

EX2 채무자의 체불임금(debtor's wages overdue)

EX3 전** 이라고 하는 과거 한국의 최고위직에 올랐던 한 인물이 자신의 비자금을 스위스 은행에 숨겨두었는데, 마침 국세청으로부터 1,000억원의 세금고지서를 발부받음. 그러나 전**는 자신은 수중에 현재 27만원 밖에 없다고 잡아 뗌. 그러나 스위스 은행의 비자금내역이 밝혀진 후 국세청이 전**에 미납세금에 대해 스위스은행을 상대로 해당자금을 소송과 국제법상의 절차에 의해 요구했을 경우, 이는 garnishment에 해당한다.

2) 채권자가 채무자가 받을 수 있는 급여를 garnish할 경우 주법과 연방법에 의하여 일정한 금액한도가 있다.

3) 채무자가 받을 수 있는 federal social security benefits는 garnishment가 될 수 없다.

4) 반면 tax lien의 경우 garnishment의 대상이 된다(the IRS guys are cruel!!!)

8 사적 채무조정

1) Composition agreement with creditors

A. **definition** : an agreement not only between the debtor and the creditors but also between the creditors themselves to accept less than what each is owed (even up to null).

2명이상의 채권자가 있는 경우에는 채권자들이 채무자들의 채무를 줄여주거나(아예 면제해주거나) 기간을 연장해주기로 합의한 것을 화의(和議 composition agreement)라고 한다.

B. It is a contract and such an arrangement is largely governed by contract law. There must be a meeting of the minds or mutual assent between the debtor and the creditors before a composition is created. The creditors themselves must also agree to the amount they will accept in satisfaction of their claims. They rely on mutual concessions of their rights to full payment in order to further the common purpose of securing their claims.

계약법의 지배를 받는다. 화의가 이루어지기 위해서는 consideration이 있어서 새로운 계약이 성립되어야 하는데 채권자들 사이의 상호약속(creditors'mutual promises to accept less than full amount)이consideration이 된다.

C. 화의에 동의하지 않는 채권자는 파산신청을 할 수 있다.

D. Composition of creditors는 debtor의 채무를 아예 release 해주거나 줄여주는 반면, assignment for the benefit of creditors는 자발적으로 debtor의 재산을 특정 트러스트에 맡겨 분배하는 것이다.

2) Assignment for Benefit of Creditors(ABC)

A. 채무자가 자발적으로 갖고 있던 전 재산을 신탁(trust)에 이전하여 채권자에게 분배하도록 한 것이다. 수탁인(trustee)는 그 재산을 처분하여 채권자에게 우선순위(priority)에 따라 배분한다.

B. Assignee takes legal title and debtor must cease all control of assets
Assignee 또는trustee가 이전된 재산의 소유권(legal title)을 갖게 되고 채무자는 더 이상 그 재산에 대한 권리행사를 할 수 없게 된다.

C. Assignment is irrevocable. Assignment를 하고나면 취소를 할 수 없게 된다.

채무자보호를 위한 그 외의 법

1) Homestead Exemption [입주주택 면제조항] under Homestead Act

Tax liens와 집에 설정된 mortgage에 의한 경우를 제외하고는 채무자의 집에 대해 채권자와 파산관재인이 채무자의 집을 팔아서 변제를 받을 수 없도록 하는 Homestead 법에서 나온 예외조항이다.

2) Fair Debt Recollectin Act :

A. fair debt recollection act basically prohibits a debt collector from harrassing a debtor.
채무자에게 부당한 방법으로 또는 권리를 남용하는 방법으로 부채상환을 독촉하지 못하도록 하는 법이다. 예를 들면 employer(사용자)의 동의 없이 채무자인 근로자를 불편한 시간에 만나거나, 불편한 장소에서 만나자고 하거나, 근무 장소에서 만나 독촉하는 경우, 늦은 밤이나 이른 아침에 독촉하는 등이다.

B. If a debtor is represented by n attorney, the debt collector may not contact the debtor directly. 만일 debtor가 변호사에 의해 대리되고 있으면, 추심업자는 debtor와 직접 접촉할 수 없다.

C. A debt collector generally may ascertain a debtor's location, continue to collect a debt, and commence a lawsuit to collect a debt. 추심업자는 debtor의 위치 파악, debt collection 지속, debt을 받기위한 소송 등을 할 수 있다.

D. 이 법은 연방법이며 연방거래위원회(fair trade commission)이 담당한다.

E. 채무자는 법위반을 이유로 채무감면을 주장할 수는 없다.

F. 채무자는 법위반을 이유로 채권자에게 민사상의 손해배상청구(civil damages)를 할 수 있다. 그러나 채무자는 법위반을 이유로 채권자에게 형사소송은 할 수 없다.

3) Truth in Lending Act [TELA]

이 법에 의해 채무자에게 대출을 하거나 소비자에게 신용판매를 하는 자는 채무자 또는 소비자에게 채무의 조건(이자율, 연체이자율) 등을 명확히 알려주어야 한다.

4) Federal Credit Card Fraud Act

The 1984 Credit Card Fraud Act punishes fraudulent use of an account number, punishes mere possession of illegal credit cards, and punishes the counterfeiting of credit cards and possession of counterfeiting equipment. Under the 1984 Credit Card Fraud Act, a credit card holder is protected from loss by limiting the card holder's liability for unauthorized use.

- B F Caminer, Credit Card Fraud - *The Neglected Crime,* Journal of Criminal Law and Criminology, Volume:76 Issue:3 Dated:(Fall 1985).

1984년에 발효된 Credit Card Fraud Act법은 계좌번호를 사기에 이용하거나, 불법카드를 소지하거나, 신용카드 위조제작, 혹은 위조 장비를 소지하는 것을 불법으로 간주하여 처벌함.

동법에 의거하여, 신용카드 소지자는 분실을 해도 불법사용으로부터 손해금액의 제한을 받게 됨.

5) 기타

이외에 소비자 대출에서 성, 인종, 결혼여부, 종교, 국적, 연령 등을 이유로 차별을 금지하는 equal credit opportunity act, 소비자의 신용에 관한 보고서의 정확성을 보장하기 위한 법인 Fair Credit Reporting Act가 있다.

 Nature of Suretyship and Guaranty

1) 보증계약(suretyship or guarantee)이란 채무자가 채권자에 대한 채무를 이행하지 않을 경우 제3자인 보증인이 채무자의 채권을 이행하겠다고 약속하는 것이다.

2) 한국어로 '보증계약'이라고 동일하게 번역되지만 영어에는 suretyship과 guaranty contract의 두 가지 종류가 있고 다음과 같은 차이점에 주의해야 한다.

〈개념정리〉

	Suretyship	Guarantee contract
Responsibility	Primary The surety is a co-debtor	Secondary
Creditor's collection	Creditor Needs **NOT attempt to** collect from **debtor**	Creditor may demand payment from debtor only after debtor defaulted
Notice requirement	Creditor needs **No Notice** of debtor's default to surety.	Notice needed to the debtor
Defenses	채무자에게 먼저 상환을 청구하라는 항변사유를 이용할 수 없다	guaranty contract에서는 채무자에게 먼저 상환을 청구하라는 그 항변사유를 이용할 수 있다.
Examples	Those assuming the mortgage, accommodation endorsement	Check endorsement,

3) 보증계약은 보증인과채권자사이에 체결되는 계약이므로 계약의 구성요건(offer, acceptance, consideration, no defenses)을 충족해야 한다.

4) 또한 보증계약은 statute of frauds가 적용되는 계약이다. 즉 writing으로 반드시 이루어져야 한다.

 보증계약과 구별되어야 할 계약

1) Third-Party beneficiary contract[3PBK]

A third party beneficiary, in the law of contracts, is a person who may have the right to sue on a contract, despite not having originally been a party to the contract. This right arises where the third party is the intended beneficiary of the contract, as opposed to an incidental beneficiary. It vests when the third party relies on or assents to the relationship, and gives the third party the right to sue either the promisor or the promisee of the contract, depending on the circumstances under which the relationship was created

제3자를 위한 계약은 promisor와 promisee사이의 계약으로 제3자인 beneficiary가 계약에서 수익을 얻는 것으로 제3자는 계약의 당사자(party to K)가 아니며 이러한 계약은 보증계약과는 다르다.

2) Indeminity contract

Type of insurance cover (such as property insurance, but not personal accident insurance) that only restores the insured to his or her original financial position. The insured cannot gain from a contract of indemnity.

자동차보험 중 손해보험의 예처럼 만일 indemnitee가 장래에 채무를 지게 되거나 손해를 입게 되면 indemnitor가 indemnitee의 그 채무 또는 손해를 부담하겠다고 indemnitee에게 약속을 하는 계약이다. Indemitor가 indemnitee의 채무 혹은 손해를 감수하는 이유는 indemnitee의 위험을 인수하였기 때문이다.

3) warranty

부동산, 상품, 권리 등을 대가를 받고 매각한 경우 매도인이 판매한 부동산, 상품, 권리 등에 하자가 있을 경우 이에 대한 책임을 부담하는 것을 의미하므로 보증계약과는 다른 것이다.

Creditor's rights and remedies

1) Creditor has right to receive payment or performance specified in contract against the principal debtor

주채무자(principal debtor)에 대하여 채권자는 계약서상에 명시된 대금의 지불이나 의무이행을 요구할 수 있다.

2) **보증인(surety)**에 대하여 채무의 변제기간이 되면 채권자는 채무자에게 그 사실을 통보하지 않고, 직접 보증인(surety)에게 채무이행을 요구할 수 있다.

3) **보증인(guarantor)**의 경우에는 채권자는 채무자에게 먼저 채무의 이행을 요구하여 채무자가 채무를 이행하지 않으면 그 사실(채무불이행 사실)을 즉시 보증인(guarantor)에게 통지한 후 보증인에게 채무이행을 요구할 수 있다.

4) 채권자가 담보권을 갖고 있는 경우(When creditor has security interest) 즉 채무에 대하여 보증인(surety)이 있고 채무자는 채무를 담보하기위해 일정한 담보물을 제공하여 담보권이 설정된 경우

5) 채권자가 담보권(security interest)을 갖고 있는 경우

채무에 대하여 보증인(surety)가 있고, 동시에 그 채무에 대한 담보물(collateral)이 제공되어있는 경우

A. 채권자는 자신의 선택에 따라 보증인(surety)에게 이행을 요구하거나 담보권을 실행하여 변제를 받을 수 있다.
B. 그러나 보증인(surety)은 채권자에게 자신에게 지급을 요구하기 이전에 먼저 담보권을 실행하여 변제받으라는 요구를 할 수 없다.
C. 단, 담보물의 가격이 급락하거나 혹은 담보물을 통해 먼저 채무를 변제받지

않으면 보증인이 부당한 어려움을 겪게 된다는 사실을 입증하면 보증인은 채권자에게 먼저 담보물로부터 채무를 변제받으라고 요구할 수 있다.

 Surety's and Guarantor's Rights and Remedies 보증인의 권리

1) Exoneration

A. Surety or guarantor can require the debtor to pay obligation if debtor is able before surety has paid. But not if creditor demands performance from surety
채무의 변제를 청구 받은 보증인은 채권자가 즉시 변제요구를 하지 않는 한 주 채무자에게 채권에 대한 의무를 다하도록 요구할 수 있다.

B. Surety or guarantor may request the creditor to resort first to collateral if surety can show collateral is seriously depreciating in value
또 담보물의가치가 급락하고 있으므로 채권자에게 우선 그 담보물을 처분하여 채무를 변제받으라고 요구할 수도 있다. 그러한 요구권리를 right of exoneration 이라고 한다.

2) Reimbursement

A. Surety or guarantor are(is) entitled to resort to collateral as satisfaction of right of reimbursement
보증인이 채권자에게 채무를 이행한 경우 보증인은 채무자에 대하여 구상권이 있다.

B. 단, 채무자가 채권자에 대한 유효한 항변을 갖고 있다는 사실을 보증인에게 통보하였는데도 보증인이 채권자에게 변제를 한 경우 보증인은 구상권을 상실한다.

3) Subrogation(대위권)

A. Upon payment, surety or guarantor obtain(s) same rights against the principal debtor that creditor used to have
보증인이 채권자에게 채무를 이행한 경우, 보증인은 채권자가 채무자에 대하여 가지고 있던 권리를 취득하게 된다.

B. 만일 그 뒤에 debtor가 bankrupt가 되면, surety는 bankruptcy proceedings에서 creditor의 권리를 부여받게 된다.

Surety's and guarantor's defenses

〈개념정리〉

personal defense by principal debtor(s)	personal defense by surety/guarantor(s)
death bankruptcy incompetency,etc.	death bankruptcy incompetency,etc.
⬇ **the surety/guarantor will NOT be released** ☞ 주채무자의 personal defense가 있어도 보증인의 보증책임은 면제되지 않는다.	⬇ **the surety/guarantor will be released.** ☞ 보증인의 personal defense가 있으면 보증인의 보증책임은 면제된다.

1) 보증계약은 보증인과 채권자간의 독립된 계약이므로 보증계약자체에 대한 항변을 채권자에게 주장할 수 있으며 또한 채무자와 채권자간의 의무가 없다면 보증인도 채권자에 대한 이행의무가 없어진다.

2) 보증계약서상의 항변

A. Fraud or duress 채권자가 보증인과 계약을 하면서 보증인에게 사기 또는 강박을 한 경우

B. Suretyship contract itself is void due to illegality

C. Failure of consideration for suretyship contract

D. Suretyship agreement is not in writings as required under SOF

E. Creditor fails to notify surety of any material facts within creditor's knowledge concerning debtor's ability to perform.

EX Mr. Mongryong Lee was not able to pay back the loan from Kookmin Bank when it was due. Kookmin refused to renew the loan unless Mr.Lee finds a surety for the loan. Mr.Lee asks her girl friend, Chunhyang, to become a surety on the loan. In the process of inducing Chunhyang to become a surety, Mr. Lee fraudulently represented his financial condition and promised Chunhyang that he would marry her as soon as his business picks up. Chunhyang agreed to act as surety and the loan was renewed. Later, Mr.Lee experienced business reversals and was discharged in bankruptcy. Kookmin now wants to hold Chunhyang liable. What shall Chunhyang do to avoid liability as surety?

➡ If Chunhyang can show that Kookmin was aware of the fraudulent representation by Mr.Lee, she is free from liability.

3) 채무자와 채권자사이에 체결된 계약상의 항변

A. Breach or failure of performance by creditors)

B. Impossibility or illegality of performance

C. Creditor obtains debtor's promise by fraud, duress, or misrepresentation.

D. Statute of limitation

4) Acts of creditor or debtor materially affecting surety's obligations

A. **Tender of performance by debtor or surety and refusal by creditor will discharge surety.**
채무자나 보증인이 이행을 했는데 채권자가 이를 거절할 경우 보증채무는 소멸한다.

B. **Release of principal debtor** from liability by creditor **without consent** of surety will also discharge surety's liability.

채권자가 보증인의 동의 없이 주 채무자의 채무를 면제해줄 경우 보증인의 책임도 면제된다.

C. **Release of surety by creditor** discharge surety's liability

채권자가 보증인의 보증채무를 면제해준 경우 보증인의 채무로부터 자유롭게 된다.

D. **Rroper performance** by debtor or satisfaction for creditor through collateral will discharge surety

채무자의 채무가 변제 혹은 담보물을 처분하여 채권자에 대한 채무를 충분히 변제한 경우 보증인의 채무는 면제된다.

E. **Surety may use any obligations owed by creditor to surety as a setoff against any payments owed to creditor by the debtor.**

채권자가 보증인에 채무가 있는 경우 동 채무와 채권자에 대한 채무자의 채무를 서로 상계하는 것이 가능하다.

5) Variance in terms and conditions of contract subsequent to surety's undertakings

채무자와 채권자사이의 계약서 내용이 변경된 경우

A. **Accommodation**(discharge of noncompensated surety)

보증인이 채무자와 친인척이나 친구간이어서 보증의 대가를 받지 않고 보증인이 된 경우에는 채무와 채권자사이에 체결된 계약에 사소한 변경이 있어도 보증인은 보증채무에서 전부 면제된다.

B. **Material Increase of Risk for Commercial Surety**

계약변경이 보증인의 위험을 현저하게 증가시킨 경우에만 보증채무가 면제되고 보증인의 위험이 일부 증가한 경우에는 증가된 위험에 대해서는 책임을 지지 않아도 된다.

No defenses for surety or guarantor

1) 주채무자의 personal defenses

A. 채무자의 사망(death of debtor)

B. 채무자의 무능력(incapacity)

C. 채무자의 지급불능(부도insolvency or bankruptcy)

2) 보증인(surety)은 채권자가 주 채무자에게 먼저 지급을 요구하지 않았다는 사실(creditor did not proceed against the principal debtor)이나 채무자의 채무불이행에 대해 채권자로부터 통지를 받지 못했다(creditor did not give notice to surety of debtor's default)는 사실을 항변으로 사용할 수 없다

3) 채권자가 담보권을 실행하여 담보물의 매각대금으로부터 변제받지 않았다(creditor did not resort to collateral)는 사실 등을 항변으로 사용할 수 없다.

16 Cosureties[연대보증인]

1) Cosureties exist when there is more than one surety for same obligation of principal debtor to same creditor

2명이상의 보증인이 **동일한 채무**의 전부 또는 일부에 대해 그 이행을 보증하는 것이다.

2) 연대보증인간 서로 몰라도 되며, 보증시기와 보증금액이 달라도 된다. 또한 굳이 같은 문서에 서명하지 않아도 된다.

3) Jointly and severally liable to creditor

채권자가 채무의 일부변제를 받았더라도 전부가 변제될 때까지 보증인들의 책임은 소멸되지 않는다.

4) right of contribution for cosureties

A. 각 보증인의 부담비율(cosurety's pro rata share)에 따라 각자의 보증한도까지는 책임을 져야한다.

B. 부담비율 계산공식

$$\frac{\text{dollar amount individual cosurety personally guaranteed}}{\text{total amount of risk assumed by all cosureties}}$$

C. 각 보증인은 자신의 부담비율이상으로 채권자에게 부담한 경우 다른 cosureties에게 그들이 부담하는 비율만큼을 구상 받을 수 있다.

D. **Discharge or release** of one cosurety by creditor results in a reduction of liability of remaining cosurety
채권자가 cosureties들 가운데 한명의 보증인의 채무를 면제해주게 되면 다른 보증인의 채무도 감소하게 된다.

EX Shinhan Bank lent Mr. Gildong Hong $50,000. At Shinhan's request, Gildong entered into an agreement with Chunhyang and Mongryong for them to act as compensated cosureties on the loan in the amount of $50,000 each. The employee of Shinhan in charge of the loan management, finding Chunhyang to be his high school sweetheart, immediately released her without Mongryong or Gildong's consent or knowledge. Later Gildong defaulted on the loan. Under this circumstances, what would be the liability of Mongryong?

➡ He will be liable only for the half of the loan balance.

E. 한사람의 보증인이 사망, 파산, 등으로 인하여 채무가 면제되었다고 해서 다른 보증인의 보증채무가 면제되는 것은 아니다. 그러나 이 경우 각 보증인의 부담비율은 사망하거나 파산으로 채무가 변제된 보증인을 제외한 나머지 보증

인들에 대해서만 계산되어야 한다.

EX Woori promised to lend John $1,000,000 if John obtained sureties on the loan. John agreed with Chunhyang, Mongryong, and Gildong for them to act as cosureties on the loan from Woori. The agreement provided that compensation be paid to each of the cosureties. It further indicated that the maximum liability of each cosurety would be as follows; Chunhyang $600,000, Mongryong $1,000,000, and Gildong $300,000. Woori accepted the commitments of the sureties and made the loan to John. After paying ten installments totalling $100,000, John defaulted. Mongryong's debts, inclusive of the surety obligation to Woori, were discharged in bankruptcy. Later Chunhyang properly paid the entire outstanding debt of $900,000. What amount may she recover from Gildong?

➠ Gildong's pro rata share of the remaining $900,000 would be determined according to the following formula;

[dollar amount guaranteed by Gildong / total amount assumed by remaining cosureties] multiplied by remaining obligation = [$300,000/$1,900,000] * $900,000

17 Surety Bonds

1) performance bonds

A surety bond issued by an insurance company or a bank to guarantee satisfactory completion of a project by a contractor.

계약의 이행을 보증하는 증권인데 보증회사가 계약의 일방대상자로부터 보증료를 받고 발행해주는 것으로 이는 계약의 상대방 당사자에게 제출된다.

2) construction bonds

건설업자의 공사를 완성할 의무를 보증하는 증권이다.

3) fidelity bonds

definition : a form of protection that covers policyholders for losses that they incur as a result of fraudulent acts by specified individuals. It usually insures a business for losses caused by the dishonest acts of its employees. While called bonds, these obligations to protect an employer from employee-dishonesty losses are really insurance policies

신원보증 증권 EX 서울보증보험 상품

Chapter 12

Federal Bankruptcy Law

〈bankruptcy 개념정리〉

Debtor				**Estate created** (priority)	
	➡ petition	**voluntary**			property rights
					admin cost
		involuntary	➡ automatic order of relief		middleman debts
					wages
assets (property rights, capital, debts-secured and unsecured)	➡ **watch out for P.T.**	12 creditors / $13,475 **uncontested**		managed by trustee ➡	employee benefits
					consumer deposits
					alimony
		contested	➡ order of relief after review		tax
		due? custodian?			NPGC

Bankruptcy is mostly based on federal law

연방법에 의한 판산법 처리절차가 정해져 있다. 파산법상의 우선순위 절차에 따라 재산이 공평하게 채권자에게 배분(equitable distribution)되도록 하여, 채권자들의 권리가 보호되고 채무자를 일정한 채무로부터 벗어날 수 있도록 하여 채무자가 새로운 출발((fresh start)을 할 수 있도록 하는 것이다.

Chapter 7(liquidation = straight bankruptcy), Chapter 11(business reorganization), Chapter 13(Debt adjustment Plan)

〈개념정리〉

Chapter 7	**Voluntary petition**채무자가 자발적으로 신청
	Involuntary petition 채권자가 신청
Chapter 11	**Voluntary liquidation** 채무자가 자발적으로 신청
	Involuntary liquidation 채권자가 신청
Chapter 13	Voluntary petition만 가능

Chapter 7. Voluntary Bankruptcy Petitions

1) 채무자가 법원에 자발적으로 자신에 대한 파산절차개시명령(order of relief)을 신청(petition)하는 것이다.

2) petition을 신청할 경우에는 채무자가 자신의 자산 및 부채목록(list of debtor's

assets and liabilities)를 보여주어야 한다. 만일 정당한 사유 없이 채무자의 장부나 기록을 감출 경우 또는 보관을 하지 못하였을 경우 적발된다.

3) **채무자가 완전히 지불불능(involvent)일 필요는 없고, 채무가 있다는 사실(the debtor has debts)만으로 충분하다.**

4) 부부가 공동으로 파산신청을 할 수도 있다.

5) 모든 사람, partnership, 또는 기업은 Chapter 7의 voluntary bankruptcy petition이 가능하다.

6) 그러나 철도회사(railroads), 보험회사, 은행 등과 같은 금융기관(insurance companies, banks, savings and loans,) 등은 voluntary bankruptcy petition은 물론 involuntary bankruptcy petition도 신청할 수 없다.

7) Order of relief(OR) : 채무자가 자발적으로 파산신청을 하게 되면 절차개시명령(order of relief)이 자동적으로 시작되게 된다(Debtor is automatically given an order of relief upon filing of petition).

4 Involuntary Bankruptcy Petitions

1) 채권자(creditors)가 채무자에 대한 파산신청을 하는 것으로 채권자는 법원에 채무자에 대한 파산 절차 개시명령(order for relief)을 신청한다.

2) Petition 요건

〈개념정리〉

Any debtor can be brought in involuntarily. § 303

- If more than 12 creditors, you need 3 or more creditors to bring the action and claims must aggregate at least $13,475 or more.

- If less than 12 creditors, only need 1 creditor to bring the action.
- Excludes employees and insiders

A. **Creditor의 수가 12명이상인 경우**

(1) 최소한 3명이상의 채권자가 함께 파산신청을 해야 하고, 세 명의 무담보채권(unsecured claims)의 합계액이 $13,475 이상이어야 한다.

- 위의 금액은 법 개정에 따라 1~2년마다 변경되므로 주의

(2) **A secured claim is simply a claim that is coupled with some form of interest in property.**
담보채권이란 재산에 담보권(secured interest, mortgage, lien)이 설정된 채권을 의미하고, 무담보채권(unsecured claim)이란 위와 같은 담보권이 없는 채권이다. 그래서 여기서의 채권은 확정된 것만을 의미하며, 유동적인 것은 포함되지 않는다(claims must not be contingent).

(3) 농부(farmes), 자선단체(charirtale organization), 보험사, 등의 금융기관 등은 Chapter 7의 involuntary bankruptcy를 신청할 수 없다. 또한 $13,475 미만의 빚을 지지 않은 사람(파트너십, 기업)은 involuntary bankrupty신청을 할 수 없다.

〈개념정리〉

RIB 철도/ 보험/ 은행 등의 금융기관	**No** Voluntary bankruptcy 자발적 파산신청 금지
RIB+CF+if less than $13,475 철도/보험/은행 등의 금융기관과 자선단체 및 자선단체와 농부와 $13,475 미만의 빚을 진 자	**No Involuntary bankruptcy** 비자발적 파산신청금지

A. Creditor 수가 12명 미만인 경우

(1) A single creditor may file the petition as long as his/her claim aggregates $13,475 in excess of any security s/he may hold
채권자는 자신의 무담보채권(unsecured claims)의 금액 총액이 $13,475 이상이면 혼자서라도 파산신청을 할 수 있다.

(2) If necessary, more than one creditor may join together to have combined debts of more than $13,475 of unsecured claims
무담보채권의 금액이$13,475 미만인 경우에는 채권자들은 그들의 무담보채권액의 합이 $13,475이상이라면 함께 파산신청을 할 수 있다.

위의 금액은 법개정에 따라 1~2년마다 변경되므로 주의

3) Order of Reflief(OR) 파산절차 개시명령

A. 채무자가 파산신청에 대하여 정해진 기간 내에 이견제시를 하지 않는 경우(이견다툼이 없는 경우, the petition is uncontested) 법원은 파산절차 개시명령(OR)을 내리게 된다.

B. 채무자가 파산신청에 대하여 이견제시가 있는 경우, 즉 다툼이 있는 경우, 다음중 하나를 만족시키면 법원은 파산절차개시명령을 내린다.

(1) The debtor is generally not paying his/her debts s they become due
채무자가 변제시기가 다 된 채무를 변제하지 못하고 있는 경우

(2) During the 120 days preceding the filing of petition, a custodian was appointed

or took possession of substantially all of the property of the debtor.
파산신청이전 120일 이내에 재산관리인(= 관재인)이 선임되어 채무자 재산의 대부분을 관재인이 점유하고 있는 경우.

If contested regarding the petition, **OR** will be **Granted when**
1) Not Paying Debts when due
2) Custodian was appointed or possesses the property

채무자가 petition에 이의를 제기하였어도 채무상환일자가 도래하였을 때 채무자가 제때 지불 하지 않거나 custodian이 지정되어 있거나 해당 부동산을 점유하고 있으면 법원은 파산개시명령을 내리게 된다.

Bankruptcy Proceedings(also called liquidation or straight bankruptcy)

4 things you need to know
- Automatic **Stay** ex. Alimony and child support
- First Creditors' **Meetings**
- **T**rustee is appointed
- **E**state is created **[SM TE]**

1) Automatic Stay 자동정지 (자동보전 처분 그냥 stay라고도 한다)

A. Gets creditors off the debtor's back : Automatic injunction. Also applies to IRS : applies to EVERYONE (also, can't evict if you don't pay rent)
유효한 파산신청이 있게 되면 대부분의 채무회수절차와 파산절차 이외의 다른 법적 절차는 중단이 된다. 즉, 채무자가 파산 신청을 하게 되면 소송, 판결문

집행 등이 자동 정지되는 것이다. 예를 들어 A가 B에게 받을 돈이 있어 소송을 진행하던 중 B가 파산 신청을 하면 A는 즉각 소송을 중지해야 한다. 이런 면에서 파산 신청은 더 이상의 채권자의 법적인 침해도 막아 주는 방패 역할을 하게 되는 것이다.

注意| A stay against creditor collection proceedings will go into effect
(채권자의 회수절차를 못하도록 하는 유예조치가 발효되게 된다)

B. 예외 : alimony and child support to be paid to the divorced spouse.
이혼한 배우자에게 지급하여야 할 alimony와 child support에 대해서는 automatic stay가 적용되지 않는다.

2) First Creditors' Meetings 제1차 채권자 모임

A. Debtor furnishes a schedule of assets, their locations, and a list of creditors (채무자는 소재지가 명시된 재산목록과 채권자의 목록을 제출하여야 한다).

B. 임시관재인은 사임하고 채권자들에 의해 정식 trustee가 선임되는데 trustee는 파산재단(representative of estate)을 대표하게 된다(Trustee may be elected by creditors in Chapter 7 Proceedings).

3) 관재인의 선임(Trustee Appointment)

A. Trustee has right to receive compensation for services rendered based on the value of those services rather than only on size of the estate
관재인은 관리업무 서비스 등에 따라 급여를 받을 수 있다. <u>관리대상이 되는 파산재단이 크고 적음에 별 상관이 없음에 유의해야 한다.</u>

4) Estate(파산재단)

A. 파산신청일 현재 채무자가 소유하고 있는 재산 중 면제(exemption)되지 않은 것은 파산재단에 편입된다.

B. 파산신청일 이후 취득하게 되는 재산은 파산재단에 편입되지 않지만, 파산신청일 이후 180일 이내에 채무자가 ① 상속(inheritance), ② 생명보험금(life insurance), ③ 이혼으로 인한 재산분할(property settlement with spouse), ④ 유증(bequest or devise), ⑤ gifts 등을 통해 취득하는 재산은 파산재단에 편입된다.

• mneumonic : GIL PD 180 day-divorce after bankruptcy

If any of the following falls within **180 days of filing for bankruptcy**

- G is gifts
- I is inheritance
- L is life insurance
- P is property settlement with spouse after divorce
- D is bequest or devise

5) Exemptions from Estate

A. 채무자는 fed bankruptcy code에 의한 면제(FBCE)와 fed bankruptcy code에 의하지 않은 면제(non-FBCE) 중 한 가지를 선택할 수 있다.

〈개념정리〉

B. fed bankruptcy code에 의한 면제(FBCE)	C. fed bankruptcy code에 의하지 않은 면제(Non-FBCE)
FMV of those principal **residence** **burial** pot, one motor **vehicle**, **trade tools,** other **home-use items**, **social security** benefits, **unemployment compensation,** **disability** benefits, **alimony**, **veteran's** benefits, prescribed **health aids**, specified personal injury up to $18,450 등.	**Exempt Property**(still need to live for fresh start 채무자도 새 출발을 위해서는 살아야 하므로 최소한의 필수품은 automatic stay하지 않고 남겨둔다) (1) 주법에 의한 면제 States can opt out of fed exemptions and use their own Ex. House(homestead exemption), transportation to work, wages earned, clothes, furniture, etc. (2) **Other Fed Code-related exemptions** Ex. 군인연금, 사회보장연금, 실업수당, 장애연금, 이혼위자료

 Duties and rights of Trustee **관재인의 의무와 권리**

• Mneumonic

the duties and rights of trustee : Record and Compensate SAME LA

- **Keep the accurate records of all transactions**
- **Compensate** for services rendered
- **Set aside** the **preferential treatment** within **90 days** immediately preceding the bankruptcy filing and **Set aside** the **transfers** within **one year of filing the petition**
- **Manage(collect, liquidate, and distribute) the estate and**
- **Employ professionals** and compensate them with court approval
- Take **any legal action**

1) Trustee has duties & responsibilities to keep the accurate records of all transactions

관재인은 파산재단의 정확한 기록 관리를 할 의무와 책임이 있다

2) Trustee has right to receive compensation for services rendered

관재인은 자신과 전문가들의 업무수행에 따른 보수를 받을 권리가 있다

3) **파산신청일 90일 이내에 이루어진 특혜성이전의 철회(set aside)**

내부자의 경우 파산신청일 1년 이전에 이루어진 재산의 이전(transfer made within one year prior to the filing of the bankruptcy petition)으로 채무자의 지급불능이 된 경우(the debtor became insolvent as a result of transfer)와 사기성 이 없는 경우 이러한 재산의 이전을 철회(set aside)하는 것이 가능하다.

4) Trustee has duties & responsibilities to collect, liquidate, and distribute(manage) the estate

관재인은 파산재단의 취합, 청산, 분배 및 정확한 기록 관리를 할 의무와 책임이 있다.

5) Trustee has right to employ professionals(e.g. accountants and lawyers)

관재인은 자신의 의무수행을 위해서 회계사나 변호사 등의 전문가를 법원의 허가를 얻어 선임할 권리가 있다.

6) Trustee may take any legal action necessary to carry out duties

관재인은 자신의 의무를 수행하기 위하여 필요한 법적조치(legal action)을 취할 수 있다.

 Preferrential Transfers 특혜성 이전

1) 특혜성이전이란 특정한 채권자에게 Chapter 7에 의한 절차에 따라 배분할 수 있는 것보다 많은 금액을 배분해 주는 효과를 가져주는 효과를 가져오는 재산의 이전을 의미한다. 이 같은 특혜성이전은 나머지 채권자들에게 불이익을 주게 되므로 이를 철회하여 채무자의 재산이 공평하게 채권자에게 배분(equitable distribution of debtor's property)되도록 하기 위한 것이다.

2) Preferential treatment

다음의 경우에 해당할 때 특혜성이전이라고 한다.

• Mneumonic : PT -AIG-90 but not OBCE CO 600

- **A** is antecedent debts
- **I** is insolvent
- **G** is greater percentage
- **90** days is if the transfer is made within 90days of bankruptcy filing(**or 1year for insiders**)

Exceptioin **OBCE CO 600**

- **OB** is ordinary course of business
- **CE** is contemporanious exchange
- **CO** is Charitable Organization
- **$600** or less

A. The transfer was on account of antecedent debts or to provide a security interest given by the debtor to secure antecedent debt.

과거의 채무를 상환하기 위해 혹은 과거의 채무를 담보하기위해서 채무자의 재산에 담보권을 설정한 것이다.

EX 채무자가 은행으로부터 빌린 대출금을 담보하기위해 자신의 냉장고에 대해 담보권(security interest)을 설정해주었고, 이러한 담보권의 설정이 파산신청 90일 이내에 이루어졌다면 Preferential treatment 가 된다.

B. The transfer was made while the debtor was insolvent.

채무자는 이미 지불불능상태(insolvency)인 상태에서 재산의 이전이 일어난 경우.

C. The transfer allows the creditor to receive greater percentage than would otherwise be received in the bankruptcy proceedings

재산의 이전으로 인해 그 재산의 이전을 받은 채권자는 파산절차를 통해 받을 수 있는 것보다 더 많은 채권을 회수하게 되었다.

EX 채무자가 장비구입의 할부금 (installments) 을 미리 지급했다면 특혜적 이전이 될 수 있다. 즉 채무의 조기상환도 특혜적 이전이 될 수 있는 것이다.

D. The transfer was made during the 90 days immediately preceding the bankruptcy filing(or within 1 year for insiders

파산신청일 직전 90일 동안 재산의 이전이 이루어진 경우(내부자의 경우 12개월)

내부자(insider)란 가까운 친척(close blood relatives), 회사직원(corporate officer), 이사(director), 지배주주(controlling shareholder), 또는 partnership의 general partner등

3) Preferential Treatment 의 예외

A. 채무자가 자선단체(**charitable organization**)에 기부(gift)하는 것은 과거의 채무 때문에 이전하는 것이 아니므로 preferential treatment로 간주되지 않는다.

B. 새로운 대가를 동반한 동시적인 맞교환 (**contemporaneous exchange** accompanied with **new value**)

EX 파산신청을 한 상태에서 파산신청 65일전에 현금으로 업무용 차를 산 경우

C. **Transfer made in the ordinary course of business**

일상적 거래를 통한 재산의 이전

 각종 공공요금(utilities bill)

D. **Security interest to secure the debt that arise from ordinary course of business if filed within 45 days of creation of the debt**

일상거래상 발생한 채무를 담보하기위해 채권자에게 담보권을 설정해준 경우로 채무발생 45일 이내에 담보권이 완성된 경우

E. **security interest given by debtor to acquire property that is perfected within 10days after such security interestattached**

물건구입을 위해 담보권이 설정된 후 10일 이내에 그 담보권이 완성된 경우

F. $600 이하의 소비채무를 상환한 경우(a **consumer debtor's payment** of **$600 or less**)

8 Filing of Claims

All claims must be filed within 6 months after the first creditors' meeting

채권의 신고

모든 채권자들은 First Creditors' Meetings (제1차 채권자 모임)개최일로부터 6개월 이내에 자신의 채권을 신고하여야 한다.

9 Claims : Property Rights(PR)

채권자가 갖고 있는 권리가 property right일 경우 이는 파산재단(estate)에서 포함되지 않는데 secured claim, trust claim, reclamation, 등이 이에 해당한다.

1) Secured claim(i.e. perfected claim and recorded claim)

채권자가 담보권(security interest, e.g, mortgage in property by creditor bank)을 갖고 있는 경우, 즉 담보채권(secured claims)을 갖고 있는 경우 담보물(collateral)은 일단 파산재단에 편입된다. 하지만, 담보물의 처분대금은 담보채권자에게 우선적으로 지급된다. 또한 담보채권자는 파산절차(liquidation proceedings)에 따라 담보물을 처분하여, 담보물의 처분대금이 우선적으로 자신에게 분배되는 것을 기다리는 대신 일반적인 담보권 실행절차를 통해 변제를 받는 것도 가능한데 이를 위해 채무의 잔액(debt balance)이 담보물의 진정한 가치(FMV)를 초과해야 하고, 담보채권자가 법원에 신청(motion for relief)해야 한다. 만약 부족분(deficiency)이 있는 경우, 이에 대해서는 무담보채권(unsecured claims)와 같은 순위로 파산재단의 분배에 참여할 수 있다.

2) Trust claim : trust claim is made by beneficiary for trust property when the trustee is bankrupt

신탁의 수탁자(trustee)가 파산한 경우 수익자(beneficiary)가 신탁재산에 대한 반환을 청구하는 것이다.

3) Reclamation : claim against specific property by a person claiming it to be his or her own

파산자가 점유하고 있는 재산의 진정한 소유자가 그 재산을 자신에게 반환하라고 청구하는 소송이다.

EX 형님이 미국주재원으로 나가면서 동생에게 집을 맡겨두었다가 동생이 파산하자, 그 집이 같이 포함된 것을 발견하고 소송을 제기한 경우

10 Priority of claims

1) property rights

A. Technically they are not a part of the priorities because they never become part of the bankrupt estate
채권의 우선순위 : property rights는 파산재단에 속하지 않으므로 우선순위와 상관이 없다.

B. 그러나 **PR의 대상이 되는 재산**이 파산재단에 포함된 채 파산재단이 청산(liquidation) 된 경우 다른 채권에 **우선하여 변제**를 받게 된다.

C. secured claim을 가지고 있는 담보채권자가 일반적인 담보권 실행절차(foreclosure)를 통해 담보물로부터 변제받지 않는 경우에는 파산재단의 청산과정에서 담보물의 처분대금에 대해 **secured creditor는 unsecured creditors보다 우선적으로 변제를 받게 된다.**

D. secured claim을 갖고 있는 채권자가 담보물을 통해서 변제받지 못한 금액은 non-priority general claim이 된다.

2) 다음의 priority 순서는 매우 중요하다. 반드시 암기할 것!!!

• mneumonic for priority : PAM WED AT NPGC

- **P** is **property rights**
- **A** is **adminstration cost**
- **M** is **middleman debt**

- **W** is **wages**
- **E** is **employee benefits**
- **D** is consumer **deposits**

- **A** is **alimony**
- **T** is **tax**
- **NPGC** is non-priority general claims (timely filed)

 Priority of General Claims

1) 여러 단계의 우선순위가 존재하는데 각 단계의 채권에 대해 지급을 마친후 그 다음 단계의 채권에 대해 지급을 하게 된다.

2) If there are insufficient assets to pay any given level then assets are prorated at that level and the next level gets nothing.

어떤 단계의 채권에 대해 모두 지급하기에 충분하지 않은 경우, 그 단계의 채권에 대해 비율적으로 지급하게 되며, 다음단계의 채권에 대해서는 한 푼도 지급을 할 수 없다.

3) **우선순위**(Levels of Priority)

A. **Administration cost(= administration expenses 파산신청이후 발생한 관리비)**

(1) **expenses paid to accountants, lawyers, trustees, appraisers, etc and the expenses incurred only in recovering, preserving, selling or discovering property that should be included in debtors' estate**
회계사, 변호사, 피 신탁인, 감정평가사 등에게 지급한 보수 및 파산재단에 속하는 재산을 회수, 보존, 매각, 발견하는데 사용된 비용

(2) 파산신청이후에 발생한 합리적 비용도 포함된다.

B. **Middlemen debts(중간처리비)**

(1) **Claims arising out of the ordinary course of debtor's business after involuntary bankruptcy petition is filed after the bankruptcy begins**
비자발적인 파산(involuntary bankruptcy) 신청이후 절차개시명령이 부여되기까지 채무자의 일상적인 사업과정에서 발생하는 채무

注意| Voluntary petition의 경우에는 자동으로 order of relief 이 시작되므로 middlemen debt이 없다.

C. **Wages of bankrupt's employees (직원급여)**

(1) 파산신청일 이전 90일 이내에 발생한 임금

(2) 종업원 1인당 한도는 $5,435

위의 금액은 법개정에 따라 1~2년마다 변경되므로 주의

(3) 한도를 초과하는 금액은 non-priority general claism

D. **Contributions to employee benefit plans**

(1) 파산신청일로부터 180일 이전에 발생한 것으로
채무자가 사용자(employer)로서 employee benefit plan에 납입해야 하는 금액

(2) 종업원 1인당 한도는 $5,435

위의 금액은 법개정에 따라 1~2년마다 변경되므로 주의

E. **Consumer deposits**

(1) **Consumer deposits for undelivered goods or services**
소비자가 상품이나 서비스를 받기 전에 그 대금으로 지불한 금액

(2) 1인당 한도는 $2,225

(3) 한도초과금액은 non-priority general claims가 된다.

위의 금액은 법개정에 따라 1~2년마다 변경되므로 주의

F. **Alimony and child support**

G. **Taxes**

H. **위의 항목에 해당되지 않는 것들은 non-priority general claims(NPGC)라고 한다.**

NPGC는 timely filing이 되는 경우와 untimely filing(late filing)이 되는 경우로 나뉘며, **untimely filing(late filing)을 한 경우 한 푼도 받을 수 없다.**

12 Discharge of a Bankrupt(DOB파산의 면제)

1) A discharge is the release of a debtor from all his or her debts not paid in bankruptcy except those not dischargeable

파산면제 되지 않은 일부 예외적 채무를 제외하고 파산자의 채무를 면제시켜주는 것이다.

2) 법원에서 order of relief를 허락해주는 것이 결국 자동적으로 파산면제 신청(automatic application for discharge)을 하는 것이라 볼 수 있다.

3) Corporation과 partnership은 파산면제 신청을 할 수 없다.

4) 채무자가 채무면제를 받기위해서는 honest debtor라는 법원의 판단을 받아야 한다.

13 Acts that bar discharge of all debts 파산면제 금지행위

다음과 같은 사유가 있는 경우, 채무의 종류를 불문하고채무자는 채무로부터 면제받지 못한다. 이를 general discharge금지사유라고도 한다.

1) Improper actions during bankruptcy proceedings

파산절차소송 진행 중에 일어난 부적절한 행위로 주로 사기 또는 기망에 의한 행위(fraud : intent to deceive creditor)로 False claims against the estate(부동산에 대한 허위주장), concealing property(자산을 은닉), fraudulent transfer(사해행위), false entry in accounting(허위장부 기재), destroying or removing property(부동산 파손 및 제거), etc. 등을 예로 들 수 있다. 그러나 using false information for credit application(신용카드

발급을 받기 위해서 허위정보를 기재하는 것)은 이에 해당하지 않는다.

2) **Failing** to satisfactorily **explain** any loss of assets

자산이 없어진 것에 대해 제대로 설명을 못하는 것

3) **Refusing to objey court orders법원명령 준수 거부**

4) Being **discharged** in bankruptcy proceedings **within past 6 years**

최근 6년 사이 파산절차에 의해 채무면제를 받은 경우

5) **Substantial abuse** of bankruptcy by individual debtor with primarily **consumer debts.**

채무의 대부분이 소비성 채무로서 채무자가 파산제도를 심각하게 남용하는 경우

Debts Not Discharged(DND) by Bankruptcy, even though general discharge allowed

(**General discharge**가 허용되어도 면제되지 않는 **파산채무 면제 금지 항목**)

• Mneumonic : LG FAIL DND with Hidden Taxes

- **LG** is **luxury goods**
- **F** is **fines**
- **A** is **alimony**
- **IL** is **intent-based liability**
- **DND** is **debts not discharged**
- with **Hidden Taxes**

1) Loading up on <u>Luxury goods</u> (사치성 채무)

사치성 재화나 서비스로 인한 건별 $1,150 이상의 소비채무나 현금서비스(cash advance)

2) Government Fines or penalties imposed within 3 prior years

파산신청일 3년 이내에 부과된 벌금

3) Alimony, separate maintenance, or child support

위자료 별거유지, 양육비 등

4) Liabilities due to the international torts(deceitful, intentional, willful, and malicious injury or intoxication

고의성 불법행위

의도적인 계약위반(intentional BOK)는 이 경우에 해당되지 않는다

5) Hidden Liabilities (unscheduled debts) unless creditor had actual notice of proceedings.

파산절차에서 누락된 채무

6) Taxes within 3 years of filing bankruptcy petition

파산신청일 3년 이전의 세금 및 연방세금을 내기위한 차입금(loans for payment of fed taxes)

 Revocation of Discharge 파산에 따른 채무면제철회(면제취소)

1) 철회사유

A. 파산절차상의 사기행위(fraud)면제가 된 날로부터 1년 이내에 면제의 철회를 신청하여야 한다.

B. 파산자가 파산재단에 속하는 재산을 취득하고 이를 기망적으로 파산관재인에게 보고하지 않은 경우(**보고누락**)

C. 파산자가 법원의 적법한 명령에 따르지 않은 경우(**명령불복종** refusal to obey lawful court order)

D. 파산petition에 대한 중요한 질문에 답변을 제대로 못한 경우(**답변실패**)

16 Reaffirmation[재승인]

1) The Debtor promises to pay a debt that will be discharged

채무자가 파산에 의해 면제될 채무를 파산이 종료한 후에도 갚겠다고 약속하는 것이다.

2) Reaffirmation요건

A. 파산자를 대리하는 변호사(lawyer)가 있는 경우에는 재승인에 관한 합의사항에 대해 변호사의 동의서약서(affidavit)가 필요하다.

B. Before the discharge granted
채무면제가 되기 전

C. Must be approved by bankruptcy court
reaffirmation에 관한 합의사항을 법원으로부터 동의 받아야 한다.

D. 소비성 부채(consumer debt)일 경우 법원은 debtor의 best interest에 부합하고 undue hardship이 없다는데 동의해주어야 한다.

4) 파산자(bankrupt)는 reaffirmation에 관한 agreement를 취소할 수 있는 권리를 갖는데 파산자는 위 agreement가 법원에 filing된 날로부터 60일 또는 discharge가 되는 날 중 나중에 도래하는 날까지 위의 agreement를 철회할 수 있다.

 Business Reorganization-Chapter 11

1) 채무자에게 사업을 계속하면서 채무와 사업의 구조를 조정하기위한 절차를 제공하는데 그 목적이 있다.

2) Can be initiated by debtors(voluntary) or creditors(involuntary)

Chapter.11에 의한 절차도 Chapter 7과 마찬가지로 채무자 또는 채권자가 신청할 수 있는데, Chapter 7의 절차를 이용할 수 없는 자(Ex. 보험회사, 은행 등과 같은 금융기관(insurance companies, banks, savings and loans) 는 Chapter 11의 절차도 이용할 수 없다.

3) 절차

A. **Committee구성**

B. 파산관재인(**trustee**)의 선임 - 채무자의 경영진이 사업수행능력이 있을 경우(if debtor's management is capable of continuing business) 꼭 선임하지 않아도 된다.

C. **Reorganization Plan작성 및 approval**

채권자로 구성된 위원회에서 채권단의 1/2이상, 채권액의 2/3이상의 동의를 얻어야 하며, 주주로 구성된 위원회에서는 주식수의 2/3이상의 동의를 얻어야 한다.

위와 같은 동의를 받지 못한 경우에도 법원은 reorganization plan을 승인할 수 있다.

D. 법원의 확정승인(confirm)과 최종명령(**final decree**)
법원이 확정승인과 최종명령을 내려 채무자는 reorganization plan이 승인되기 이전에 발생한 모든 채무와 책임으로부터 면제를 받게 된다. 다만 다른 예외 규정이나 파산법에서 예외로 되어있는 경우는 면제는 받지 못한다.

18 Debts Adjustment Plans-Chapter 13

Any individual, even if self-employed or operating an unincorporated business, is eligible for chapter 13 relief as long as the individual's unsecured debts are less than $336,900 and secured debts are less than $1,010,650. 11 U.S.C. § 109(e). These amounts are adjusted periodically to reflect changes in the consumer price index. A corporation or partnership may not be a chapter 13 debtor.(UScourts.gov)

1) Chapter 13의 채무조정계획은 다음과 같은 요건을 충족하는 개인(그중에서도 채무자)만이 신청가능하다. 즉 채권자는 신청할 수 없다.

A. 정기적 수입
B. **$336,900** 미만의 무담보채무(unsecured debts)
C. **$1,010,650** 미만의 담보채무(secured debts)을 부담하고 있는 채무자가 voluntary 신청하는 것이다.

위의 수치는 1~2년마다 변경되므로 주의할 것

2) Chapter 13의 장점

Chapter 13 offers individuals a number of advantages over liquidation under chapter

7. Perhaps most significantly,

① **chapter 13 offers individuals an opportunity to save their homes from foreclosure.** By filing under this chapter, individuals can stop foreclosure proceedings and may cure delinquent mortgage payments over time. Nevertheless, they must still make all mortgage payments that come due during the chapter 13 plan on time. Another advantage of chapter 13 is that it ② **allows individuals to reschedule secured debts** (other than a mortgage for their primary residence) and extend them over the life of the chapter 13 plan. Doing this may lower the payments. Chapter 13 also has a special provision that protects third parties who are liable with the debtor on "consumer debts."

This provision may ③ **protect co-signers.** Finally, chapter 13 acts like a consolidation loan under which the individual makes the plan payments to a chapter 13 trustee who then distributes payments to creditors.

④ **Individuals will have no direct contact with creditors** while under chapter 13 protection.**(출처 : UScourts.gov)**

Chapter 13

Federal Securities Regulations

모든 증권법의 주요목적은 시장에서 유가증권에 투자를 하는 모든 사람들에게 충분한 정보(sufficient information to the investing public who purchases securities in the market place)를 제공해주는데 있다.

〈개념정리: 증권시장의 흐름〉

Primary Market(발행시장) under 1933 Act			Secondary Market(유통시장) under 1934 Act
pre-filing period		⬅ filing +20days(waiting period) ➡	- post effective period
발행사issuer	➡ 등록서류 등 관련서류제출	SEC(증권거래 위원회) ⬅ 필요시 제출서류 수정 및 보완지시	
		① 접수일(filing)로부터 20일 이내에 증권발행 가능여부를 결정해야 한다.	④ 투자자들의 증권매매 허용
mandate ⬇		② 재무제표에 대한 내용의 정확성을 보장(no guarantee of accuracy)하는 것은 아니다	⑤ 철저한 시장감독 및 공시(disclosure) 활동 감독
		③ 특정증권을 평가하거나 권고하지 않는다.	
증권회사(securities company)			
registration statement 준비 (Due diligence meeting)		ⓐ oral offer만 가능	ⓔ final prospectus배포
financial statements		ⓑ preliminary prospectus(red herring) 배포가능	ⓕ free writing by analyst허용
prospectus draft 준비		ⓒ tombstone ad를 게재하여 발행이 임박했음을 알림	ⓖ 매매중개(brokerage)
underwriting group(인수단) 구성		ⓓ road show 등을 통해 기관투자자들에게 증권매입 권고(oral offer)	ⓗ 자기매매(dealing)

1 The Securities Act of 1933 [1933 Act]

The securities Act of 1933 is a landmark law primarily regulating the issuance of securities by corporation, a general or limited partnership, an unincorporated association or an individual.

1) Purpose목적

A. To provide full and fair disclosure of all material information relating to issuances of securities
증권 발행시장과 관련하여 중요정보의 full &fair disclosure

B. To prevent fraud or misrepresentation
사기행위방지

2) 목적달성방법(accomplished by)

A. requiring registration statement to be filed with SEC before either a public sale or an offer to sell securities in interstate commerce
주간통상(interstate commerce)을 통해 증권을 매도하거나 매도청약을 할 경우 발행인은 등록신고서를 SEC에 등록하도록 하고 있다

B. 증권의 매도(sale)나 교부(delivery)이전에 투자자에게 prospectus(사업계획서)를 교부하여야 한다.

C. 증권의 발행과 관련된 fraud(사기)나 misrepresentation(부실표시)을 막기 위하여 민・형사상의 책임(civil and criminal liabilities)을 규정한다.

D. Deciding whether the issuer has met the disclosure requirements
발행사가 공시의무를 다하고 있는지 감시 및 판단한다.

3) U.S. Securities and Exchange Commission

미국증권거래위원회(SEC)

The mission of the U.S. Securities and Exchange Commission is to protect investors, maintain fair, orderly, and efficient markets, and facilitate capital formation(SEC homepage).

고객보호, 공정하고 질서 있고 효율적인 시장추구, 자본형성 촉진이 주요임무이다.

구체적으로는

A. The SEC oversees the key participants in the securities world, including securities exchanges, securities brokers and dealers, investment advisors, and mutual funds. Here the SEC is concerned primarily with promoting the disclosure of important market-related information, maintaining fair dealing, and protecting against fraud(SEC homepage).
증권거래소, 증권중개회사, 자기매매회사, 자문사, 뮤츄얼 펀드 등의 증권세계에 참여하는 관계자들을 감독하며, 주로 시장과 관련된 중요정보를 공시가 잘 이루어지도록 하고, 공정한 거래를 하도록 하며, 사기를 방지하기 위해 노력한다.

B. 연방의 증권관련법들을 규율하는 정부기관으로서 법률을 해석(interpret)하고 법위반사실을 조사(investigate)하며 관련규칙을 제정(rule-making function)한다.

C. 증인소환권한(can subpoena witness), 법규위반 증권의 판매정지를 법원에 신청(can obtain injunction preventing sale of securities)할 수 있다.

D. 사법기관이 아니므로 직접적인 벌금(monetary penalties)을 부과하거나 법이나 규칙을 위반한자를 기소할 수는 없다(cannot prosecute criminal acts).

E. The SEC does not evaluate the merits or values of securities. It just enforces that full and fair disclosure.
SEC는 증권의 가치나 장점 등을 평가하는 것이 아니고 완전하고 공정한 공시(full and fair disclosure)를 강제하여 일반인들이 증권의 가치를 평가할 수 있도록 한다.

F. No guarantee of the accuracy about the facts stated in registration statement
SEC는 registration statement에 담겨있는 사실에 대해 정확한지 여부를 보장하는 기관이 아니다.

2 Definitions

1) Security

Securities are defined as any ① interest in a scheme where a person invests in a ② common enterprise and is led to expect ③ profits from the ④ efforts of others(S=IPCE). They include an interest or instrument that is common stock, preferred stock, a bond, a debenture, or other derivatives; an interest or instrument that is expressly mentioned in securities acts, or an investment contract.

증권인지 여부를 판단하는 중요한 기준은 "① 공동의 사업에 ② 타인(제3자)의 노력을 통하여 ③ 수익을 얻을 것을 기대하고 ④ 자금을 투자하는 것"으로 보통주, 우선주, 채권, 후순위 채권, 파생상품, 증권 법에 나와 있는 각종 상품들, 그리고 투자계약을 의미한다.

A. Partnership은 "voluntary Association of 2 or more persons carrying on as co-owners of business for profit sharing"(두 명 이상이 자발적으로 참가하여 이익분배를 위해 두 사람의 공동소유주가 비즈니스를 영위하는 것).

B. 'general partnership'은 경영에 본인이 직접 참가하여 이익을 얻는다는 점에서 증권이 아니고, 'limited partnership interest'는 limited partner가 경영에 참가하지 않고 general partner의 노력을 통해서 이익을 얻는 다는 점에서 증권이다.

C. Neither the certificate of deposit nor the agreement in question is a security within the meaning of § 10(b) of the Securities Act of 1934-*Marine Bank v. Weaver(1982).*
certificate of deposit은 증권의 IPCE요건을 충족하지 못했으므로 증권이 아니다

(Marine Bank v. Weaver(1982)).

D. 증권을 인수할 권리(rights and warrants to subscribe), 자기주식(treasury stock)등도 주식이다.

2) controlling person

소유관계(ownership), 계약, 지위 등에 의해 발행인(issuer, 즉 발행회사)의 경영과 정책에 직간접적으로 영향력을 행사할 수 있는 자를 의미하는데 51%의 지분을 가진 주주(51% stockholder), 10%의 지분을 갖고 있으며 경영에 주도적 역할을 하고 있는 이사 등을 들 수 있다.

3) Insider

A. "Insider" is a shareholder who owns more than 10% of a corporation, or an officer or director. "내부자" 란
이사(director), 임직원(officer) 및 지분(equity securities)을 10%이상을 소유하고 있는 자(owner)에 해당한다.

> **注意|** equity securities중에서 convertible bond는 전환된 보통주로 간주되어 지분증권인 반면에 무담보장기채권(debentures)은 지분증권이 아니다. 즉 debenture는 아무리 많이 갖고 있어도 insider로 간주되지도 못한다.

B. Beneficial ownership rule

A person shall be deemed to be the beneficial owner of a security if that person has the right to acquire beneficial ownership of such security including but not limited to any right to acquire:

- through the exercise of any option, warrant or right;
- through the conversion of a security;

- pursuant to the power to revoke a trust, discretionary account, or similar arrangement; or
- pursuant to the automatic termination of a trust, discretionary account or similar arrangement, etc.

법적인 소유자는 아니지만 편법으로 법망을 빠져나가는 것을 막기 위해issuer의 equity securities의 10%이상에 대한 beneficial owner(실질적 소유자)도 insider에 포함된다. 즉 beneficial ownership을 결정하기 위해서는 관련 equity stock 소유자의 배우자, 소유자의 미성년자녀, 소유자의 친인척 중 함께 거주하는 자, 수혜자를 소유자로 해서 신탁에 맡긴 소유자의 equity stock도 전체 지분에 포함된다.

4) Underwriter [인수회사]

발행인(issuer)로부터 증권을 구매하거나, 인수단(=underwriting group or syndicate)에 참여하여 증권을 인수받아 일반대중에게 distribution하고자 하는 회사.

5) sales of securities 유가증권의 판매

기업구조조정, stock warrant(신주인수권), ESOP(employee stock ownership program우리사주제도)에 의하여 주식을 매입하는 경우에도 sales of securities에 해당하므로 모두 1933 Act에 의거하여 SEC등록대상이 된다.

注意| stock dividends(주식배당)나 stock splits(주식분할)은 sales of securities에 해당되지 않는다.

6) Registration Statement 등록서류

A. In general, securities offered or sold to the public in the U.S. must be registered by filing a registration statement with the SEC. The prospectus, which is the document through which an issuer's securities are marketed to a potential investor, is generally filed in conjunction with the registration statement. The SEC prescribes the relevant forms on which an issuer's securities must be registered.

Registration statements and the incorporated prospectuses become public shortly after they are filed with the SEC. Registration statements are subject to SEC examination for compliance with disclosure requirements. It is illegal for an issuer to lie in or to omit material facts from a registration statement or prospectus.

B. 주간통상의 방법으로 증권매매(to sell, offer to sell, or offer to purchase securities)를 하고자 할 경우 반드시 등록신고를 먼저 하여 신고한 날로부터 그 효과가 발효되는 20일 뒤부터 증권을 매매 해야만 하며 그렇지 않을 경우 위법이다.

C. 그러나 등록신고 발효이전이라도 발행인(issuer)은 등록신고를 하자마자
(1) Oral offers [서면으로 offer하는 것은 불법]
(2) Tombstone ads
(발행계획에 관한 기본사항(Ex. 발행가격, 사업설명서의 교부방법 등)이 담겨 있으며 “묘석(墓石)광고”라고도 함)
(3) 예비사업설명서(preliminary prospectus = red herring붉은색잉크로 표시된 예비사업설명서) 등은 배포할 수 있다.

〈개념정리〉

	filing date	effective date
Pre-filing period	Filing + 20days(waiting period)	Post-effective period
No sales of securities	구두판매만 허용	매매허용
청약금지(no offers)	Oral offers, red herrings (preliminary prospectus), tombstone ads	서면청약(written offer)도 허용, finalized prospectus 배포& free writing 기간

7) Prospectus(사업설명서)

A prospectus is a legal document that institutions and businesses use to describe the securities they are offering for participants and buyers. A prospectus commonly provides investors with material information about mutual funds, stocks, bonds and other investments, such as a description of the company's business, financial statements, biographies of officers and directors, detailed information about their compensation, any litigation that is taking place, a list of material properties and any other material information.

A. Prospectus include any written communication which "offers any security for sale or confirms the sale of any security it can be radio or televised communication (증권의 매매 및 매매권유 및 매매사실을 확인하는 관련된 모든 문서와 자료)

B. 증권의 인도와 동시 또는 그 이전에 1933 Act의 section §10에 따른 모든 정보를 포함하는 사업설명서를 매수인에게 교부하여야 한다(Final prospectus delivered before final sale). 단, 요약본만 제공하는 것도 가능하다.

3 Registration Requirement under Section §5 of 1933 Act

1) 증권이 각종 형태의 주간통상(trade, commerce, mail, transportation, communication (including telephone calls))을 통해서 청약, 매매, 또는 인도되는 경우에는 등록이 필요하다.

2) 주간통상이란 둘이상의 주에서 거래, 운송, 지불, 또는 보고 등이 일어나는 것을 의미했는데, 이 개념이 폭넓게 확대되어 한 주에서 거래 등이 일어났지만 다른

주에도 영향을 미치는 것도 광범위하게 포함하게 되었다.

3) 법적으로 등록의무자는 발행인(issuer)이지만, 실제로는 발행업무의 위임(mandate)을 받은 증권회사에서 총괄업무를 한다.

4) 등록신고서의 주요내용

A. 재무제표(financial statements audited by independent CPAs)
B. 발행인, 임원현황, 대주주 현황, 사내변호사 등

注意| 속임수문제로 "대주주(major shareholders)"가 아닌 "모든 주주(all the shareholders)" 혹은 "임원(executives)현황"이 아닌 "전 직원(every employee)현황" 등의 오답을 제시하는 경우가 있으므로 주의가 필요하다.

C. 관련 위험
D. 발행인의 부동산소유현황, 자본금 현황, 비즈니스 현황
E. 발행인의 경영정보에 관한 사항
F. 매도할 증권에 대한 설명과 증권발행을 통해 조달한 자금의 사용목적(용도)

5) 사업설명서(prospectus)는 등록신고서와 함께 제출해 등록해야 한다(In a securities offering in the United States, a prospectus is required to be filed with the Securities and Exchange Commission (SEC) as part of a registration statement)

6) SEC는 사업설명서와 등록신고서를 검토하며, 20일 동안의 대기기간(waiting period)동안 시장상황의 변동에 따라 발행인은 등록신고서의 기재사항에 변경할 필요가 있는 경우 정정을 할 수 있다.

7) 발행인은 주식판매 여부에 상관없이 등기책임이 있다

 Shelf Registration Rule 일괄등록제도

Allows the issuer to register security and take it off shelf at short notice for distribution at some later point.

1) 일반적으로 등록신고서는 그 신고서에 발행될 것으로 기재된 증권에 대해서만 효력을 가지므로 등록절차를 거쳐 증권을 발행한 후 다시 증권을 발행하고 싶은 경우에는 다시 등록을 해야 한다.
   그러나 일괄등록 신고서를 제출하여 당해증권발행과 관련하여 근본적인 변경사항이 있다면 추가적으로 수정신고서만 제출하면 된다)발행인이 처음 발행인 그대로일 필요는 없다.

2) Registration Forms 등록신고서 양식

A. Form S-1
   Most used form, filing initial public offering
   기본적인 양식으로 발행인과 발행증권에 관하여 가장 많은 정보를 기재하여야 한다.

B. Form S2 and Form S3
   SEC에서 disclosure requirements에 따라 registration statement를 작성하는데서 오는 부담을 줄여주기 위해 만들어낸 form으로서 S1보다 적은 양의 정보를 기재하면 충분하다.

C. Form SB-1 and SB-2 for small business issuers(generally under $25 mn) under the Regulation

 Exempt Securities 면제대상 증권

• mneumonic for exempt securities : CIGAREST

- ☑ C is commercial paper
- ☑ I is insurance contract, ICC-controlled commercial carriers' securities, some of intra-state securities
- ☑ G is government or quasi-government
- ☑ A is annuity contract or issuance under Regulation A
- ☑ R is religious, educational, or charitable organizations' issuance
- ☑ E is exchanged securities
- ☑ S is savings & loans, banks,
- ☑ T is trustee-issued securities

1933 Act에 따라 등록을 할 필요는 없지만 증권의 종류에 상관없이 만일 사기행위를 할 경우 1933 Act의 antifraud provision(사기방지조항)의 규제를 받는다.

1) Commercial Paper(note, draft, check, etc) with a maturity of 9 months or less 만기가 9개월 이하의 약속어음, 환어음, 수표 등의 commercial paper로서 투자목적이 아니고 상업목적상 발행된 경우에 한한다(Must be for commercial purpose and not investment)

2) ① Insurance Contracts 보험회사 계약증서

보험회사에서 발행한 증권(securities issued by insurance companies)은 반드시 SEC에 등록해야 한다.

② ICC-regulated Common Carriers' securities.
주간통상위원회(Interstate Commerce Commission)의 규율을 받는 운송업체에서 발행한 증권

③ some of intra-state securities

주간 통상을 통해서 발행되는 증권이 아니고 1개 주안에서 발행되는 증권 중 일부

3) Government Securities, Quasi-government securities, etc. 정부, 지방자치단체, 또는 유사 정부기관 등이 발행하거나 보증한 증권

4) ①Annuity contracts(연금계약)

② Regulation "A" (small issues)

소액규모로 발행하는 경우의 증권으로서 12개월 동안 5백만 불을 초과할 수 없다(issuance by issuers up to $5,000,000 in 12-month period). Regulation A에 의한 약식등록절차는 일반적인 등록절차와 유사하지만 등록신고서와 사업설명서 대신에 약식인 모집신고서(offering circular)를 사용한다. 또한 일반적인 권유와 광고(general solicitation and offering 일반인에게 무작위로 편지를 발송하거나 인터넷에 발행관련 자료를 올리는 행위 등)를 허용하기 때문에 인터넷을 통한 증권발행에 많이 이용되고 있다.

5) Religious, educational, or charitable organization's securities or receiver-issued certificate 종교, 교육, 자선단체가 발행하는 증권

6) Security exchanged by issuer exclusively with its existing shareholders so long as no commission is paid and both sets of securities are issued by the same issuer. 기존주주에게만 배타적으로 주식을 교환해주는 경우로서 두 종류의 증권모두가 동일발행인이 발행하고, 수수료나 다른 보상이 없어야 한다. 주식분할(stock split), 주식배당(stock dividend) 등이 이에 해당한다.

7) Savings & loans, banks, farmers, co-ops, 은행, 협동조합, 농협 등이 발행하는 증권

8) Certificates issued by trustee in bankruptcy 파산관재인이 발행하는 증서 등이다

 Exempt Transactions or Offerings

1933 Act의 Section 4에 따라 등록을 할 필요는 없지만 antifraud provision의 적용대상이 된다.

1) 발행인, underwriter, or dealer가 아니고, 다른 사람에게 이루어지는 거래(sale or offer to sell)로 주로 개인투자자(individual investors)가 증권을 매각하거나 증권회사가 중개업무(brokerage)를 하는 경우에 해당된다.

> **注意|** 단, controlling person은 issuer(발행인)나 underwriter로 간주되므로 controlling person이 한 거래는 exemption되지 않는다.

2) Transaction by an issuer not involving any public offering

사모발행(=private placement)은 등록이 면제된다.

3) Postregistration transaction by dealers(i.e. dealer is not required to deliver prospectus)

등록 후 거래로 해당거래가 증권공모일로부터 40일 이후에 이루어진 경우나, 발행인의 신규공모(IPO)도 등록인 경우에는 90일 이후에 해당한다.

4) Broker's transaction executed upon customers'orders

고객의 주문에 따른 브로커의 거래

5) Regulation D

소규모발행에 관한 Rule 504, Rule 505및 사모발행에 관한 Rule 506에 대한 규정을 담고 있다. 아래의 하나에 해당할 경우 SEC에 등록할 의무를 면제해줌으로써 증권발행을 촉진하는 데 그 목적이 있다.

〈개념정리 : Regulation D Exemption〉

		Rule 504	Rule 505	Rule 506
Dollar(amount) limit 금액제한		up to $1 million	more than $1 million up to $5 million	more than $5 million and up to unlimited amount.
Time Limit 발행시간 제한		within 12 months	within 12 months	no time limit
investors	accredited	any number	unlimited	unlimited
	unaccredited		35 or less	35 or less
general solicitation and advertisements 무작위 주식구매권유 및 판매홍보		permitted with limitations 원칙적으로 금지하나 예외허용	not permitted 금지	not permitted 금지
resale within first 2 years 전매제한		permitted with limitations 원칙적으로 금지하나 예외허용	Must hold 2 or more years (encouraging long-term investments)2년간 전매금지	Must hold 2 or more years(encouraging long-term investments)2년간 전매금지
notice of offering to SEC		Must send notice of offering to SEC within 15 days of first sale of securities. 증권을 처음 판매한 날로부터 15일 이내에 SEC에 통지해야 한다.		

[sources] 이동욱『미국비즈니스법의 핵심』; Nathan Bisk, *Regulation*, p.40-7

注意 1 | Rule 505와 Rule 506은 유사하다.
다만 Rule 506에는 사모발행(private placement)에 따른
a) 발행금액의 제한이 없다(no limitation to $)는 점,
b) safe-harbor(안전조항)이 들어있다는 점과
c) accredited investors들이 전문지식이 있어야 한다는 요건 (sophisticated investors rule)이 들어있다.

Accredited investors들이란 은행, 신용금고, 신용협동조합, 보험회사, 개인 혹은 공동으로 1백만 불 이상의 자산을 갖고 있고, 최근 2년 동안 20만 불 이상의 순익을 얻은 개인 등을 포함하는데 이에 대한 규정은 Rule 215에 포함되어있다.

注意 2 | Despite the stringent registration requirements imposed by the 1933 Act, most US securities are not sold through public, registered offerings. Instead, one or more exemptions are used. Under Section 4(2), private placement may be made to institutions or "accredited investors." Regulation D codifies this statutory principles and offers more clearly defined safe harbor rules for those seeking a private placement exemption. Section 3(a)(11) offers the little used exemption allowing issues made only within one state to avoid registration. Rule 147 creates a clearly defined safe harbor for intra-state offerings.

7 Antifraud Provision under 1933 Act

〈개념정리 : Comparative Elements of Fraud under common law and under 1933 Act〉

fraud under common law	constructive fraud(= gross negligence) under common law	fraud under 1933 ACT
misrepresenation of materials facts	좌동	좌동
intent to deceive, intent to mislead, or scienter	reckless disregard of truth	NO NEED
reasonable reliance	좌동	NO NEED
injury or damage(economic loss)	좌동	좌동
causation	좌동	좌동
rescission of K, monetary damages 등의 remedy 청구가능	rescission of K, monetary damage 등의 remedy 청구가능	Only monetary damages are available. Rescission of K or restitution 등의 remedy 청구 불가

1) 구매자를 기망할 목적을 갖고(to defraud purchasers) 수단, 계획, 혹은 술책을 사용하는 것,

2) 중요한 사실(material facts)에 대해 허위로 표시(untrue statement)하거나 중요한 사실을 누락(omission of material facts)하여 금전적 이익을 얻는 것

3) 매수인에게 사기(fraud)나 기망(deceit)이 되거나 될 수 있는 거래(transaction), 관행(practice), 혹은 사업(course of business)을 하는 것은 위법(unlawful)이다.

4) Protects the purchaser defrauded, not seller.

Both the person defrauded and the SEC can challenge the fraud committed in the course of selling the securities.

사기를 당해 증권을 매입하게 된 purchaser를 보호하는데 주목적이 있는 조항이며 ① 사기를 당한 피해자와 ② SEC모두 사기에 대한 손해배상 소송을 제기할 수 있다.

8 Civil Liability(private actions brought by purchasers of securities/SEC)

1) Purchaser(SEC) may recover if s/he can establish that it was a purchaser of security issued under a registration statement containing a misleading or omission of material fact.

증권의 매수인(SEC)은 등록신고서에 중요한 사실을 부실기재 했거나 누락했을 경우 손해배상을 받을 수 있다.

注意 1 | 여기서 중요한 사실이란 평균적으로 신중한 합리적 투자자(average prudent or reasonable person)가 알아야만 하는 사실을 의미한다.

注意 2 | 회계사의 경우 Section 11에 의거하여 등록신고서(registration statement)에 포함된 감사받은 재무제표(audited financial statements)에 중요사실에 대한 허위 기재나 누락(misstatement or omission of material facts)이 있을 경우이다.

2) 요건

원고는 피고의 고의성(scienter), 원고에 대한 의존(reliance)을 입증할 필요가 없고 다만 중요사실의 부실기재 및 누락, 그리고 경제적 손실을 입은 사실만 증명하면 된다. 즉 입증책임이 원고에서 피고에게로 넘어가게 되는 것이다(the burden of proof is shifted to defendant)

A. No reliance on registration statement needed
B. No intent to deceive(scienter) to be proved
C. No K privity to be proved
D. Suffered economic loss
E. by misstatement or omission of material facts

3) Plaintiffs

Section 11에 의해 원고가 될 수 있는 사람은 등록신고서에 의해 발행된 ① 증권을 매입한 사람과 ② SEC가 소송제기를 할 수 있도록 되어있다.

4) Defendants 피고는 아래의 누구라도 될 수 있다.

A. 발행인(the issuer)
B. any directors, partners, or underwriters of issuer
C. anyone who signed the registration statement

D. experts of authorized statements(e.g. lawyers, accountants, engineers, appraisers)

5) Defendants' defenses

A. Due diligence항변
회계사가 합리적인 조사(reasonable investigation)를 한 후 중요사실에 대해 허위 기재나 누락이 없다고 믿을만한 합리적 이유(reasonably believe)가 있었다면 회계사의 책임은 면제된다. 원고가 증권을 매입할 때 부실기재나 누락을 알고 있었다는 항변

B. 원고가 증권을 매수할 때 그러한 부실기재 혹은 누락을 알고 있었다.
(Plaintiff's knowledge of misrepresentation or omission when purchasing securities)는 항변

C. lack of causation항변: 즉 손실(loss)이 부실기재나 누락에 의한 것이 아니라 다른 요인들에 의한 것이라는 항변

D. GAAS(generally accepted auditing standard)에 따랐다는 항변

GAAP(generally accepted accounting principle)에 따랐다는 항변은 사용불가

E. 원고가 등록신고서를 신뢰하지 않았다((Plaintiff did not rely on the information of the registration statement)라는 항변과 privity of contract이 없다는 항변은 할 수 없다.

6) Remedies

Monetary damages only 원고에게 가능한 구제수단은 금전적인 손해배상(monetary damages)뿐이고, 계약취소(rescission)나 원상회복(restitution)은 불가능하다.

7) Statute of Limitation(SOL)

A. 사기(fraud)나 기망(deceit), 혹은 증권법위반과 관련된 조작(manipulation involving contravention of securities laws)에 관해 알게 된 날로부터 2년 (2 years after discovery)or

B. 사기, 기망, 조작과 관련된 증권법 위반일로부터 5년(five years after such violation) 중 빠른 쪽(Sarbanes Oxley Act)

9 Criminal Liability

1) 고의적으로(intentionally or willfully) 1933 Act와 SEC regulation을 위반하거나 고의적으로 부실기재나 누락을 한 자는 징역(imprisonment) 혹은 벌금(fines)의 형벌을 받을 수 있다.

2) Reckless Disregard of the Truth도 고의로 간주될 수 있다.

3) 타인을 속이거나 기망하여 주간통상 혹은 우편을 이용하여 증권을 팔려고 한 자도 징역이나 벌금에 처한다.

4) 등록이 면제되는 증권의 경우나 등록이 면제되는 transaction의 경우에도criminal liability는 적용될 수 있다.

10 Securities Exchange Act of 1934(1934 Act)

1934 Act는 유통시장(trading of securities)을 규제하는데 주로 적용된다.

1) The Purpose of 1934 Act 법의 목적

A. To prevent unfair use of info by insiders.

내부자의 불공정한 정보이용 방지

B. To prevent fraud and deceptive practices.

사기와 기망적 관행 방지

C. To require adequate info be provided in various transactions.

다양한 거래에 적절한 정보를 제공

D. To required periodic disclosure by issuer of equity securities.

주식발행인에게 정기적인 공시를 하도록 규정

E. To federally regulate securities exchanges and securities traded thereon.

증권거래소와 증권거래를 연방차원에서 규율

2) 1934 ACT에 따라 반드시 등록해야 하는 증권

A. 장외시장에서 거래되는 주식 중 회사의 자산(corporate assets)이 1천만 불 ($10M)이상이고 주주의 수가 500명 이상인 경우

속임수 문제로 자주 시가총액(market capitalization)이 1천만 불 이상이라고 하거나, 종업원이 500 명 이상이라고 하여 오답을 유도하기도 한다.

B. National securities exchanges에서 거래되는 증권

C. Securities exempted under 1933 Act may still be regulated under 1934 Act

3) 등록 시 공개되어야 하는 정보[required disclosure in registration]

A. financial structure of the firm

B. nature of business

C. any bonus and profit-sharing provision

D. names of officers and directors

4) Sanctions Available to SEC under the 1934 Act

SEC는 1934 ACT에 따라 등록의 철회 (revocation)및 정지(suspension), 등록거부(denial of registration), 영구적 혹은 일시적 정지(permanent or temporary suspension of trading),

불법취득 이익 반환(disgorgement of gains made illegally)등의 조치를 취할 수 있다.

5) Exempt Securities under 1934 ACT 등록이 면제되는 증권

A. ICC의 규제를 받는 운송업자(ICC-regulated common carriers)가 발행하는 증권
B. 연방정부(US Govt), 주(state),시(municipal)나 정치관련 단체가 발행하거나 보증하거나 이해관계를 가진 증권
C. 연방에 등록한 은행 및 금융기관(federally chartered bank or savings banks)이 발행한 증권
D. 비영리법인(non-profit organization)이 발행한 증권
F. 산업개발채권(Industrial development bonds)

〈개념정리〉

Exempt Securities under 1933 Act	Exempt Securities under 1934 Act	Remarks
Commercial paper	Not exempt	상업어음 등은 1933년 법에 의해서만 면제
Insurance K, ICC-regulated common carriers, and intrastate securities issues	ICC-regulated common carriers	
Government, quasi-government	Government, state, and municipal bonds	
Annuity K, issue under Regulation A	Not exempt	Annuity K, issue under Regulation A는 □1933년 법에 의해서만 면제
Religious, educational, and charitable organization's securities	Non-profit organizations' securities	
Exchanged securities	Not exempt	주식맞교환의 경우 1933년 법에 의해서만 면제
Savings & loans, banks	Federally chartered bank or savings banks	1934년 법은 연방법에 의해 등록된 은행만 면제, 1933년 법은 모든 은행 등록면제
Trustee	Not exempt	법정관리인(파산관재인)은 1933년 법에 의해서만 면제
	Industrial development bonds	산업개발채권은 1934년 법에 의해서만 면제한다는 점에 주의

6) Periodic Reporting 정기공시의무

〈개념정리〉

1/4분기 (1st Quarter)	2/4분기 (2nd Quarter)	3/4분기 (3rd Quarter)	4/4분기 (4th Quarter)
10 Q report	10 Q report	10 Q report	10 K report audited by independent CPA

A. 1934 ACT에 의한 등록여부에 상관없이 1933 ACT에 의해 등록을 한 경우에는 정기보고 의무를 부담한다.

1934 ACT에 따라 등록을 한 회사는 SEC에 정기적으로 보고서를 제출해야 하는 의무가 있는데 이를 '정기공시의무'라고 한다. 이러한 의무에 의해 SEC에 제출해야 하는 보고양식은 다음과 같다.

B. Annual report(form 10K) 연차보고서

A Form 10-K is an annual report required by the U.S. Securities and Exchange Commission (SEC), that gives a comprehensive summary of a public company's performance. The 10-K includes information such as company history, organizational structure, executive compensation, equity, subsidiaries, and audited financial statements, among other information.

- "연차보고서"라고도 하며 그 내용에는 기업사, 조직구조, 임원보상현황, 지분, 자회사, 감사받은 재무제표 등이 10K report에 포함되어야 한다. 특히 독립성을 갖춘 공인회계사의 인증을 받아 SEC에 제출해야 한다.

C. Quarterly reports(form 10Q) 분기보고서-공인회계사의 인증을 받을 필요가 없다.

D. Current reports(form 8K) 수시보고서

① 회사지배구조의 변경(corporate control), ② 자산재평가(asset revaluation), ③ 발행증권수의 변화(change in amount of issued securities), ④ 새로운 임원 및 직원의 신규선임(changes in newly appointed directors and officers) 등의 사항이 발생하면 이를 SEC에 보고해야 한다.

참고 Form 8-K

In addition to filing annual reports on Form 10-K and quarterly reports on Form 10-Q, public companies must report certain material corporate events on a more current basis. Form 8-K is the current report companies must file with the SEC to announce major events that shareholders should know about.

The instructions for Form 8-K describe the types of events that trigger a public company's obligation to file a current report, including any of the following:

Section 1 -- Registrant's Business and Operations
Item 1.01 Entry into a Material Definitive Agreement
Item 1.02 Termination of a Material Definitive Agreement
Item 1.03 Bankruptcy or Receivership

Section 2 -- Financial Information
Item 2.01 Completion of Acquisition or Disposition of Assets
Item 2.02 Results of Operations and Financial Condition
Item 2.03 Creation of a Direct Financial Obligation or an Obligation under an Off-Balance Sheet Arrangement of a Registrant
Item 2.04 Triggering Events That Accelerate or Increase a Direct Financial Obligation or an Obligation under an Off-Balance Sheet Arrangement
Item 2.05 Costs Associated with Exit or Disposal Activities
Item 2.06 Material Impairments

Section 3 -- Securities and Trading Markets
Item 3.01 Notice of Delisting or Failure to Satisfy a Continued Listing Rule or Standard; Transfer of Listing
Item 3.02 Unregistered Sales of Equity Securities
Item 3.03 Material Modification to Rights of Security Holders
Section 4 -- Matters Related to Accountants and Financial Statements

Item 4.01 Changes in Registrant's Certifying Accountant
Item 4.02 Non-Reliance on Previously Issued Financial Statements or a Related Audit Report or Completed Interim Review

Section 5 -- Corporate Governance and Management
Item 5.01 Changes in Control of Registrant
Item 5.02 Departure of Directors or Certain Officers; Election of Directors; Appointment of Certain Officers
Item 5.03 Amendments to Articles of Incorporation or Bylaws; Change in Fiscal Year
Item 5.04 Temporary Suspension of Trading Under Registrant's Employee Benefit Plans
Item 5.05 Amendment to Registrant's Code of Ethics, or Waiver of a Provision of the Code of Ethics
Item 5.06 Change in Shell Company Status

Section 6 -- Asset-Backed Securities
Item 6.01 ABS Informational and Computational Materials
Item 6.02 Change of Servicer or Trustee
Item 6.03 Change in Credit Enhancement or Other External Support
Item 6.04 Failure to Make a Required Distribution
Item 6.05 Securities Act Updating Disclosure

Section 7 -- Regulation FD
Item 7.01 Regulation FD Disclosure

Section 8 -- Other Events
Item 8.01 Other Events (The registrant can use this Item to report events that are not specifically called for by Form 8-K, that the registrant considers to be of importance to security holders.)

Section 9 -- Financial Statements and Exhibits
Item 9.01 Financial Statements and Exhibits

 Tender Offers 공개매수

1) 공개매수자(buyer, bidder)가 대상회사(target company)의 주주들에게 일정기간 동안 미리 정해놓은 가격으로 주식을 팔도록 유인하는 것이다(buyers'invitation to SH of targeted company to tender shares they own for sale for price specified over a period of time).

2) 법에 따라 공개매수자와 대상회사 모두 주주에게 공시를 해야 할 의무가 있다.

A. 대상회사는 공개매수가 시작일로부터 10일 이내에 주주들에게 회사가 공개매수에 대해 찬성, 반대, 중립 또는 아직 아무런 의견을 갖고 있지 않은지에 대해 입장표명을 해야 할 할 의무가 있다(10-day Rule).

B. 공개매수자는 전체지분의 5%를 초과하여 실질적으로 보유하는 자는 5%를 초과한 보유일로부터 10일내에 매수자의 신원 및 실질적 보유주식의 수, 자금원, 매수목적, 향후계획 등을 공시하여야 한다(5% Rule).

〈개념정리〉

Bidder(bidding company)	→ Disclosure duty on the purpose, funding sources, buyer details, etc of tender offer (5% rule)
Target company	→ Duty on express their position about the tender offer

 Proxy (위임장)

1) Proxy(위임장)란 주주들로부터 투표권(즉 의결권)을 이전받는 것(assignment of voting rights)을 의미하는데 proxy를 받은 사람은 주주총회(주총)에서 이에 근거하여 의결권을 행사하게 된다.

2) 주간통상 혹은 우편으로 주주로부터 위임장을 이전받고자 할 경우 이를 "proxy solicitation(위임장 요청서)"이라고 하고, 1934 ACT의 Proxy rule에 따라야 한다.

3) 위임장 요청을 하고자 할 경우 주주에게 주주총회 의안에 관한 중요한 사실(all material facts concerning matters to be voted upon)을 기재한 위임장 설명서(proxy statement)를 주주에게 위임장 요청서(proxy solicitation)와 함께 발송해야한다.

4) 위임장에는 누구를 대신하여 위임장을 요청하는지(on whose behalf solicitation is made), 위임장을 통해 취하려고 하는 조치에 대해 분명하고 객관적(identify clearly and impartially each matter to be acted upon)으로 설명되어야 한다.

5) 위임장 요청서에는 다음과 같은 관련서류를 첨부할 수 있다.

A. 현 경영진에 반대하는 주주가 자신이 비용을 부담하여 위임장 요청과 관련한 서류를 주주들에게 발송해달라고 요청한 경우 현경영진은 그에 따라야 한다(Incumbent management is required to mail proxy materials of insurgents to SH if requested and expenses are paid by the insurgents).

B. 위임장 요청이 현경영진을 위한 것 (solicitation is on behalf of management) 이거나 이사가 선임되는 정기주총에서 위임장요청(for annual meeting at which directors are to be selected)인 경우

6) 만일 중요사실에 대해 부실기재(misstatement)를 했거나 누락(omission)이 있을 경우 proxy rules위반이 된다.

7) 위임장 설명(proxy statement), 위임장(proxy itself), 위임장 요청서(proxy solicitation)의 관련서류는 모두 SEC에 제출해야 한다.

8) Remedies for Violation of Proxy Solicitation Rules

위임장 권유에 있어 중요사실에 대한 부실기재나 누락이 있는 경우 주주는

A. 손해배상청구(civil action by aggrieved shareholder for damages caused by material misinformation or omission of material facts),
B. 위임장과 관련된 모든 서류배포를 중단하도록 법원명령(injunctions)을 청구하는 방법,
C. 위임장규칙을 위반하여 결정된 주총결의 사안을 무효로 하고 완전하고 공정하게 정보공개(full and fair disclosure)를 한 상태에서 새로 주주총회를 개최하도록 하는 판결을 법원에 청구할 수 있다.

13 Short-swing profits 단기매매차익 반환제도

A Securities & Exchange Commission regulation that requires company insiders to return any profits made from the purchase and sale of company stock if both transactions occur within a six-month period. A company insider, as determined by the rule, is any officer, director or holder of more than 10% of the company's shares.

1) 회사내부자가 6개월 이내에 자신이 속한 회사의 주식을 매매하여 이익을 얻은 경우, 그 이익을 회사에 반환하도록 하는 제도이다(corporation is entitled to recover profits from any insider who sells stocks of company within 6 months of its purchase)

2) 내부자의 고의성이나 과실에 상관없는 무과실책임 원칙이라는 점에서 주의해야 한다.

Insider Trading Requirements

증권등록(when securities are registered under 1934 ACT), 등록신고서 효력발생(when registration statement becomes effective under 1933 ACT) 및 내부자가 된 후 10일 이내(within 10 days of person attaining insider status)에 SEC에 수량보고에 대한 보고서를 제출해야 한다.

15 Antifraud Provision

1934 ACT section 10(b) 에는 증권의 매매와 관련하여 SEC가 제정한 규칙을 위반하여 시세조작과 기망적 수단을 사용하는 것은 위법이라고 되어있는데 여기서 나온 규칙이 Rule 10(b)-5이다. 이 규칙은 예외가 없으며

A. 거래과정을 조작하거나 거래가 활발한 것처럼 보이도록 하는 것은 불법이며 (unlawful to manipulate process and create appearance of active trading)

B. 모든 증권매매와 관련하여 증권의 등록여부에 관계없이 모두 적용된다(applies to all securities whether registered or not).

1) SEC Rule 10(b)-5

It shall be unlawful for any person, directly or indirectly, by the use of any means or instrumentality of interstate commerce, or of the mails or of any facility of any national securities exchange, 주식매매와 관련하여 주간통상, 우편, 혹은 전국적 증권거래소라는 수단을 이용하여 직간접적으로

A. To employ any device, scheme, or artifice to defraud, 사기를 위한 수단, 계략, 혹

은 술책을 사용하거나

B. To make any untrue statement of a material fact or to omit to state a material fact necessary in order to make the statements made, in the light of the circumstances under which they were made, not misleading, or

중요사실에 관하여 허위표시를 하거나 또는 표시가 된 당시의 상화에 비추어 오해가 유발되지 않도록 하기 위하여 필요한 중요사실의 표시를 누락하거나

C. To engage in any act, practice, or course of business which operates or would operate as a fraud or deceit upon any person, in connection with the purchase or sale of any security.

타인에게 사기나 기망이 되거나 될 수 있는 행위, 관행, 또는 거래방법에 관여하는 것은 위법이다.

16 Civil Liabilities under Rule 10(b)-5

1) 성립요건(when the D does in connection with the purchase and sales of securities 증권매매와 관련하여 피고가 다음을 했을 경우)

A. Intentionally(willfully, with scienter)

의도적으로 [고의를 갖고]

注意| "의도적"이라 함은 오류가 있다는 것을 알면서도 강행했거나(knowledge of falsity), 조금만 주의했더라면 그런 무모한 실수를 하지 않았을 경우(reckless disregard for truth)를 의미하며 단순과실(negligence)만으로는 부족하다.

B. Manipulates a security and/or makes misleading(false, untrue) statements or omission

잘못된 증언을 하거나, 누락을 하거나, 주식을 조작

C. About material facts

중대한 사실에 대하여

注意| 어떤 사실이 중대한지 여부는 ordinary reasonable person standard가 적용된다.

D. Plaintiff's reliance on the statements of defendant

원고는 피고의 말/표시/설명에 의존함.

E. Damages to the Plaintiff

원고에게 손해를 끼침.

F. Causation 피고의 행위와 원고의 damages간에 인과관계가 있어야 한다.

〈개념정리 : Comparative Elements of Fraud under common law, 1933 Act, and 1934 Act〉

fraud under common law	constructive fraud(=gross negligence) under common law	fraud under 1933 ACT	fraud under 1934 ACT
misrepresenation of materials facts	좌동	좌동	좌동
intent to deceive, intent to mislead, or scienter	reckless disregard of truth	NO NEED	intent to deceive, intent to mislead, or scienter
reasonable reliance	좌동	NO NEED	reasonable reliance
injury or damage (economic loss)	좌동	좌동	좌동
causation	좌동	좌동	좌동
rescission of K, monetary damages 등의 remedy 청구가능	rescission of K, monetary damage 등의 remedy 청구가능	Only monetary damages are available. Rescission of K or restitution 등의 remedy 청구 불가	rescission of K, monetary damages 등의 remedy 청구가능; 또한 SEC는 증권사기를 당한 피해자를 위하여 liability fund를 받아낼 수 있다.

2) Defendants can be

증권매매와 관련한 관계자(즉 seller and purchaser는 물론 주식관련 보고서 작성자 등) 모두가 피고가 될 수 있다. 피고가 여러 명일 경우 Joint and several liability 를 물을 수 있다.

3) D's Defenses: The party sued can avoid liability if s/he can prove s/he

A. Acted in good faith
"행위상 고의성이 없다"는 뜻이므로 willful 하거나 intentionally 잘못한 것이 아니라는 의미이다.

B. Had no knowledge that the statements were materially misleading or false
내용이 잘못된 것인 줄 몰랐다는 것도 고의성을 부정하는 defense로 사용된다.

C. 그 외에 lack of causation, materiality 부인, reliance부인 등의 방법이 있다.

4) Remedies for the P

원고는 금전적인 손해배상(monetary damages)을 요구하거나 거래를 취소(rescind the transaction)하고 원상회복(restitution)을 받을 수 있다. 또한 SEC는 증권사기를 당한 피해자를 위하여 liability funds를 받아낼 수 있다.

 17 Criminal Liability

1) Sarbanes Oxley Act (SOA,2002)의 도입으로 처벌이 강화되었다.

A. Rule 10(b)-5위반자에 대해서도 개인의 경우 20년 imprisonment or $5백만까지 벌금

B. 1934ACT를 고의적으로 위반(willful violation)할 경우 25년 imprisonment or fines

C. 기업이나 partnership은 $25 백만까지 벌금

18 State "Blue-Sky" Laws

American law term that refers to government controls, through statutes, of the sale of securities to the public.

State securities laws, commonly known as Blue Sky Laws after the word was used by a Supreme Court justice (McKennan) in 1917, Hall v. Geiger-Jones Co., 242 U.S. 539. Blue sky laws are designed to protect investors against fraudulent sales practices and activities. While these laws can vary from state to state, most states laws typically require companies making small offerings to register their offerings before they can be sold in a particular state. The laws also license brokerage firms, their brokers, and investment adviser representatives."

1) 증권발행과 유통에 관한 각 주의 증권관련법을 총칭하며 antifraud조항과 registration조항을 포함해야 한다.

2) 연방법률과 함께 추가적으로 준수하여야 한다.

3) 연방법에서는 등록 면제가 되는 경우에도 blue sky laws에서는 면제가 안 될 수도 있다.

19 Foreign Corrupt Practices Act

〈개념정리 : 외국공무원 부패방지법〉

Foreign Corrupt Practices Act (주요내용 정리)

The FCPA makes it unlawful to bribe foreign government officials to obtain or retain business. With respect to the basic prohibition, there are five elements which must be met to constitute a violation of the Act:

A. Who -- The FCPA potentially applies to any individual, firm, officer, director, employee, or agent of a firm and any stockholder acting on behalf of a firm. Individuals and firms may also be penalized if they order, authorize, or assist someone else to violate the antibribery provisions or if they conspire to violate those provisions.(대상은 반부패법을 위반하거나 위반하기 위해 음모를 꾸민 개인, 기업, 임직원, 근로자, 기업대리인, 주주 등임)

Under the FCPA, U.S. jurisdiction over corrupt payments to foreign officials depends upon whether the violator is an "issuer," a &"domestic concern," or a foreign national or business. (위반자는 증권발행사, 미국기업, 외국인이나 외국 기업체)

B. Corrupt intent -- The person making or authorizing the payment must have a corrupt intent, and the payment must be intended to induce the recipient to misuse his official position to direct business wrongfully to the payer or to any other person. You should note that the FCPA does not require that a corrupt act succeed in its purpose. (부패를 저지를 의도, 반드시 행동으로 이어지지 않아도 무관)

C. Payment -- The FCPA prohibits paying, offering, promising to pay (or authorizing to pay or offer) money or anything of value(돈이나 무엇이든 가치있는 것을 지불)

D. foreign political party or party official, or any candidate for foreign political office. (외국공무원, 정당, 정치가, 정치지망자)

E. Business Purpose Test -- The FCPA prohibits payments made in order to assist the firm in obtaining or retaining business for or with, or directing business to, any person. The Department of Justice interprets "obtaining or retaining business" broadly, such that the term encompasses more than the mere award or renewal of a contract. (비즈니스 신규유치 및 유지목적)

출처:US Department of Justice: Layperson's Guide to Foreign Corrupt Practices Act

1) 미국기업의 직원이 해외에서 그 나라 공무원, 정치단체, 정치가, 등에게 의사결정 상의 영향을 미치기 위해 무엇인가 가치 있는 것(something of value)을 줄 경우 위법이다. [가치의 기준은 굳이 거액일 필요도 없고 단 $1도 해당한다]

Prior to 1998, foreign companies, with the exception of those who qualified as "issuers," and foreign nationals were not covered by the FCPA. The 1998 amendments expanded the FCPA to assert territorial jurisdiction over foreign companies and nationals. A foreign company or person is now subject to the FCPA if it causes, directly or through agents, an act in furtherance of the corrupt payment to take place within the territory of the United States. There is, however, no requirement that such act make use of the U.S. mails or other means or instrumentalities of interstate commerce.(1998년 이후 외국인및 외국기업으로 대상범위 확장)

2) 미국의 증권거래소에 상장된 기업들(외국기업포함)은 내부통제제도를 유지하고 정확한 회계처리 및 독립적인 감사가 이루어지도록 하여야 한다.

Chapter 14 Professional Responsibilities (Legal Issues)

1 회계사의 민사상 법적책임

〈개념정리〉

under common law(판례법)				under statutory liabilities(제정법)		
K law	torts law					
	negligence	strict liability	intentional torts	1933 act	1934 act	PSLRA
				section11	rule10b5	
Breach of K	duty, breach, causation, injury(damage)	strict duty breach, causation, injury(damage)	intent(scienter) +reliance+misre presentation of material facts+causation (fraud)	원고:증권매수인 misrepresentation of material facts+ causation	원고:증권 매수인 또는 증권매도인intent (scienter) + reliance+ misrepresentation of material facts+causation (fraud)	1933 Act와 1934 Act를 amend.고의성이 있는 경우에만 joint and several liability인정
privity 필요	privity 불필요	privity 불필요	privity 불필요	privity 불필요	privity 불필요	
punitive damage 불인정	punitive damage불인정	punitive damage인정	punitive damage인정	punitive damage인정	punitive damage인정	

<출처 : 이동욱, 『미국비즈니스법의 핵심』, Robert E. Meines, et al. *The Legal Environment of Business*>

 회계사의 의뢰인에 대한 CL상의 책임 중 계약위반에 따른 책임 (Common law liability for the breach of contract by the accountant)

1) 회계사와 의뢰인간의 계약상의 의무에는

A. 아무런 과실 없이(in nonnegligent manner) 계약을 이행하겠다는 묵시적 의무(implied duty)

B. 계약조건을 제대로 이행하겠다는 명시적 의무(express duty)

C. 특히 명시적 의무는 업무의 성격과 범위, 절차 및 방법에 대한 구체적인 내용을 담은 engagement letter를 통해 표시된다.

D. engagement letter에는 회계사가 아닌 <u>의뢰인의 서명이 있어야 하는 것이 원칙</u>이나 감사계약은 구두(oral contract for audit)로 해도 engagement letter없이 enforceable하다.

2) 의뢰인과 회계사간 계약이 체결된 경우 양자사이에 계약상의 견련관계(Privity of contract)가 생겨나게 된다.

3) 일반적으로 회계사는 재무제표의 보증인(insurer of financial statements)이 아니므로 사기로 인한 손실(loss from frauds)에 대해서는 책임을 지지 않는다.

4) 일반감사(normal audit)의 목적은 부정을 발견하기 위한 것이 아니라(not to uncover frauds), 재무제표에 대한 의견(opinion on fairness of financial statements)을 표명하기 위해 감사증거(audit evidence)를 필요로 하는 것이다.

5) 다만, 일반감사나 검토(normal audit or reviews)를 통해 부정을 발견할 수 있거나, 감사계약서에 부정을 적발해주기로 약속한 경우, 감사보고서에 부정을 적발해내기로 약속하는 문구(wordings of audit report indicates greater responsibility)가 있는 경우에는 예외로 한다.

EX A CPA is hired by a client to perform an audit. During the audit, the CPA could not find any signs of embezzlement by one of the client's employees. The CPA is not liable for the losses unless a typical, reasonable audit should have resulted in the discovery of the embezzlement scheme.

6) 조사의무(duty to investigate) : 회계사는 재무제표를 감사하거나 검토하다가 부정에 대한 의심이 생기면(discovers of becomes aware of suspicions) 조사할 의무가 생긴다.

7) 계약위반에 따른 배상(When breach of contract(BOK) occurs)

〈개념정리〉

중대한 계약위반(major BOK)	회계사는 보수를 받을 수 없고, 추가적인 계약위반에 대해 손해배상을 할 수도 있다.
경미한 계약위반(minor BOK)	회계사는 보상을 받을 수 있지만 minor breach에 대한 손해배상을 해야 한다.
징벌적 배상(Punitive damages)	인정되지 않는다.

참고

Sample engagement letter - AUDIT ENGAGEMENT LETTER

FIRM NAME
Certified Public Accountants

DATE
COMPANY NAME
COMPANY ADDRESS
CITY STATE ZIP

Dear CONTACT PERSON :
This will confirm our understanding of the arrangements for our audit of the financial statements of COMPANY NAME, for the year ending BALANCE SHEET DATE.
We will audit the Company's balance sheet as of BALANCE SHEET DATE, and the related statements of income, retained earnings, and especially cash flows for the year then ended, for the purpose of expressing an opinion on them. The financial statements are the responsibility of the Company management. Our responsibility is to express an opinion on the financial statements based on our audit.
We will conduct our audit in accordance with generally accepted auditing standards. Those standards require that we plan and perform the audit to obtain reasonable assurance about whether the financial statements are free of material misstatement. An audit includes examining, on a test basis, evidence supporting the amounts and disclosures in the financial statements. An audit also includes assessing the accounting principles used and significant estimates made by management, as well as evaluating the overall financial statement presentation. We believe that our audit will provide a reasonable basis for our opinion. Our procedures will include tests of documentary evidence supporting the transactions recorded in the accounts, and direct confirmation of receivables and certain other assets and liabilities by correspondence with selected customers, creditors, legal counsel, and banks. At the conclusion of our audit, we will request certain written representations from you about the financial statements and matters related thereto.
Although the audit is designed to provide reasonableassurance of detecting errors and irregularities that are material to the financial statements, it is not designed and cannot be relied upon to disclose all fraud, defalcations, or other irregularities. However, we will inform you of any material errors, and all irregularities or illegal acts, unless they are clearly inconsequential, that come to our attention.
If you intend to publish or otherwise reproduce the financial statements and make reference

to our firm, you agree to provide us with printers' proofs or masters for our review and approval before printing. You also agree to provide us with a copy of the final reproduced material for our approval before it is distributed.

As part of our engagement for the year ending BALANCE SHEET DATE, we will review the federal and state income tax returns for COMPANY NAME.

Further, we will be available during the year to consult with you on the tax effects of any proposed transactions or contemplated changes in business policies.

Assistance to be supplied by your personnel, including the preparation of schedules and analyses of accounts, is described in a separate attachment. Timely completion of this work will facilitate the completion of our audit.

Our fees will be billed as work progresses and are based on the amount of time required plus out-of-pocket expenses. Invoices are payable upon presentation. We will notify you immediately of any circumstances we encounter that could significantly affect our initial estimate of total fees, which will range from $XX,XXX to $XX,XXX.

The working papers for this engagement are the property of NAME OF AUDITOR and constitute confidential information. However, we may be requested to make certain working papers available to NAME OF REGULATOR pursuant to authority given to it by law or regulation. If requested, access to such working papers will be provided under the supervision of NAME OF AUDITOR personnel. Furthermore, upon request, we may provide photocopies of selected working papers to NAME OF REGULATOR. The NAME OF REGULATOR may intend, or decide, to distribute the photocopies or information contained therein to others, including governmental agencies.

If this letter correctly expresses your understanding, please sign the enclosed copy where indicated and return it to us.

We appreciate the opportunity to serve you and trust that our association will be a long and pleasant one.

Sincerely,
FIRM NAME

____

[Engagement Partner's Signature]
Accepted and agreed to:

____

[Client Representative's Signature]

____

[Title]

____

[Date]

 회계사의 과실에 따른 책임(Liability to Clients based on Negligence)

다음의 요건이 성립되어야만 회계사의 과실을 묻는 것이 가능하다.

〈개념정리 : Negligence〉

Duty of care 주의의무	적어도 평균수준의 회계사가 갖고 있는 정도의 판단력과 기술(average accountant's judgment and skills)을 갖고 이행할 의무로 이러한 의무는 주법과 연방법(state and federal law), customs of profession, GAAS, GAAP(persuasive, not conclusive)법원의 결정(court decisions), 의뢰인과의 계약(contract with client), 에서 나온 것이다.
Breach of that duty 의무위반	회계사가 duty of care를 위반한 경우로 주의의무위반은 감사는 물론 대차대표 발생이후의 사건들을 검토(reviews)하는데도 발생할 수 있다.
Causation 인과관계	회계사의 과실(faults)와 원고가 입은 손해사이에 인과관계가 있어야 한다. 여기에는 foreseeable and proximate cause가 있어야 한다.
Injuries Damages, or Resulting Losses 손해	회계사가 주의의무를 다했더라면 피할 수 있었던 실질적인 손해(actual losses)를 의미하며 징벌적 손해배상은 인정되지 않는다.

1) 회계사는 의뢰인에게도 잘못이 있다는 항변을 제기할 수도 있다. 이것을 contributory negligence라고하며 대부분의 주에서 인정된다.

2) 회계사가 단순한 판단실수(honest errors of judgment)로 책임을 지는 것이 아니라, 최소한 CL상의 과실(negligence)가 있어야 책임을 지는 것이다.

4 회계사의 사기에 따른 책임(Liability to clients based on Fraud)

회계사의 사기, 중과실, 또는 추정적 사기에 대한 책임(Liability to client for fraud, gross negligence, or constructive frauds)

1) 성립요건

〈fraud : 개념정리〉

Misrepresentation of material facts [중요사실에 대한 부실표기]	피고의 중요한 사실이나 회계사 의견의 부실표시
Intent to mislead-"scienter"	기망의 의도 또는 고의성 또는 중과실(reckless disregard for truth, reckless disregard of truth, gross negligence, constructive fraud)
Reasonable reliance	상대방의 합리적인 신뢰
resulting Injuries or damages	손해발생
Causation	인과관계

A. 계약상의 견련관계(privity of contract)는 사기나, 중과실 등을 입증하는 데는 불필요하다.

B. 원고(의뢰인)에게도 과실이 있다는 contributory negligence나 comparative negligence는 defense로 사용할 수 없다.

C. 징벌적 손해배상(punitive damages)은 실제손해액(actual damages)에 추가될 수 있다.

 제3자에 대한 CL상의 책임(CL Liability to Nonclients)

1) 회계사 - 의뢰인간에는 계약상의 견련관계(privity of contract)가 있지만, 제3자의 경우에는 3PB를 제외하고는 제3자와 회계사간의 견련관계가 형성되지 않는다.

2) 제3자와 회계사간의 계약상의 견련관계가 없으므로 회계사는 제3자에게 계약위반에 대한 책임을 부담하지 않는다.

3) 일반적인 회계사의 과실에 관한 사건에서는 제3자에 대하여 계약상의 견련관계(privity of contract)가 없다는 것이 좋은 방어논리가 될 수 있다.

6 회계사의 제3자에 대한 CL상의 과실책임 (CL Liability to Nonclients Based on Negligence)

1) Ultramares Corp v. Touche, Niven & Co(1931,이하 Ultramares Decision)

In Ultramares, plaintiff (Ultramares) was a lending agency which agreed to loan money to Fred Stern & Co. (Stern), contingent upon Stern providing Ultramares with a financial report. Stern hired the accounting firm of Touche, Niven and Company (Touche) to perform a full audit of Stern's books and to provide the required report. Stern ultimately provided the report prepared by Touche to Ultramares; however Touche had no knowledge that the report would be relied upon by Ultramares, and when Stern hired Touche, Ultramares was never mentioned. The report furnished by Touche turned out to be incorrect because Stern had falsified its books. After Stern defaulted on the loans made by Ultramares, and subsequently filed for bankruptcy, Ultramares sought damages against Touche for preparing report.

Justice Cardozo determined that a more intensive review of Stern's books by Touche would have revealed the fraud, and that it appeared that Touche was negligent; however, he dismissed Ultramares' action against Touche because of a lack of privity. In reaching his decision, Justice Cardozo stated that, essentially, an accountant's duty runs only to those with whom there is privity or a bond is so close as to approach that of privity, if not completely one with it. Thus, Ultramares could not recover against Touche because there was no contract between them, and Touche was not on notice, oral or otherwise, as to any possible duties owed to Ultramares.

A. 회계사는 자신을 피고로 제3자가 제기한 과실소송(negligence action)에서 "견련관계로 인하여 회계사는 견련관계가 있는 의뢰인이나 3PB에게만 책임을 져야한다(Accountant is held liable only to clients and 3rd party beneficiaries since these were in privity of contract with the accountant)"라고 판시하였다.

B. 그러나 Ultramares Decision에서도 사기, 혹은 중과실에서는 lack of privity의 항변을 할 수 없다[현재 소수의견].

2) 최근의 판결(Rosenblum Inc. vs. Adler 등의 다수의견)

Rosenblum v. Adler, 461 A.2d 138 (N.J. 1983).

The Rosenblum decision greatly expanded the scope of accountant liability by adopting a "foreseeability" standard for cases involving accountant negligence. Rosenblum placed New Jersey law in direct conflict with the position taken by the New York Court of Appeals in the case of Ultramares Corp. v. Touche Niven & Co. 255N.Y.170 (1931), which position was followed by the vast majority of other jurisdictions. The Uitramares decision rejected negligence claims brought by third parties due to the lack of privity of contract between the plaintiff and the accountants.

The New Jersey Supreme Court in Rosenblum rejected the New York Rule and allowed a recovery without a lack of privity, by finding that an independent auditor owes a duty to all parties who the auditor could reasonably foresee would be recipients of and rely upon from the financial statements prepared.

A. 제3자라 할지라도 회계사가 재무제표를 사용하는 사람이 누구인지를 알고 있고, 재무제표를 읽을 당사자라는 것을 안다면(forseen, known or intended class of financial statements), 회계사에게도 책임을 묻게 되었다.

EX For example, if the accounting firm knew that the financial statements were to be used to obtain a bank loan, then the accounting firm would be liable to any bank that they specifically knew would rely on the financial statements or could be expected to rely on the financial statements.

B. 예측된 당사자(forseen party)와 예측가능한 당사자(foreseeable party)간의 차이

〈개념정리〉

Foreseen party 예측된 당사자	Forseeable Party예측가능한 당사자
특정한 거래를 하는데 있어 재무제표에 의존할 사람(혹은 제한된 집단의 구성원) 이라는 것을 회계사가 알고 있었던 경우, 즉 intended user class of financial statements	회계사가 자신이 작성한 재무제표를 사용할 사람이라는 것을 합리적으로 예측할 수 있는 경우(reasonably foreseeable third parties)로 투자자(investors), 공급업자(suppliers), 정부 등이 사용할 것이라고 예측되는 경우 그들이 해당된다. 아직 단순한 회계사의 negligence에 대해서는 foreseeable party에게 까지 회계사의 책임을 물을 수 없다는 것이 다수의견이다.

7 회계사의 사기, 중과실, 혹은 추정적사기에 대한 책임 (Liability to nonclient for fraud, gross negligence, or constructive fraud)

1) 회계사의 제3자에 대한 사기, 중과실, 또는 추정적 사기의 책임에서는 견련관계(privity of contract)가 필요 없다. 즉, 회계사는 제3자가 예측된 당사자의 여부에 관계없이 책임부담.

2) 제3자에게 과실이 있다는 항변도 사용할 수 없다.

3) 징벌적 손해배상은 실제손해액에 추가될 수 있다.

4) 만일 제3자(예를 들면 회계사가 작성한 재무제표를 읽어본 해당기업의 주식투자자)가 회계사를 상대로 소송을 제기했을 경우에는 회계사도 책임을 져야한다. 이 경우 회계사는 "the false statement is immaterial"라고 하거나 아니면 "the damages is not caused by the false statements"이라고 하여 인과관계를 부인하는 것이 최선의 방어가 된다.

〈개념정리〉

Accountant is liable for		Under the Ultramares Decision	Under the recent decisions 최근의 동향
Negligence to	Clients	Yes	Yes
	3PB	Yes	Yes
	Forseen Party	No	Yes
	Foreseeable party	No	Yes & No. No under majority rulings, but yes under minority rulings
Fraud, gross negligence, constructive negligence to	Client, 3PB, Foreseen party, Foreseeable party	Yes	Yes

8 Negligent Misrepresentation

1) '과실표시'란 negligence와 fraud의 구성요건중의 하나인 misrepresentation 이 뒤섞인 일종의 hybrid형의 상황을 의미한다.

2) negligent misrepresentation requires proof of a

A. misstatement of

B. material fact and

C. reliance upon it.

과실표시란 ① 중요사실(material fact)에 대해 피고가 과실에 의해

② 잘못 언급(misstatement)을 하고
이에 대해 원고가 ③의존(reliance)했을 경우에 성립된다.

9 Statutory Civil Liability to 3P under 1933 Act

1) 1933 Act에 따라 처음에 주식을 발행할 때(initial issuance of securities) SEC에 등록해야 한다.

2) 등록할 때 등록서류나 prospectus[사업설명서]에 untrue material fact를 포함하거나, material fact를 누락하면 불법이다.

3) 유가증권이 발행되고 난 뒤에 SEC에 정기적으로 제출하는 보고서(periodic report)나 주주들에게 배포하는 연차보고서(annual report)는 1933 ACT의 적용을 받지 않고, 유통시장에 관한 건이므로 1934 ACT의 적용대상이다.

4) Section 11 of 1933 ACT에 따라 주식을 매입한 매수자가 중요사실에 대해 untrue statements or omission of material facts로 손해를 입었을 경우 소송제기 가능하다.

5) CPA는 due diligence, reasonable belief under reasonable investigation, plaintiff's knowledge of financial statements, lack of causation, GAAS 등의 항변이 가능하다.

 Statutory Civil Liability to 3P under 1934 Act

1) 적용대상

National securities exchange에 거래되는 주식들의 유통시장의 문제에 대해 다룬다. 장외거래 종목이라도 자산기준 1000만 달러($10 million)이상이고, 500명이상의 주주가 있다면 적용대상이 된다.

"자산기준"이란 용어대신 "자본금 기준", "주주"라는 용어대신 "직원" 등의 용어를 대신 사용하여 오답을 유도하므로 주의가 필요하다.

2) Section 10(including Rule 10(b)-5)

A. 속이기 위하여 여하한 장비(device, scheme, or artifice to defraud)를 사용하든지 간에

B. 중요사실에 대해 거짓으로(untrue statement or omission of material facts)

C. 주식의 매매와 관련하여 fraud or deceit을 하는 행위를 할 경우 불법이다.

3) 1934 ACT에 따르면 회계사는 due diligence항변을 할 수 없다.

〈개념정리〉

CL negligence	CL fraud	CL constructive fraud	fraud under 1933 ACT	fraud under 1934 ACT
duty of care	misrepresentation of material facts			
breach of duty	intent to deceive	reckless disregard of truth	불필요	intent to deceive
causation	reliance		불필요	reliance
injury or damages	injury or damages			
causation	causation			
when raised by 3rd Party against CPA, privity matters under Ultramares while foreseeability matters under Rosenblum	privity does not matter at all			

11 Auditor's defenses under 1933 Act and 1934 Act

〈개념정리〉

Auditor's defenses	Under 1933 Act	Under 1934 Act
Due diligence	Yes	No
Due care	Yes	Yes
Immaterial misstatement	Yes	Yes
P's prior knowledge of financial statements	Yes	Yes
P did not rely on information	No	Yes
No causation	Yes	Yes

[source] Debra R. Hopkins, Northern Illinois Univ

 Private Securities Litigation Reform Act(PSLRA)

1) 이 법은 1933 ACT와 1934ACT의 내용을 수정한 것이다.

2) 감사인은 만일 감사를 하다가 불법사항이 발견되었을 경우 audit committee 또는 이사회(board of directors)에 알려야 할 의무가 있다.

3) 감사인이 이 법을 제대로 준수하지 못한 경우 민사소송 대상이 된다. 한편, 감사인이 법에 따라 SEC에 보고서를 제출했다면 민사소송으로부터 보호받을 수 있다.

4) 이 법은 안전조항(safe harbor)을 통해 민사소송에 대한 두려움 없이 투자자들에게 보다 의미 있는 정보를 제공할 수 있도록 예측보고서(forward-looking statements)를 작성할 수 있도록 하기 위한 것이다. 예측보고서는 회사의 소득, 수익, EPS추정 등과 회사제품 및 서비스에 대한 계획 등이 포함된다. 안전조항을 충족하기 위해서는 예측보고서에 주의문구(cautions), 가정(assumptions), 조건(conditions) 을 명시해야 한다.

5) 하찮은 목적을 위해(for frivolous purpose) 집단소송(class actions)을 하지 못하도록 하기위해 엄격한 소송요건을 규정하고 이러한 요건을 충족시키지 못하는 소송에 대해서는 원고로부터 소송비용 및 변호사비용(litigation costs and attorneys' fees)을 보상하도록 함으로써 하찮은 목적의 집단소송을 방지할 수 있다.

6) **연대책임규정(joint and several liability)변경**
1933 ACT와 1934 ACT에서는 연대책임원칙(deep pocket rule)이었는데, PSLRA에서는 이를 변경하여 피고들이 자신들의 과실에 비례하여(proportionate to their degree of faults) 책임을 부담하도록 하였다.

7) 단, 공동피고들이 알면서 규율을 위반하였을 경우(knowingly committed violation)

여전히 연대책임원칙이다.

〈개념정리〉

knowing violation under PSLRA	unknowing violation under PSLRA
joint and security liability	liability proportionate to the degree of faults

8) 1934 ACT의 적용을 받는 회사의 재무제표를 감사한 감사인은 다음과 같은 절차를 수립하여야 한다.

A. 중요한 불법행위의 발견(detect direct material illegal acts)
B. 특수관계인과 회사사이의 중요거래의 인식(identify material related-party transactions)
C. 기업의 계속성 평가(evaluate ability of firm to continue as going concern)

13 회계사의 형사상의 책임(Criminal Liability)

1) 1933 ACT와 1934 ACT에서 형사상의 책임을 져야하는 경우는 고의성(willfully)이 있는 경우로서 다음과 같다.

A. 고의로 등록신고서에 중요사실을 누락(omission of material facts)
B. 고의로 등록신고서에 잘못된 정보(false information) 기재
C. 회계사가 경영진의 사기행위(fraudulent scheme)를 도운경우
D. 회계사가 전기재무제표의 잘못된 부분을 은닉한 경우(cover up prior year financial statement misstatements)

→ $10,000이하의 벌금 and/or 5년 이하의 징역에 처해질 수 있다.

2) Internal Revenue Code의 형벌규정을 위반한 경우

고의적으로 false tax return을 작성(perjury)하거나, 탈세(tax evasion)를 고의적으로 도운 경우

3) Racketeer Influenced and Corrupt Organization(RICO) Act 위반

The Racketeer Influenced and Corrupt Organizations Act (commonly referred to as RICO Act or RICO) is a United States federal law that provides for extended criminal penalties and a civil cause of action for acts performed as part of an ongoing criminal organization. Under the law, racketeering activity means:

Any violation of state statutes against gambling, murder, kidnapping, arson, robbery, bribery, extortion, dealing in obscene matter, or dealing in a controlled substance or listed chemical (as defined in the Controlled Substances Act);Any act of bribery, counterfeiting, theft, embezzlement, fraud, dealing in obscene matter, obstruction of justice, slavery, racketeering, gambling, money laundering, commission of murder-for-hire, and several other offenses covered under the Federal criminal code (Title 18); Embezzlement of union funds; Bankruptcy or securities fraud; Drug trafficking; Money laundering and related offenses; Bringing in, aiding or assisting aliens in illegally entering the country (if the action was for financial gain); Acts of terrorism.

A. 조직범죄, 범죄조직에 의한 강탈, 도박, 공갈, 증권사기, 우편을 이용한 사기 등의 반복적 범죄행위에 대하여 처벌대상이 된다. 이 같은 범죄에 연루된 회계사도 벌금이나 징역형의 대상이 된다.

B. RICO법은 민사소송에도 적용되어 손해액의 세배까지 손해배상(treble damages)청구가 가능하다.

14 Sarbanes Oxley Act of 2002

〈Sarbanes Oxley Act (개념 정리)〉

In response to the Arthur Anderson, Enron and WorldCom debacle, the Sarbanes-Oxley Act seeks to:

- Restore the public confidence in both public accounting and publicly traded securities

- Assure ethical business practices through heightened levels of executive awareness and accountability

1) Creation of the Public Company Oversight Board (상장기업감시위원회 설립)
   - Created as a non-profit organization, the Board will oversee audits of public companies; it is under the authority of the SEC but above other professional accounting organizations such as the AICPA

2) AUDITOR INDEPENDENCE STRENGTHENED(회계사 독립성 강화)
   - Prohibits registered public accounting firms who audit an issuer from performing specific non-audit services for that issuer, including but not limited to: bookkeeping, financial information systems design, appraisal services, actuarial services, internal audit outsourcing services, management/human resource functions, broker/dealer, legal/expert services outside the scope of the audit
   (감사업무를 하는 기업에 대해 다른 서비스를 겸해서 제공하지 못하도록 함)

3) CORPORATE RESPONSIBILITY REINFORCED(기업책임 강화)
   - Audit Committee (committees est. by the board of a company for the purpose of overseeing financial reporting) Independence
   - Establishes minimum independence standards for audit committees
   - CEOs and CFOs must certify in any periodic report the truthfulness and accurateness of that report → creates liability

1) 모든 상장기업에 적용되는 법이다.

2) 이법의 Section 906에 따르면 CEO와 CFO는 회사의 재무상태에 관한 중요사항이 fairly present되었다고 certify하는 내용의 서명을 해야 한다.

3) 만일 회사의 임직원이 SEC 요건과 부합하지 않는다는 것을 알면서 certification에 서명을 할 경우 $1백만의 벌금 and/or 10년 형의 처벌을 받을 수 있다. 또한 willful violation of certificate requirements일 경우 $5백만의 벌금 and/or 20년 형의 처벌을 받을 수 있다.

4) 이법의 Section 302에 따르면 임원은 효과적인 내부통제제도를 유지할 책임이 있으며 주요임원과 재무담당 임원은 내부통제제도의 중요한 취약점(all significant internal control deficiencies)을 감사 혹은 감사위원회(audit or audit committee)에 알려야 한다.

5) 상장기업 회계감시위원회(Public Company Accounting Oversight Board)를 설립하여 상장기업의 감사를 하는 회계법인을 규율하도록 하였다(The SOA established the Public Company Accounting Oversight Board to regulate CPA firms that audit public companies).

상장기업 회계감시위원회(PCAOB)에서 상장기업들의 감사표준(auditing standards)를 제정한다.

6) 상장기업을 감사하는 회계법인(issuer's public accounting firm)은 설령 감사위원회(audit committee)에서 동의를 하더라도 다음과 같은 제공해줄 수 있는 서비스와 제공해줄 수없는 서비스가 있으므로 유의해야 한다.

〈개념정리〉

수행불가	수행가능
- Bookkeeping or other services relating to financial statements or accounting records - Financial information system design and/or implementation - Appraisal services - Internal audit outsourcing services - Management functions - Actuarial services - Investment or Brokerage-Dealing Services	tax service

7) 독립성확보를 위해 상장법인을 감사하는 모든 회계법인은 감사담당파트너를 5년마다 rotation 해야 한다.(5 year Partner rotation rule5 P RO Rule)

15 기타 법적인 고려사항(Legal Considerations)

1) 회계사의 감사조서(working papers)

의뢰인과 별도계약이 없는 한 기밀유지(preserve confidentiality)와 회계사가 실시한 감사의 범위와 특정 등을 입증하기 위한 법률상의 목적 및 기타목적을 고려하여 회계사가 보관(retention by accountant)하는 것이 원칙이다.

2) 회계사의 기밀유지의무(duty to preserve confidentiality)

A. 의뢰인의 동의 없이(absent client consent) 감사조서에 담긴 내용을 타인에게 전달해서는 안 된다(no transmission of information in working papers). 단, 감사조서를 작성한 동일회계법인의 partner는 별도의 고객허락이나 법원 명령 없이 감사조서를 볼 수 있다.

B. 의뢰인의 동의가 없는 한 회계영업(CPA practice)을 구매한 다른 회계사에게도 감사조서는 넘길 수 없다.

C. 단, 법원 또는 정부기관으로부터 감사조서에 대한 합법적 문서제출명령(enforceable subpoena)을 받은 경우에는 제출해야 한다.

D. 문서제출명령이 지나치게 광범위하거나 지나치게 부담이 되면(too broad or unreasonably burdensome) 이를 다툴 수 있다.

3) Code of Professional Conduct

A. Code of professional conduct에 의하면 회계사는 의뢰인에 관한 비공개자료(confidential client data)를 외부에 공개할 수 없다.

B. 공개가 허용되는 경우

(1) enforceable subpoena에 의한 경우

(2) AICPA나 state trial board(주의 심리위원회)에서 공개를 요구한 경우

(3) quality review under AICPA authorization

(4) GAAS를 따르기 위한 경우

(5) 의뢰인이 동의한 경우(consent)

• Mneumonic: STRG CD

- ☑ S is <u>s</u>ubpoena
- ☑ T is state <u>t</u>rial board
- ☑ R is quality <u>r</u>eview
- ☑ G is <u>G</u>AAS compliance
- ☑ C is <u>c</u>onsented
- ☑ D is <u>d</u>isclosure is mandatory

注意| 국세청(IRS)이라고 해서 함부로 고객정보를 회계사에게 요구할 수는 없다. 국세청등과 같은 문구를 넣어 혼돈을 유도하므로 주의할 것!

16 의뢰인의 불법해위(Clients'Illegal Acts)

1) 의뢰인의 과거 불법행위는 공개하지 않는 것이 원칙이다.

2) 다음과 같이 회계사가 의뢰인의 불법행위를 외부에 공개할 의무가 (duty to notify parties outside the client)있는 경우

A. Form 8-K disclosure(감사인 변경)
B. 후임감사 변경(disclosure to successor auditor)
C. Subpoena
D. Disclosure to government funding agency under GAO standard

17 회계사의 사용자책임(employer's liability)

A. 회계사의 고용인(EE)이 제3자에게 torts를 가한 경우 그 행위가 엄무상(in the course of business) 발생했다면 회계사는 제3자에 대하여 책임을 져야한다.
B. 회계사의 고용인과 회계사는 제3자에 대하여 연대책임(joint & several liability)을 진다.

18 회계사와 의뢰인간의 privileged communication

〈개념정리〉

Privileged communication recognized			privileged communication not recognized	
doctor	attorney	attorney	CPA	CPA
		CPA		attorney
patient	client	client	client	client

A. CL가 아닌 statute에 의거하여 생겨난다.

B. 연방법이 아닌 소수의 주법에 의거하여 생겨났다. 대부분의 주에서 인정되지 않고 극히 일부의 주에서만 인정된다.

C. 미연방대법원 탈세관련사건에서 회계사와 의뢰인 사이의 accountant-client privilege를 인정하지 않았다.

D. 회계사가 privileged commuication의 권리를 가진 변호사의 agent로서 행위를 할 경우에는 회계사에게도 privileged communication이 인정된다.

E. 그러나 변호사가 회계사의 agent로 활동할 경우에는 privileged communication이 인정되지 않는다.

Chapter 15

Professional Responsibilities(Code)

1 Code of Professional Conduct 전문가행동강령

1) Public practice(공적인 회계실무)를 하는 것과 상관없이 모든 CPA에 적용된다.

2) 회계사들의 이해(understanding)와 자발적인 행동(voluntary actions)에 따라 본 행동강령을 준수하는 것을 원칙으로 하며 2차적으로

A. reinforcement by peers 동료들에 의한 보강
B. public opinion 여론
C. disciplinary proceedings 징계절차 등의 방법에 의존한다.

3) AICPA Code는 6개의 principle과 여러 개의 rules로 이루어져있다.

2 Principle은 AICPA Code가 지향하는 목표이다.

6개의 principle의 구성은 다음과 같다.

- Public interest(공익)

- Responsibility(책임)
- Objectivity and independence (객관성과 독립성)
- Due care (합당한 주의)
- Scope and nature of services (서비스의 범위와 성격)
- Integrity (신의성실성)

3 AICPA Code of Professional Conduct의 구조

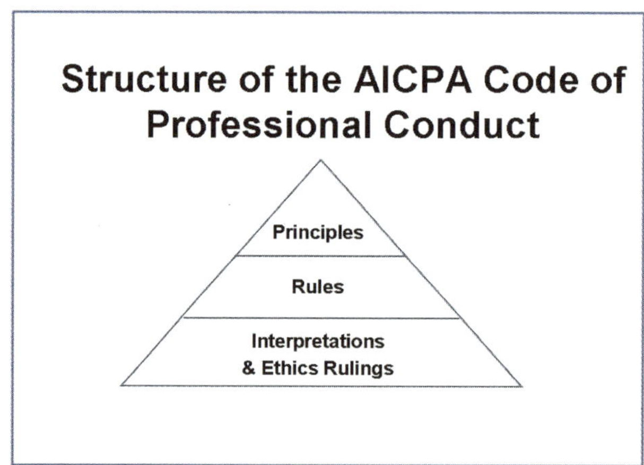

1) AICPA code는 원칙, 규칙, 해설, 윤리관련 판례로 구성된다(The Code of Professional Conduct of the AICPA consists of 3 parts: Principles, Rules, Interpretations and Ethics Rulings).

2) 원칙은 Rule의 기본구조를 구성한다(Principles provide the framework for the Rules)

3) 규칙은 AICPA회원들의 각 업무수행 여부를 관할한다(Rules govern the

performance of professional services by members of the AICPA)

4) 해설은 관련 규칙들의 범위와 적용사례에 대한 가이드라인을 제공한다 (Interpretations provide guidelines as to the scope and application of the Rules)

5) 윤리관련 판례들은 특정사안에 대한 각 규칙과 해설을 요약한 것이다(Ethics Rulings summarize the application of the Rules and the Interpretations to particular set of factual circumstances).

4 AICPA Code of Professional Conduct의 구성

101 Independence (독립성)
102 Integrity and Objectivity (성실성과 독립성)
201 General Standards (일반기준)
202 Compliance with Standards (일반기준 준수)
203 Accounting Principles (회계원칙)
301 Confidential Client Information (고객비밀정보)
302 Contingent Fees (성공불)
501 Acts Discreditable (불명예행위)
502 Advertisement and other forms of solicitation (광고 및 기타 유치행위)
503 Commissions and Referral Fees (수수료 및 소개비)
505 Forms of Organizations and Names (조직형태와 명칭)

Governing Entities(집행기관)

1) 정부기관

A. State Board of Accountancy (주 회계위원회)

각 주별로 회계사에게 개업을 할 수 있도록 license를 발급해주고, 문제가 있는 회계사에게는 license를 정지(suspend)하거나 취소(revoke)시켜버릴 수 있는 기관이다.

설령 AICPA(미국회계사협회)에서 발급받은 certificate을 취소당한 회계사라 할지라도 license가 있기만 하면 해당 주에서 영업을 할 수 있다.

Certified public accountants(CPAs) are licensed to practice by individual state boards of accountancy. Note that the right to practice public accounting requires only a valid CPA license issued by State Board of Accountancy <references :Bisk, Regulation>

B. Securities & Exchange Commission (증권거래위원회)

The SEC has rules governing the proper/improper conduct of accountants and other securities-related professionals performing audits for public companies or otherwise practicing before the commission. Improper conduct requires greater than simple negligence. For example improper conduct includes

(1) intentional(deliberate, conscious, knowing, willful, purposeful) conduct resulting in various violations of applicable professional standards.

(2) repeated instances of unreasonable conduct that indicate a lack of competence to practice before the commission, etc.<references :Bisk, Regulation>

증권과 관련된 상장기업의 감사업무나 증권거래위원회와 연관된 실무를 하는 경우를 규율하는 규정을 두고 있음. 전문가로서 부적절한 행동에 대한 규정을 갖고 있으며 부적절한 행동이란 단순한 과실보다 큰 잘못을 의미함.

예를 들면,

(3) 의도적인 (일부러 하는, 의식적인, 알면서 하는, 의도를 갖고 하는, 목적을 갖고 하는) 행동으로 인하여 전문가로서 기준을 위반할 경우

(4) 능력부족임을 보여주는 비이성적인 행동을 거듭하는 경우 등을 포함함.

C. Public Company Accounting Oversight Board(PCAOB 상장기업 회계감시위원회)

The Sarbanes-Oxley Act established the PCAOB and charged it with the responsibility of overseeing the audits of public companies by including the duties to PCAOB as follows;

(1) registering accounting firms that audit public companies 상장기업을 감사하는 회계법인 등록의무 부여

(2) establishing auditing, quality control, ethics, independence, and other standards relating to public company audits. 상장기업 감사와 관련된 각종 감사, 품질관리, 윤리, 독립성, 등의 기준마련

(3) conducting inspections, investigations and disciplinary proceedings of registered accounting firms 등록 회계법인의 검사, 조사, 징계활동 실시

(4) enforcing the compliance with the Sarbanes-Oxley Act. 사베인즈 옥슬리 법을 준수하도록 집행업무 담당

(5) requiring management to support its evaluation of ICOFR(internal control over financial reporting) with sufficient evidence. If auditor concludes that management has not fulfilled these responsibilities, the PCAOB requires the auditor to report in writing the management and the audit committee that the audit of ICOFR cannot be completed and that the auditor must disclaim an opinion. 경영진이 재무보고서에 서명을 하도록 함으로써 내부통제를 확실하게 유지하도록 의무화하고 있으며, 만일 감사가 경영진이 이 같은 의무를 준수하지 않는다고 판단할 경우, 감사는 경영진과 감사위원회에 ICOFR이 되지 못하고 있다고 서면통보하고, 감사의견제출을 거부하여야 함

(6) requiring the auditor to communicate in writing with the management and the audit committee all

① significant deficiencies and

② material weakness and the communication should ③ distinguish clearly between significant deficiencies and material weakness

회계감사는 경영진과 감사위원회에 서면을 통하여 ① significant deficiencies ② material weakness를 알려주고, ③ 양자의 차이점을 분명하게 구분해서 통보해야 함

〈개념정리〉

significant deficiency	control deficiency	material weakness
control deficiency, or combination of control deficiencies that adversely affects the company's ability to initiate, authorize, record, process, or report external financial data in accordance with GAAP such that there is more than a remote likelihood that a misstatement will not be prevented or detected. Deficiencies that are less than material weaknesses are required to be disclosed to the audit committee or the board of directors, and management may disclose them in its report on ICOFR.	when the design or operation of a control does not allow management or employees to prevent or detect misstatements on a timely basis in the normal course of performing their assigned function.	a significant deficiency or combination of significant deficiencies, that results in more than a remote likelihood that a misstatement of the company's annual or interim financial statements will not be prevented or detected. The PCAOB standards generally don't use the term material deficiency. If a material weakness in ICOFR exists, management and the auditor must conclude that ICOFR is not effective.
통제결여로 인하여 기업이 각종 재무기록을 GAAP에 따라 작성하는 것이 어려워져 오기가 발생하는 것을 막기 어려운 심각한 결여 상태로 중대한 약점에 이르지 않은 결여상태는 감사위원회 혹은 이사회와 경영진에 ICOFR관련 보고서를 통해 공개될 수도 있음.	통제의 디자인 혹은 운영상의 문제로 인하여 경영진이나 직원이 오기를 시의 적절하게 막거나 발견하기 어려운 경우의 통제결여 상태	기업의 재무제표 혹은 중기 재무제표상의 오기를 막거나 적발하기 어려운 심각한 결여상태를 중요한 약점이라고 하며, 일반적으로 중요한 결여라는 용어는 사용하지 않음. 만일 ICOFR에 중대한 약점이 존재할 경우 경영진과 감사는 반드시 ICOFR이 effective 하지 않다고 보고해야 함.

(7) requiring the auditor to document the identification of the points at which misstatements related with relevant financial statements assertions could occur within significant accounts and disclosures and major classes of transactions. 회계감사는 재무제표 상 중요한 계정에서 발생할 수 있는 오기를 지적하고, 발생상황, 주요거래 내역을 표시해야 함.

(8) the date of the reports on the company's financial statements and on internal control over financial reporting(ICOFR) should be the same, as the auditor cannot audit ICOFR without also auditing the financial statements. 재무제표를 감사하면서 재무보고서에 대한 내부통제가 적절히 잘 이루어지고 있는지 감사하여야 하므로 재무제표 보고서와 내부통제 보고서는 날짜가 일치되도록 하여야한다. <references :Bisk, Regulation>

Internal Control over Financial Report 재무보고서 관련 내부통제

In its Auditing Standard 2 (AS 2), the PCAOB defined ICOFR as a process designed by management to provide reasonable assurance regarding the reliability of financial reporting and the preparation of financial statements in accordance with GAAP. 경영진이 기업의 재무보고서에 대해 GAAP에 따라 이루어져 상당히 신뢰도가 높다는 것을 reasonable assurance 하도록 한 것

1. ICOFR is a subset of internal control specific to financial reporting objectives.

A. The PCAOB's definition requires ICOFR to provide reasonable assurance regarding the **reliability of financial reporting and the preparation of financial statements.** Reasonable assurance represents a high level of assurance, but it is not absolute. It recognizes that, even when ICOFR is effective, misstatements may occur, being neither prevented nor detected on a timely basis. (합리적인 assurance 수준)

B. In deciding whether the ICOFR is effective, AS 2 requires that a company's management and its independent auditor consider the likelihood and magnitude of a potential misstatement. 기업의 경영진과 회계감사가 재무보고서 작성 상 오기를 할 가능성에 초점을 맞춤

2. When an internal control deficiency is identified, management and the auditor should decide whether this deficiency is **a significant deficiency** or whether it is **a material weakness** in ICOFR. 내부통제 결여상태가 발견될 경우 경영진과 회계감사는 심각한 결여상태(significant deficiency)인지 중대한 약점(material weakness)인지 여부를 판단하여야 함

A, If the likelihood of a misstatement is more than remote and its magnitude is more than inconsequential but less than material, the control deficiency is deemed to be significant. 오기의 가능성이 중대하지는 않으나 상당한 정도일 경우, 통제결여상태가 심각한 것으로 판단함.

B. If the control deficiency's likelihood of causing a material misstatement is more than remote, it is considered a material weakness in the ICOFR. 만일 통제결여의 정도가 중대한 오기를 낳게 될 경우 중대한 약점이 있는 것으로 판단함.

C. The PCAOB requires that management and auditors base their assessment of the effectiveness of the company's ICOFR on a suitable, recognized control framework. AS 2's performance and reporting directions are based on the 1992 framework published by the Committee of Sponsoring Organizations (COSO) of the Treadway Commission, "Internal Control-Integrated Framework." Most companies have adopted the COSO internal control framework as a basis for their assessment of ICOFR.

3. Reports on ICOFR

A. **If a material weakness in ICOFR exists, management and the auditor must conclude that ICOFR is not effective.** All identified material weaknesses that exist at year-end must be disclosed in the reports on ICOFR.
ICOFR상의 중대한 약점이 있을 경우 경영진과 감사는 ICOFR이 효율적이지 않다고 결론을 내리게 됨. 연말에 존재하는 모든 중대한 약점은 ICOFR에 관한 보고서에 모두 게재하여야 함

B. Deficiencies that are less than material weaknesses are required to be disclosed to the audit committee or the board of directors, and management may disclose them in its report on ICOFR.
중대한 약점은 아니나 발견된 결점들은 감사위원회 혹은 이사진과 경영진에게 ICOFR보고서를 통해 공개될 수도 있음

4. The SEC requires management to disclose the following information in its report on

ICOFR:미국 증권위원회는 다음사항을 공개하도록 하고 있음

A. A statement of management's responsibility for establishing and maintaining adequate ICOFR; 경영진이 적절한 ICOFR체계를 수립하고 유지하는 것에 관한 경영진이 책임 있다는 내용의 statement

B. A statement identifying the framework used by management to evaluate the effectiveness of ICOFR; 경영진이 ICOFR의 효율성을 평가하기 위해 사용하는 framework에 관한 statement

C. Management's assessment of the effectiveness of the company's ICOFR as of the end of its most recent fiscal year, including an explicit statement as to whether that control is effective, and disclosure of any material weakness identified; 각 회계연도 말에 회사의 ICOFR의 효율성에 관한 경영진의 statement로 통제가 효율적인지, 중대한 약점이 발견되었는지 여부를 공시하는 내용이 포함된 statement.

D. A statement that the registered public accounting firm that audited the financial statements has also issued an attestation report on management's internal control assessment. 등록 회계법인이 재무제표를 감사하고 또한 경영진의 내부통제에 관한 평가에 관한 인증보고서를 발행한다는 내용의 statement.

5. The auditor's report on ICOFR includes two opinions:
회계감사의 ICOFR에 관한 보고서는 다음 두 가지를 담고 있음.

A. **Management's assessment of the effectiveness of ICOFR. ICOFR의 효율성에 대한 경영진의 평가서**
The auditor will issue an unqualified opinion on management's assessment of the effectiveness of ICOFR under two circumstances:
① If the auditor did not find material weakness in ICOFR; or
② If the auditor and management have both identified material weakness in ICOFR.
③ On the other hand, if the auditor found material weakness in ICOFR and management did not, the auditor must issue an adverse opinion on management's assessment of the effectiveness of ICOFR.

B. The auditor's independent assessment of the effectiveness of the company's ICOFR. 회계감사의 독립된 기업 ICOFR의 효율성에 관한 평가서

① An unqualified opinion on the assessment of the effectiveness of ICOFR if there were no material weaknesses in ICOFR, or ICOFR was effective;

② An adverse opinion on the assessment of the effectiveness of ICOFR if there are one or more material weaknesses in ICOFR; or

③ A disclaimer if management has in any way restricted the auditor's scope of work needed to assess the effectiveness of ICOFR.

6. Impact on the Auditor's Report

A. A company can receive an unqualified (clean) opinion on its financial statements from an independent auditor even if management or the auditor identifies a material weakness in ICOFR.

B. If a material weakness in ICOFR is found, **management and the auditor should take the necessary steps to compensate for the material weakness** in the financial statement preparation process by expanding the scope of testing account balances or altering the audit approach and procedures in the area of weakness.

C. If, after expanding the scope of the audit, the auditor can conclude that the financial statements are fairly stated, the auditor may issue an unqualified opinion on the financial statements. <references: Abdel M. Agami, *Reporting on Internal Control Over Financial Reporting*>

D. International Revenue Services(IRS)국세청

The IRS may bar an accountant from practicing before the IRS based upon incompetency or noncompliance with tax rules and regulations. IRS regulations also provide for assessing fines for various violations. <references :Bisk, Regulation>

국세청은 세금관련 법규에 따라 무능(incompentency) 혹은 미준수(noncompliance)가 발견될 경우 해당 회계사의 업무를 중단시키거나 혹은 벌금을 규정할 수 있다.

2) 민간기관

A. American Institute of Certified Public Accountants(AICPA, 미국회계사협회) 회계사 시험에 합격하여야만 회원이 될 수 있으며, 회원들의 잘못이 있을 경우 자율규정을 두어 징계처리를 한다.

B. State CPA Society 주 단위 회계사 협회

6 Independence(Rule 101-1)

A member in public practice should be independent in fact and appearance when providing auditing and other attestation services - *Article IV-AICPA Code of Professional Ethics*

A member in public practice shall be independent in the performance of professional services - *Rule 101-AICPA Code of Professional Ethics*

1) definition

A. Independence means freedom from control or influence of others. 독립성이란 업무수행상 타인의 통제나 영향으로부터 자유로운 것을 의미한다.

Individuals with independence:	Individuals without independence are:
Are self-controlled Make their own opinions Set their own course of conduct Are not ruled by others	Subjective Influenced by emotions or personal prejudices Biased Opinionated Not free from conflicts of interest Subordinating their judgments to others

[source] : Jane Zhang and Debra Grace, *Integrity, Objectivity and Independence*

B. 독립성이 필요한 이유는 attestation services를 제공하는 데 객관성을 훼손하는 것을 피하기 위해서이다(Why is independence necessary? To avoid impairing one's objectivity in performing attestation services (Article IV.01)

attestation이란 audit, compliance, review, examination의 4가지 업무를 의미한다.

attestation(attest engagement 인증업무)	non-attestation
audit compliance review examination 을 통해 신뢰도에 관한 결론을 내는 것 (expressing conclusion about reliability via ACRE)	compilation preparation filing tax return services 등은 attestation업무가 아니다.

2) 전문적인 서비스를 제공하는 기간 동안(during the period of professional engagement) 회계사나 회계사가 속한 법인(a covered member)은 다음의 경우에 독립성을 훼손당하게 된다.

A. 의뢰인과 직접적인 혹은 중요한 간접적인(any direct or material indirect) 금전적인 이해관계(financial interest)를 갖는 경우

注意| 금전적인 이해관계(financial interest)에 대해서 "직접적인(direct)" 경우에는 무조건 금지된다. 그리고 간접적인 경우에는 "중요한 간접적인(material indirect) 경우"에만 적용된다.

- covered member가 attest service를 제공해주는 대상인 고객회사의 주식소유, 고객에게 직접적인 대출관계를 구성하는 등과 같이 금전적인 이해관계를 갖게 될 때 "직접적인(direct)"이란 용어를 사용한다

("direct" results when a covered member has a financial interest in an attest client, such as ownership of stock or a loan to or from a client.

- covered member가 attest service를 제공해주는 대상인 고객회사와 금전적인 이해 관계가 있는 법인(Ex. 뮤츄얼 펀드) 등을 통해 주식을 소유하는 경우 "중요한 간접적인(material indirect)"라는 용어를 사용한다.
  ("material indirect results when a covered member has a financial interest in an entity that is associated with an attest client, e.g.mutual fund investment which owns the stocks of the client corporation)

B. 의뢰인과 직접 혹은 중요하게 간접적인 금전상의 이해관계를 갖는 신탁 관리인 (trustee)이나 상속유산의 유언집행인(executor of any estate)인 경우

C. 의뢰인 혹은 의뢰 회사의 임원과 공동으로 covered member가 joint closely held investment를 한 경우

참고 joint closely held investment : an investment in an entity or property by the member and the client(or the client's officers or directors, or any owner who has the ability to exercise significant influence over the client) that enables them to control

D. Interpretation 101-5에서 허용되는 것을 제외하고 의뢰인, 의뢰회사의 임원, 지분증권을 10%이상 소유한 주주 등과의 loan 거래관계(loan financial transaction)를 갖는 경우로 여기서의 loan이란 보증관계도 포함된다(10% Loan Rule).

E. 계약기간동안, 회계법인의 partner 혹은 전문적 종사자(professional employees), 그들의 가족, 또는 그들이 공동으로 의뢰회사의 지분증권의 5%이상을 소유한 경우(5% Rule)

3) 재무제표상의 해당기간동안(during the period covered by financial statements) 혹은 계약기간동안 (during the period of professional engagement)혹은 회계법인의 파트너 또는 전문직 종사자가 아래와 같은 직위를 동시에 겸직해서 갖고 있을 경우 독립성이 훼손된다.

A. 이사, officer, employee, 혹은 경영진과 동일한 지위

B. promoter(발기인), underwriter, voting trustee,etc.

C. trustee for any pension or profit-sharing trust of the client

4) 다음 예외사항을 제외하고는 covered member의 직계가족(immediate family = spouse, spouse equivalent, dependent whether or not related)도 Rule 101이 적용된다.

A. Covered Member의 정의

(1) Attest engagement를 하는 개인회계사 혹은 회계법인의 파트너 및 직원,

(2) GAAP의 적용대상이 되는 기업

(3) attest client를 위해 10시간 이상 활동하는 회계법인의 파트너나 직원 (nonattest 담당 포함)

B. Covered member 의 직계가족이 의뢰인의 종업원이지만 중요한 위치(key position)를 갖고 있지 않은 경우(참고로 director는 key position holder로 간주되므로 주의할 것.

C. 의뢰인의 직계가족이 의뢰인의 종업원 자격으로서 어떤 plan의 혜택을 받고 있지만 그러한 혜택이 특별한 우대혜택이 아니고 일반적으로 모든 종업원들에게도 제공(normally offered to all EEs)되는 경우

5) 가까운 친척관계(close relatives)가

A. 의뢰인회사에서 중요한 위치에 종사(key position holder)하고 있을 경우,

B. 의뢰인과 금전적인 이해관계(financial interest)가 걸려있으며 이에 대해 파트너나 개인이 알고 있는 경우

C. 가까운 친척이 의뢰인에게 상당한 영향(significant influence)을 행사할 수 있는 경우에는 독립성이 훼손된 것으로 간주된다.

참고 CR(close relatives) = parent, sibling, or nondependent child 가까운 친척이란 부모, 형제, 혹은 nondependent 자녀를 의미한다.
☞ 사촌(cousin)은 가까운 친척(close relative)에 해당되지 않는다.

〈개념정리〉

covered member	immediate family	close relative
Attest engagement 를 하는 개인회계사 혹은 회계법인의 파트너 및 직원	Spouse	Parent
GAAP의 적용대상이 되는 기업	Spouse equivalent	Siblings
Attest client를 위해 10시간 이상 활동하는 회계법인의 파트너나 직원	Dependent, whether or not related	Non-dependent child
☞ Attest client에게 tax service를 제공하는 경우에는 covered member에 해당되지 않는다.		☞ 사촌(cousin)은 해당되지 않는다.
☞ A covered member's immediate family is subject to rule 101 and its interpretations and rulings		☞ when a close relative has a material financial interest in the client and CPA participating in the engagement is aware of the interest, close relatives can impair independence of the CPA 회계사의 가까운 친인척이 지분을 갖고 있는 기업에 대해서 회계사가 알면서 attest engagement를 할 경우 회계사의 독립성은 훼손된다.

Interpretation 101-2 Former Partners and Firm Independence (전임 파트너와 firm의 독립성)

다음의 경우 전임파트너(주주 또는 유사한 위치에 있는 자)가 독립성을 훼손한다고 볼 수 없다.

1) 퇴직연금액이 확정(retirement benefits fixed)된 경우

2) Reasonable transition[사임, 퇴임, 전직…] 이후 firm의 비즈니스 활동에 참여하지 않은 경우(not participate)

3) Firm의 비즈니스 활동에 외관상 참여하고 있는 것처럼 보이지 않는 경우(do not appear to participate in the firm's business)

A. 예를 들어 이전 파트너의 이름이 회계법인 사무실안내판에 기재되어있다면 외관상 참여하고 있는 것임

B. 전임 파트너에게 사무실(비서, 전화 포함)을 제공하는 것은 이러한 외관을 갖고 있다고 보지 않는다.

8 Interpretation 101-3 여타서비스의 실행 (performance of other services)

본 규정에 관한 해석은 SEC, GAO(General accounting office), Department of Labor에서 한다.

다음 사항은 독립성을 훼손하는 것으로 본다.

1) 경영진을 대신하여 이사회에 보고하는 것(reporting to the board of directors on behalf of management)

2) 의뢰인의 주식매매이전, escrow agent, registrar, general counsel, or its equivalent가 되는 것

3) 회계법인 또는 그 구성원의 제안에 관한 실행여부를 결정하는 것(determining which recommendations of the member should be implemented)

4) 의뢰인의 자산보관(having custody of client assets)

5) 의뢰인을 위하여 거래행위를 대신해주는 행위 (authorizing, executing, or consummating transaction)

6) 의뢰인을 위하여 source documents를 제공해주는 행위 (preparing source documents): 예를 들면 purchase orders, payroll time records, and customer orders 등을 대신해서 준비해주는 행위.

7) 의뢰인의 종업원이 수행하는 일상적인 활동을 감독하는 것(supervising client EEs in the performance of their normal recurring activities)

9 Interpretation 101-4 비영리단체 이사

회계법인의 CPA가 비영리단체의 이사(director)인 경우, 그 직위가 순수한 명예직(purely honorary position)이고, 외부자료에도 명예직임이 표시가 분명하게 되고(identified as honorary on external materials), 경영관련 안건의 의결에 참여하지 않으며

(not vote or participate in management affairs), 이름만 사용하도록 제한된 경우(restricted to use of name) 독립성이 훼손된다고 보지 않는다.

Interpretation 101-5 금융기관 대출(Loans from Financial Institutions)과 예외조항

앞에서 '의뢰인의 주식 10%이상을 가진 사람과 대출관계를 갖게 되면 독립성이 훼손된다(10% Loan rule)'고 했는데 그 예외조항으로서 다음과 같은 것들이 있다.

1) Grandfathered loans

home mortgage, secured loan 등이 다음의 경우 에 해당할 경우 회계사의 독립성을 훼손하지 않는다.

A. 1992년 1월1일 이전에 받아 당시 유효하던 기준에 따른 경우(obtained prior to Jan. 1, 1992 under standards then in effect)

B. 금융기관의 일반대출과정과 조건(normal lending procedures, terms and requirements)을 통해 이루어졌을 경우

C. Covered member가 된 이후에도 금융기관의 각종 대출조건이 그대로 유지되는 경우(kept current and not renegotiated afterwards)

D. 독립성이 요구되지 않는 금융기관에서 대출을 받았고, 나중에 그 금융기관이 의뢰인이 된 경우(obtained from the financial institutions prior for which independence was not required, and the financial institutions subsequently became an attest client)

E. 어떤 회계사가 2002년 5월31일 이후 금융기관으로부터 대출을 받았는데 나중에 그 CPA가 그 금융기관에 대해 covered member가 된 경우(obtained after May 31, 2002 from a financial institution client requiring independence by a borrower prior to his or her becoming a covered member with respect to that client)

2) Other Permitted Loans

A. 자동차 대출(autolease)과 자동차를 담보로 한 리스(leases collateralized loans)

B. 보험증서를 담보로 중도해약 환불금에 대한 대출
(loans fully collateralized by the cash surrender value of an insurance policy)

C. 동일한 금융기관에 예치되어있는 현금예금을 담보로 하는 대출(loans fully collateralized by cash deposits at the same financial institutions)

D. $5,000 이하의 신용카드 부채 및 현금서비스(credit cards and cash advances on checking accounts of $5,000 or less)

11 Interpretation 101-6 소송협박과 분쟁

1) 의뢰인과 회계사간 실제소송 혹은 소송협박(actual or threatened litigation) 은 독립성을 해친다.

A. 감사의 부족한 점을 주장하며 현경영진이 이의를 제기(commenced by present management alleging audit deficiencies)하면 독립성이 훼손된다.

B. 현 경영진의 사기, 속임수에 대한 감사인의 제기(commenced by auditor against present management for fraud and deceit)

C. 감사 작업의 부족한 점을 제기하려는 현 경영진의 의도적 주장이(감사인의 생각에) 이길 가능성이 크다고 생각한다면 독립성이 훼손된다(expressed intention by present management alleging deficiencies in audit work impairs if auditor believes strong possibility of claim).

D. 감사와 관련되지 않은 중요하지 않은 사항에 관련된 소송 및 소송가능성은 대체로 독립성을 훼손하지 않는다(Ex. Billing disputes 청구서에 대한 다툼).

2) 의뢰인 회사의 주주(client security holder)나 다른 제 3자간의 소송은 중요의뢰인과 회계사간의 맞소송 (material client-CPA cross-claim)으로 발전하지 않는 한 독

립성을 훼손하지 않는다.

3) 만약 독립성이 훼손된 경우 CPA는 관계를 단절하거나 독립성이 없다는 이유로 의견을 거절해야 한다(If independence is impaired, CPA should disassociate and/or disclaim an opinion for lack of independence).

12 Interpretation 101-8

CPA가 의뢰인이 아닌 회사의 주식을 보유하고 있고, 그 회사가 CPA의 의뢰인회사의 주식을 보유하고 있다면 독립성이 훼손된다(A CPA's financial interests in nonclients may impair independence when those nonclients have financial interests in the CPA's clients).

〈개념정리〉

☞ independence impaired despite the indirect ownership scheme of client's corporate stocks by the CPA	**CPA**		☞ indirect material financial interest
	⬇⬇⬇	**ownership**	
	corporate stocks		
	⬇⬇⬇	**ownership**	
	client's corporate stocks		

13 Interpretation 101-12

1) 계약기간동안(during the period of professional engagement)이나 의견을 도출하려는 시점(while expressing an opinion) 회계사 혹은 회계법인이 의뢰인에게 중요한 협력관계(material cooperative arrangements)를 갖는 경우 독립성이 훼손된다.

2) 다음과 같이 MCA에 해당하는 경우와 해당하지 않는 경우를 구분해 볼 수 있다.

〈개념정리〉

MCA에 해당하는 경우	MCA에 해당하지 않는 경우
Joint venture to develop or market a product or service	Separate agreements 기업참여자와 고객간의 별도계약
Arrangements to provide services or products to a 3P	No responsibility o respective party (상대방에 대해 책임질 필요 없다)
Arrangement to combine one or more services or products (의뢰인의 제품 혹은 서비스와 회계법인이 제품 혹은 서비스를 결합하여 판매하기 위한 계약)	No agent to each other(상호간의 대리인이 아님)
Distribution of other's products or services between clients and CPAs (회계법인과 의뢰인간 상호제품 및 서비스를 distribution 하는 계약)	

14 Interpretation 101-14

If a firm is organized in an alternative practice structure, in which the attest function is part of a larger organization that leases the staff to the attest function, the independence provision of the AICPA Code of Professional Conduct must be adhered to by all staff and management on attest engagement and every individual that is a direct superior of attest partners or managers.

[인력조달회사 등과 같이 회계법인의 형태를 갖지 않더라도 만일 attest function에 회계사등과 같은 인력을 파견할 경우 attest engagement를 하는 동안 AICPA code of conduct를 준수하여야 한다]

〈개념정리〉

윤리강령상 독립성 준수의 잠재적 위협(Threats to Independence under the Code)

① 이기적 위협(self-interest threats) : 감사의 결과가 감사인 자신의 이익에 영향을 주는 위험
generally as a result of the financial or other interests of a professional accountant or of an immediate or close family member

② 자기검토위협(self-review threats) : 감사인의 중요한 판단이나 의사결정이 반영된 재무정보에 대해 자신이 인증업무를 수행함으로 발생하는 위험
re-evaluation of a previous judgement

③ 변호위협(advocacy threats) : 의뢰인, 의뢰인의 이해관계자 또는 감사인 자신을 변호해야 하는 상황에서 발생하는 위협
promotion of a position or opinion to the point that subsequent objectivity may be compromised

④ 유착위협(familiarity threats) : 의뢰인 등 특수관계인에 대한 동정심, 친밀성에서 기인하는 위협

as a result of a close relationship one may become to sympathetic to the interest of others

⑤ 압력위협(intimidation threats) : 의뢰인 및 의뢰인의 임직원 또는 기타 제3자 등으로부터의 압력, 위협에 기인하는 위험
objectivity affected by actual or perceived threats

⑥ 반이익 위협(adverse threats)-actions or interests between the member and the client that are in opposition

⑦ 부적절한 영향력 위협(undue influence threat)-attempts by a client's management to coerce the member or exercise excessive influence over the member

⑧ 경영진참여 위협(management participation threat) - assuming the role of management or performing management functions for the attest client

15 Ruling 101 Ethics Rulings: Impairing Cases

Impairing cases 회계사의 독립성을 훼손하는 케이스

1) 회계사가 의뢰인으로부터 단순한 선물이상의 것(more than a token gift)

2) 회계사가 재단의 관리인(trustee of foundation)인 경우 독립성이 훼손된다.

3) 회계사가 비영리사교단체(non-profit social club)의 이사회의 일원으로 활동하고, 그 이사회가 그 사교단체업무(affairs of the club)에 궁극적으로 책임을 지는 경우라면 독립성이 훼손된다.

4) 회계사가 의뢰인 회사직원용 조합아파트(a member's ownership of an apartment

in a coop apartment)를 소유하는 것은 독립성을 훼손시키는 것이다.

5) 보고서의 날짜 전 1년 이상 전문적인 서비스에 대한 보수가 청구되었든 않되었든 미지급 상태인 경우(when prior year fee for professional services, whether billed or not, remain unpaid for more than one year to the date of the report)

注意| 1년(one year)이면 12개월(12 months)인데 주어진 지문에서는 흔히 19 months 등과 같이 나오므로 착각하거나 속임수에 넘어가지 않도록 주의할 것

6) Public practice를 하지 않는 변호사는 재무제표와 관련해서 그리고 자신의 고용주에 대한 관계에서 회계사라는 명칭을 사용할 수 있다. 또한 회사의 직책(employment title)과 함께 쓴다면 명함에 회계사라는 명칭을 사용할 수 있다. 회계사는 고용주로부터 독립을 암시해서는 안 된다. 독립이 된 듯 한 암시를 주면서 회계사라는 명칭을 사용함(transmittal)으로써 GAAP를 따르는 것이라고 언급해서는 안된다.

7) 회계사는 blind trust의 경우라도 의뢰인에 대한 attestation에 대해 직접적으로 금전적 이해관계(direct financial interest)를 가져서는 안된다.

8) limited partnership의 상당한 지분(material interest)을 갖고 있는 회계사는 그 limited partnership의 general partner가 general partner로 있는 다른 limited partnership에 대해 독립성을 갖지 못한다(A member with a material limited partnership interest is not independent of other limited partnerships that have the same general partner).

9) 회계사(회계법인)가 의뢰인(의뢰회사)의 advisory board의 일원으로 활동하는 경우

A. 진정으로 권고만의 기능을 행하거나,

B. 의사결정을 할 수 있는 실제 또는 외관상의 권한이 없거나,
C. 경영진과 이사회의 확실하게 구별되는 경우가 아니라면 독립성을 훼손한다.

10) 회계사가 의뢰인에 대한 투자를 하는 general partnership의 general partner인 경우 혹은 의뢰인에 대해 투자를 하는 limited partnership의 limited partner인 경우 독립성을 훼손하게 된다.

11) 회계사가 전문가 증인(expert witness)으로 선임된 경우, 회계사는 변호인이 아닌 단지 전문지식과 교육, 그리고 경험을 가진 사람(as one having specialized knowledge, training, and experience)로서 전문가 증인이 된 것이므로 개관적인 입장(objective position)이어야 한다. 편들기(advocate) 금지.

소송에서 재무제표가 쟁점이 되는 경우, 회계사를 전문가 증인으로 법원에서 선임할 수 있다

Non-impairing cases 회계사의 독립성을 훼손하지 않는 케이스

12) 회계법인의 구성원이 고객(의뢰인)의 trade association에 참여할 경우 만일 그 구성원이 officer, director, 혹은 경영진(member of management)으로 참여하지 않는다면 회계사의 독립성이 훼손되지 않는다.

13) 재무제표의 해석, 예측을 포함하여 광범위한 회계 및 컨설팅 서비스(advisory service 포함)는 독립성을 훼손하지 않는다.

14) Country club(골프클럽)의 회원이 되기 위해서는 equity securities(주식)이나 debt securities(채권)을 구입해야 하는 경우 이러한 증권을 갖고 있는 것은 독립성을 훼손하지 않는다(골프클럽 회원권을 살 경우 흔히 의무적으로 구입해야 하는 채권이 있기 때문이다).

15) 회계사가 의뢰인의 주식을 소유하는 뮤추얼 펀드에 투자(a member's ownership of shares in a mutual investment fund which owns stock in the CPA's clients)하는 것은 독립성을 훼손하지 않는다. 의뢰인이 아닌 regulated mutual fund를 소유하는 것은 당연히 회계사의 독립성을 훼손시키지 않는다.

Indirect financial interest라고 할 수 있으나 material하지 않으면 독립성과는 무방하다.

16) 주나 연방이 보장하는 예금을 금융기관에 갖고 있는 것은 독립성을 훼손하지 않는다. 보장되지 않는 예금(uninsured deposits)은 그 금액이 immaterial하다면(즉 중요하지 않다면) 독립성이 훼손된다고 볼 수 없다.

17) 회계사가 의뢰인의 advisory board구성원으로서 순수하게 제안(충고)만 하는 경우에는 독립성이 훼손되지 않는다.

18) 회계사가 감사의견(audit opinion)이나 review report를 발행하기 위해서는 독립적이어야 하지만, compilation report를 발행하기 위해서는 꼭 독립적이어야 할 필요는 없다.

19) 회계사가 금융기관에 $5,000을 초과하는 신용카드 채무(outstanding credit card loans to a financial institution of over $5,000)가 있는 경우, 만약 회계사가 그 채무를 $,5000 이하로 줄이게 되는 경우 독립성이 훼손되지 않는다.

20) 의뢰인과 회계사(혹은 회계법인) 사이에 리스가 존재할 경우, 그 리스가 operating lease라면 독립성이 훼손되지 않고, capital lease라면 독립성이 훼손된다.

21) 의뢰인과 회계사사이에 소송을 대신해서 ADR(alternative dispute resolution 대안분쟁해결 혹은 갈등중재(Conflict Mediation)라고도 하며 전통적인 소송 방식에 대한 대안으로, 중재자에 의해 강제성 없이 상호 관심사항을 기반으로 분쟁을 해결하려는 시도)을 통해 분쟁을 해결하려 하는 것은 독립성을 훼손하지 않는다.

16 Interpretation 102. Integrity and Objectivity

To maintain and broaden public confidence, members should perform all professional responsibilities with the highest sense of integrity.
-Article III-AICPA Code of Professional Ethics

A member shall not knowingly misrepresent facts.
-Rule 102-AICPA Code of Professional Ethics

1) 모든 전문직을 수행하는 회계사는

A. objectivity와 integrity를 유지해야 하고,

B. 이해의 충돌을 피해야 하며(avoid conflicts of interests),

C. 고의로 사실과 다르게 표시해서는 안 된다(not knowingly misrepresent facts or subordinate judgment)

2) Integrity is necessary to maintain the public's trust(Article III.01). integrity는 대중의 신뢰를 유지하기 위해 필수적이다.

Individuals with integrity	Individuals without integrity
Follow strict moral or ethical codes Are honest, good and honorable Accept responsibility for their actions Do the right thing at all times Tell the truth	Are dishonest Act in questionable manners Are corruptible Tell lies Blame others Avoid taking responsibility for their actions Only do the right thing if they are watched

[source] Jane Zhang and Debra Grace, *Integrity, Objectivity and Independence*

3) examples of integrity

Situation	Answer
Janet knows her company's financial statements are materially misstated, yet she signs a representation letter to her company's external auditors saying that the statements are true and correct. Has Janet violated the Code of professional Conduct?	➡ Yes, Janet has violated the Integrity principle. Under Rule 102, a member must not sign a document with materially false and misleading information. Interpretation of Rule 102-1(c)
John, a new accountant, realizes that an entry on his company's books is false and will materially affect the financial statements. He did not change the entry. Has John violated the Code of Professional Conduct?	➡ Yes, John has violated the Integrity principle. Under Rule 102, a member must correct materially false and misleading financial statements or records. Interpretation of Rule 102-1(b)
Shana, the company's CEO, directs the accounting department head to record an entry that she knows to be fictitious and materially false. Has Shana violated the Code of Professional Conduct?	➡ Yes, Shana has violated the Integrity principle. Under Rule 102, a member cannot make, or direct others to make, materially false and misleading entries to financial statements or records Interpretation of Rule 102-1(a)

[source] Jane Zhang and Debra Grace, *Integrity, Objectivity and Independence*

4) Objectivity is necessary to perform services free from conflicts of interest.

객관성은 이해충돌을 피해서 업무를 수행하는 데 필수적이다.

A member should maintain objectivity and be free of conflicts of interest in discharging professional responsibilities. -**Article IV-AICPA Code of Professional Ethics**

A member shall be free of conflicts of interest and shall not subordinate judgment to others-**Rule 102-AICPA Code of Professional Ethics**

5) Examples of objectivity

Situation	Answer
Carmen, a senior accountant, was directed by her supervisor to enter a journal entry different from the original one. What should Carmen do to avoid subordinating her judgment?	➡ Carmen must determine whether her supervisor's entry represents a correct alternative. If it does, she need not do anything further. Interpretation of Rule 102-4(1)
Rosalie is directed by her supervisor to enter a journal entry different from the original one. Rosalie's research indicates the new entry would result in a material misrepresentation in the financial statements and records. What should Rosalie do to avoid subordinating her judgment?	➡ Rosalie must make her concerns known to higher management. She should document her understanding of the facts, the accounting principles involved and the parties with whom she discussed the matters. Interpretation of Rule 102-4(2)
Aaron is directed by his supervisor to enter a journal entry different from the original one, which would result in a material misrepresentation in the financial statements and records. Aaron has brought this to the attention of higher management but no action was taken. What should Aaron do to avoid subordinating her judgment?	➡ Aaron should consider whether to continue with his employer. He may wish to consult with legal counsel. Interpretation of Rule 102-4(3)

[source] Jane Zhang and Debra Grace, *Integrity, Objectivity and Independence*

 Rule 201. General Standards for CPA회계사의 일반기준

회계사는 다음과 같은 기준을 따라야 한다.

1) Due professional care 회계사는 전문가로서 due care를 해야 한다.

注意| A CPA is strictly liable for failure to exercise due professional care. 회계사에게는 업무수행(Ex. detect fraud, detect illegal acts 등)과 관련하여 일반적으로 엄격책임(strict liability)을 묻지 않고 다른 일반적인 회계사처럼 합리적인 수준으로 일을 했는지 만 묻는다. 다만 due care를 하지 않은 것에 대해서는 strictly liable하다.

Auditor는 다른 전문가의 판단을 그대로 받아들일 게 아니라 이를 엄밀히 검토하여야한다.

2) Planning and Supervision: 모든 engagements를 적절하게 계획하고 감독하여야 한다.

회계사가 의뢰인에게 전문적인 서비스를 제공하면서 회계사가 아닌 다른 분야의 전문가(예. 변호사, 의사, 컴퓨터전문가) 를 고용할 경우 이들을 감독하고 작업결과를 제대로 평가하여야 한다.

3) Sufficient relevant data: 결론과 제안에 대한 합리적인 기준을 마련하기 위하여 충분하고 관련된 자료를 수집하여야 한다.

4) Professional competence: 전문적 능력을 갖추어야 한다.

5) 그리고 추가로 Rule202에 따라서

A. Client interest를 위하여 integrity and objectivity를 갖고 봉사(serve)하도록 하고,

B. 의뢰인과공동의 이해를 갖도록 하고(understanding with client) 그것을 서면이나 구두(writing or oral)로 확실하게 해두어야(establish) 한다.

C. 또한 이를 고객이 알도록 반드시 대화(communication with client)를 해야 한다.

18 Rule 203. Accounting Principles

회계사는 GAAP과는 거리가 멀어도 재무제표가 제대로 되어있다고 해서는 안 된다. 특히 그러한 departure(회계원칙에서의 이탈 또는 괴리)가 중대한 영향을 미칠 경우 보고서를 통해서 그러한 departure, effects, and reasons를 설명해야만 한다.

19 Rule 203-1. Departures from Established Accounting Principles.

GAAP을 따를 경우 재무제표에 오해를 하게 되는 비정상적인 상황에서는 GAAP에서 이탈하는 것이 허용된다. 그러한 비정상적인 상황은 evolution of new form of business transaction(새로운 거래형태의 발전) 이나 new legislation(새로운 입법) 등이다.

20 Rule 301 Confidential Client Information

회계사로 활동하는 사람은 의뢰인의 명시적 동의없이(without specific consent of the client) 의뢰인에 관한 비밀정보(any confidential client information)를 공개해서는 안 된다.

단, 예외적으로

1) compliance with Rule 202 and 203 obligations

2) 법정수배나 소환장(enforceable subpoena and summons)

3) AICPA review of professional practice

4) 소송제기(initiating complaint) 또는 조사위원회나 징계위원회에서의 inquiry에 대한 응답의 경우(response to inquiry made by a recognized investigative or disciplinary body)

5) voluntary quality control review by AICPA or state CPA society

미국회계사협회(AICPA)나 주의 회계사협회에서 자발적인 quality control 목적상 회계사의 자료를 보고자 할 경우 고객의 동의 없이 제공가능하다.

21 Rule 302 Contingent Fees 성공보수

1) 회계사는 다음과 같은 경우 성공보수를 받으면 안 된다.

A. 재무제표의 감사나 리뷰(audits or reviews)
B. 회계사가 독립적이고 제3자가 재무제표를 사용할 수 있을 가능성이 있는 경우의 compilation
C. examination of prospective financial statements 추정재무제표의 examination

2) 의뢰인에게 성공보수를 받고 세금신고서(tax return)를 작성해주거나 수정해주거나 세금환급신청(claims for a tax refund)을 해서는 안 된다.

3) Financing한 금액의 많고 적음에 따라 성공보수를 받아서는 안 된다(fee for a review that varies depending on the amount of financing)

4) 단, 법원이나 다른 공공기관이 확정한 보수(fees fixed by courts or other public authorities), 혹은 세금문제(tax matters)에 있어서 회계사의 노력으로 인하여 재판 혹은 정부의 결정결과(judicial proceedings or findings of governmental agency)에 따라 변동되는 보수를 받기로 하는 것은 허용된다.

22 Rule 501 Acts Discreditable [불명예행위]

1) Interpretation 501-1.의뢰인의 요구에도 불구하고 고객정보를 계속해서 보관(retention of client records)하면 discreditable.

A. 회계사는 회계사를 위하여 의뢰인이 작성해준 analyses 와 schedules를 보관해도 무방하며 이걸 굳이 다시 고객에게 제공하지 않아도 된다.

B. 회계사는 받을 비용을 다 받을 때까지(until payment of fee is received) 고객의 장부에 반영되지 않은 정보를 work papers에 정리해두어도 된다.

Rule 502 Advertising and other forms of solicitation

회계사의 misleading, deceptive or false한 광고가 금지되며[MIDOFA rule] 특히

1) 보통사람이 오해(mislead)하거나 속아 넘어가게(be deceived) 하면 안 되고

2) 미래에 발생할 비용을 현실성 없게 추정하거나(unrealistic estimates of future fees)

3) 법원, 규제당국, 혹은 유사기관에 영향력을 행사할 수 있는 능력이 있다고 암시하거나(implies ability to influence a court, tribunal, regulatory agency, or similar body or official)

4) 거짓 혹은 정당화될 수 없는 기대감(false or unjustified expectations)을 만들어내선 안된다.

 Rule 503. Referral Services

회계사 혹은 회계법인이audit or reviews, compilations of financial statements, examination of prospective financial information을 하도록 추천을 해주거나 소개를 해준 경우 수수료나 소개비(No commissions or referral fees)를 받아서는 안 된다.

 Rule 505 Form of Practice and Names

1) 회계법인의 파트너와 주주모두가 회계사가 아닌 한 AICPA라는 용어를 회사명으로 사용하지 못한다.

2) 회계법인이라는 용어를 사용하려면 supermajority인 66 2/3의 회사지분이 회계사 소유이어야 한다.

 Responsibilities in Consulting Services

1) 1991년 1월에 발효된 Statements on Standards for Consulting Services(SSCS)에 따라 컨설팅 서비스를 하여야 한다.

A. SSCS에 따르면 CPA는 고객에게 engagement 과정 중에 어떤 업무를 제공해주

는지, 어떤 업무가 포함되지 않는지 여부를 명확하게 알려주어야 할 의무가 있다.

Under the Statements of Standards for Consulting Services, a CPA is responsible to inform the client of significant reservations concerning thc benefits of the engagement.

B. SSCS에 따르면 CPA는 고객에게 자신의 engagement service내용에 대해 구두 혹은 서면으로 전달하면 되고, 반드시 서면으로 할 필요는 없다.

The SSCS do not require a CPA to obtain a written understanding with the client concerning the engagement inclusive of the time for completion of the engagement.

C. SSCS에 따르면 CPA는 고객과의 합의에 의해 합의내용을 수정할 수 있다

2) Consulting services 컨설팅서비스란 의뢰인의 이용과 이익(for the use and benefits of the client)을 위한 것이 주목적이다.

3) Consulting service 업무의 성격은 오로지 의뢰인과 서비스제공자(회계사, the practitioner)사이의 계약에 의해 결정된다.

4) Consulting service를 제공하면서 객관성을 유지해야 하지만(objective), 독립성이 요구되지는 않는다. 다만, 해당고객에게 attest service[인증서비스]를 제공하는 경우 (예. 감사업무)에는 독립성(independence)이 요구된다.

〈개념정리〉

Attest service	- Independence
Consulting service	- Objectivity [aico rule]

3) 의뢰인에게 attest service를 하면서 동시에 consulting service를 제공하는 경우 독립성이 필요하지만, 컨설팅 서비스를 제공했다고 해서 그 자체만으로 독립성이

훼손되지는 않는다.

4) consulting service의 유형(types)

〈개념정리〉

consultations: 의뢰인에 대한 기존의 개인적인 지식(based mostly on existing personal knowledge) 에 의거하여 단기(short time frame)조언을 해주는 것	Ex. Reviewing and commenting on client's business plans
advisory services: 의뢰인의 의사결정을 돕기 위해 연구하여 결론을 도출해내고 제안하는 것(develop findings, conclusions, and recommendations)	Ex. Analysis of accounting system
transaction services: 의뢰인과 제3자간의 거래에 관련된 서비스를 제공하는 것	Ex. Insolvency services, valuation services, litigation services, etc.
product services: 제품과 관련된 부수적 서비스제공	Ex. 제품판매 후 training programs of computer software
implementation services: 계획을 이행에 옮기는 것	Ex. Installing computer system, executing steps to improve productivity(i.e. 6 sigma, BSC)
staff and other support services	Ex. Data processing facilities management, bankruptcy trusteeship, controllership services

27 Responsibilities in Personal Financial Planning

개인재무계획수립(personal financial planning)이란 개인의 재무목표(personal financial goals)를 정의하고 성취하도록 하기위하여 의뢰인에 대한 보조목적상 전략수립 및 제안(developing strategies and making recommendations) 하는 것에 참가하는 것을 의미한다.

1) 개인재무계획 수립(personal financial planning)은 다음활동을 포함해야 한다(shall involve all of the followings).

A. defining engagement objectives
B. planning engagement objectives
C. developing basis for recommendation
D. communicating recommendations to client
E. identifying tasks for taking action on planning decisions.

2) 기타 다음활동을 포함할 수 있다(may involve).

A. updating recommendations and helping clients revise planning decisions
B. assisting client to take action on planning decisions
C. monitoring client's progress in achieving goals

28 Responsibilities in Business and Industry

1) operational auditing:기업이나 정부의 효율성과 실적평가 감사

2) compliance auditing:구체적인 법규준수여부감사

3) Internal auditing 내부감사활동

A. do financial, operational, and compliance audits

B. in financial auditing, evaluate effectiveness of internal audit procedures[금융감사에서는 특히 내부감사절차의 효율성에 대한 평가]

C. compliance with Foreign Corrupt Practices Act that requires companies to have effective internal control.

4) 내부감사인은 CPA가 될 필요는 없지만 certified internal auditor(공인내부감사인 CIA) 자격을 얻을 수 있다.

5) 내부감사인에 관한 Institute of Internal Auditing의 업무표준(standards for professional practice of internal auditing)

A. Independence 독립성[해당기관이 auditor가 판단을 내리는데 대하여 제한을 가하지 말아야 한다(no restrictions on auditor's judgment)

(1) internal auditor의 독립성은 AICPA와는 다르며 현업으로부터의 독립성이 주로 강조된다.

(2) reporting is often directly to audit committee or BOD. 내부감사는 감사위원회나 이사회에 직접 보고하여야 한다.

B. professional proficiency

C. Scope of work

D. Performance of audit works 감사작업수행

E. Management of internal audit department 회사내 감사부서의 운영을 할 경우 외부감사인(AICPA)과의 업무를 조정하게 되는데, 내부감사(internal auditor)가 행한 감사로 외부감사인이 행해야 하는 감사를 대신할 수는 없다.

29 Responsibilities in Government Auditing

1) 정부기관은 물론이고 정부기관을 감사하는 기관(Ex. Government Accounting Office)도 적용대상이 된다.

2) 감사인은 AICPA GAAS와 GAO에서 만든 GAS(Government auditing standard 정부감사기준)를 준수해야 한다.

3) GAS, 즉 정부감사기준은 "Yellow book standards"라고도 한다. 일부예외를 제외하고는 GAAS와 대체로 동일하다.

4) 만일 AICPA회원이 GAS(정부감사기준)을 위반할 경우 동시에 AICPA Code of Professional Conduct을 위반하는 것임에 주의해야한다.

5) GAS에서는 continuing education을 필요로 한다.

30 Single Audit Act

The Single Audit Act of 1984 (Public Law 98-502, amended in 1996) was passed by Congress to improve auditing and management for federal funds provided to state and local governments.

The act created a single organization-wide financial and compliance audit for state and local governments receiving federal funds equal to or greater than $300,000 in any fiscal year (a fiscal year is any twelve-month period). There are four major purposes of the act.

① To promote the efficient and effective use of audit resources
② To establish uniform requirements for audits of federal funds provided to state and local governments
③ To ensure that federal funds, to the greatest extent practicable, are audited in accordance with the requirements of the Single Audit Act
④ To improve state and local government's financial management of federally funded programs through more effective auditing

1) 여러 연방정부기관으로부터 자금지원을 받는(get funding from several federal government sources) 주정부 등은 이법을 통해 여러 번 감사를 받는 것을 한번으로 줄일 수 있도록 하는 법안이다.

2) 1회기년도(1 fiscal year)중에 연방으로부터 $300,000 이상을 받는 state government 나 local governments(Ex. City government, county government)는 이 법을 통해 한 번의 감사를 받을 수 있다.

 Statements on Responsibilities in Tax Practice

1) 세무와 관련하여 회계사는 의뢰인에게 overpaying이나 underpaying을 하도록 해서는 안 되며 세법에 따른 legal minimum만 납부하도록 해야 한다.

2) 회계사가 tax return(세금신고서)에 서명을 하는 경우, 거기에 기재된 정보가 자신이 아는 한 true, correct, and complete하다고 단언하는 것이다.
회계사가 모든 자료를 다 조사할 필요는 없지만, 만일 정확하지 않거나 불완전하거나 모순 된 정보(incorrect, incomplete, or inconsistent information)가 있다고 믿을 만한 이유가 있는 경우에는 조사(investigation)를 하여야 한다.

3) 회계사가 tax return을 작성하는 것을 도와줄 때 의뢰인이 만일 의도적으로 수입원을 작게 얘기해주어 이를 합리적으로 믿고 tax return을 작성해 회계사가 서명을 했다면, 회계사는 willful understatement of tax liability책임은 없다(A preparer is not required to audit or examine a client's books and records).

4) 회계사는 당연히 tax return작성을 도와준 의뢰인의 비밀을 보장해주어야 할 책임이 있다. 외부인에게 유출하고자 할 경우 반드시 의뢰인의 명시적 동의를 얻어야 한다. 단, quality review를 위하여 동료나 같은 회계회사의 파트너에게 자료를 보여주는 경우(peer review)에는 의뢰인의 별도의 동의가 필요 없다.

5) Reporting & Correction duty: 회계사가 의뢰인의 tax return을 도와주다가 만일 다른 회계사가 한 전회계년도의 tax return이 잘못되었음을 발견했을 경우, 고객에게 오류가 있음을 통보(inform)하고, 적절한 corrective action조치를 취해야 한다.

 Disciplinary System of the Profession and State Regulatory Bodies

1) 징계위원회는 다음과 같은 조치를 CPA를 상대로 할 수 있다.

A. acquittal-해당사항 없음

B. admonishment-훈계

C. suspension up to 2 years 2년 이하의 자격정지

D. expulsion from AICPA 제명

AICPA에서 제명당했더라도 주에서 발행한 license가 있다면 계속 회계사로 활동할 수 있다. 그러나 state code를 위반했다면 license와 certificate이 취소당하고, 회계사로 활동을 할 수 없게 된다.

2) Automatic expulsion from AICPA자동제명사유

A. 중죄가 선고된 회원(member convicted of felony)

B. 회원의 CPA certificate 이 주의 회계 위원회(State Board of Accountancy) 또는 권한 있는 다른 기관에 의해 취소(revoked)된 경우

C. 자신이나 의뢰인의 세금신고서를 허위작성 혹은 작성을 도와준 경우(preparing fraudulent tax return)

D. 고의로 세금신고서를 제출하지 않은 경우(intentional failure to file tax return)

• Mneumonic: intentionall FAST automatic expulsion

- ☑ Intentional failure to submit tax return
- ☑ Felony
- ☑ other authorized bodies
- ☑ state accountancy board
- ☑ fraud in tax return ➡ automatic expulsion

| 저자약력 |

미국 워싱턴 대학교 로스쿨 졸업(JD & LL.M)
미국 뉴욕주 변호사
쌍용투자증권, 국제금융센터, 한국은행 등 근무
연락처 : lovedolee2@hanmail.net

| 주요저서와 논문 |

『영어증권금융용어사전』,
『왜 힐러리는 르윈스키를 잡아넣지 못했을까? - 가족, 성, 사랑으로 읽는 미국가족법과 문화』,
『미국법정에 선 한국기업들』,
『전자금융거래법』,
『북한의 시장경제 모델찾기 - 중국과 북한의 금융개혁』,
『미국비즈니스법의 핵심』

- "Broken Homes and Juvenile Delinquency - A Case Study of St. Louis, MO, USA"(International Family Law)
- "Learning from China's Experience for the Reform of North Korean Central Bank" (Australian Journal of Asian Law, vol.6, no3
- "Legal Problems of the Two Koreas in the WTO Structure"(Asia Law Review, vol.2
- "Chinese Banking Market for the Foreign Investors after the WTO Accession"(Harvard Asia Pacific Review(vol.8, no.1)

U.S. Business Law

초판인쇄 • 2009년 5월 4일
초판발행 • 2009년 5월 11일
저　　자 • 이 동 욱
발 행 인 • 정 성 열
발 행 처 • 도서출판 ONE
주　　소 • 서울특별시 마포구 망원1동 458-31
등　　록 • 제 312-2003-000037호
전　　화 • 02-323-8536
팩　　스 • 02-323-8531

저자와의
협의하에
인지생략

ISBN 978-89-91115-69-9

정가 20,000원